GW00750548

Hoodoo, Voodoo, and Conjure

A Handbook

Jeffrey E. Anderson

Greenwood Folklore Handbooks

GREENWOOD PRESS
Westport, Connecticut • London

Library of Congress Cataloging-in-Publication Data

Anderson, Jeffrey E., 1974–
   Hoodoo, voodoo, and conjure : a handbook / Jeffrey E. Anderson.
      p. cm. — (Greenwood folklore handbooks, ISSN 1549–733X)
   Includes bibliographical references and index.
   ISBN 978–0–313–34221–9 (alk. paper)
1. Hoodoo (Cult)—Handbooks, manuals, etc.   2. Magic—Handbooks,
manuals, etc.   3. Voodooism—United States—Handbooks, manuals, etc.
I. Title.
BL2490.A65   2008
133.4'308996073—dc22   2008020832

British Library Cataloguing in Publication Data is available.

Library of Congress Catalog Card Number: 2008020832
ISBN: 978–0–313–34221–9
ISSN: 1549–733X

First published in 2008

Greenwood Press, 88 Post Road West, Westport, CT 06881
An imprint of Greenwood Publishing Group, Inc.
www.greenwood.com

Printed in the United States of America

The paper used in this book complies with the
Permanent Paper Standard issued by the National
Information Standards Organization (Z39.48–1984).

10   9   8   7   6   5   4   3   2   1

To Lynn, Michael, and David—my family

Contents

Preface

Rerences to hoodoo, Voodoo, and conjure seem to be everywhere these days. They appear in works by prominent authors, including some by Toni Morrison, Alice Walker, and Ishmael Reed—to name but the most prominent. Articles on the doings of Voodoo practitioners are common in newspapers and magazines. Marie Laveau, the "Voodoo Queen of New Orleans," has become a celebrated figure in scholarly circles. Three different Laveau biographies have hit the shelves in recent years. Several movies, most notably *The Skeleton Key,* have introduced African American magic to an even broader audience. One prominent hoodoo practitioner, Catherine Yronwode, now offers an e-mail- or paper-based correspondence course for aspiring practitioners through her business, the Lucky Mojo Curio Company (Pryse and Hortense).

The only problem with all the attention hoodoo and related practices have garnered from the media is that the average American does not have much context in which to situate references to African American magic. It is doubtful that most could give straightforward definitions of *hoodoo, Voodoo,* or *conjure* or explain why *hoodoo* and *Voodoo* are not quite synonymous. Even less expected is that more than a handful could properly situate these systems of belief within African American history, folklore, and everyday life.

Just as important to Americans' cloudy ideas of hoodoo, conjure, and Voodoo are the stereotypes that surround supernaturalism. Magic, especially the variety introduced into America by Africans, has long been associated with superstition, ignorance, or downright devil worship. These stereotypes have been present since the days when New Englanders were hanging witches, as evidenced by the fact that at least one of the accused was a believer in and possible practitioner of Voodoo. True, the number of executions of accused magic workers has significantly declined over the centuries, but African American believers and practitioners still receive more than their fair share of disparaging remarks in the popular press. The very presence of hoodoo often makes news, as was true in early 2003 when word got out that Michael Jackson allegedly used Voodoo to hex his enemies (Breslaw; "Magazine: Jackson Resorts to Voodoo"). In addition, one's race often has little impact on these stereotypes. African Americans are almost as likely to see Voodoo and hoodoo as diabolic practices as are whites. Folktales current in black society that accuse conjurers of causing illness and death bear out this contention (for examples of such tales, see Kulii, 214–217, 225–230).

In addition to the lack of knowledge and stereotypes with which most people approach hoodoo and Voodoo, many assume them to be a part of the past, never realizing that they are alive and well. To them, Voodoo conjures up images of nineteenth-century queens leading midnight ceremonies along the Bayou St. Jean outside New Orleans. Likewise, hoodoo might appear to be a fit subject for the blues singers of the early twentieth century but not a serious presence today. Conjure seems simply a quaint word, aptly associated with antebellum slavery.

Hoodoo, Voodoo, and Conjure: A Handbook is a unique work that seeks to fill gaps in public knowledge and to provide much-needed correctives when public perception diverges from facts. In recent years, a few books have attempted similar tasks. Carolyn Long's *Spiritual Merchants: Religion, Magic, and Commerce,* Yvonne Chireau's *Black Magic: The African American Conjuring Tradition,* and Jeffrey E. Anderson's *Conjure in African American Society* are the most prominent examples. Unfortunately for general readers, all of these were written with scholarly audiences in mind. As such, each can be somewhat inaccessible to nonspecialists. The present work, in contrast, has been written with students and the general public in mind. Although in no way "dumbed-down," it was written with more than a small cadre of professionals in mind.

The most logical way for a book of this sort to begin is by clearly defining what it is all about. Most important, what exactly are Voodoo, hoodoo, and conjure, and how do they differ from one another? Voodoo proper is an African creole religion, meaning that it is a faith that began in African and adapted to new conditions in the American South. As a developed system of belief, it has its own gods, priests, sacred ceremonies, and magic. At the same time, just which religion the term designates varies significantly by context. For instance, scholars frequently use *Voodoo* to refer to a West African religion that is more properly called *Vodu* or *Vodun.* More often, however, one sees *Voodoo* used to indicate a folk religion of Haiti, the preferred term for which is *Vodou.* In North America, *Voodoo* means a religion once popular along the banks of the Mississippi River, especially in the city of New Orleans. To further complicate matters, Voodoo is sometimes called *Voudou* or *Vaudou* in the United States. A more detailed analysis of the relationship between these religions and the reasons for the multiplicity of similar terms must await a later chapter.

Hoodoo, in modern parlance, does not refer to a religion. On the contrary, it designates a body of magical beliefs, with little reference to deities and the trappings of religious worship. Practitioners generally limit their duties to telling fortunes, casting spells, and making charms for paying clients; however, this has not always been the case. Hoodoo has long been associated with the Mississippi Valley, as has Voodoo. Evidence strongly indicates that the two share a common ancestry and may once have been synonyms. For purposes of clarity, *hoodoo* will typically be used to refer to both African American magic and African creole religion in general, a practice in keeping with historical usage that will also prevent the conflation of conjure and Voodoo.

Whereas *hoodoo* refers to the brand of African American supernaturalism found along the Mississippi, *conjure* properly denotes the variety found elsewhere in the United States. The term is rarely used today and was already in decline by the early twentieth century. Most modern writers treat it as a synonym for hoodoo, a trend this handbook will adopt except in those instances where the historical development of black folk supernaturalism is discussed.

Is it true that Voodoo and hoodoo are really just devil worship? The answer is a clear-cut *no.* From at least the late nineteenth century on, the vast majority of conjurers have confidently described themselves as Christians. The same has also been true of Voodoo practitioners, who often saw no insurmountable conflicts between their African-derived faith and the Catholicism prevalent along the Mississippi. Satan does sometimes appear as part of Voodoo and hoodoo, to the extent that African American folklore has preserved numerous formulas for selling one's soul to him in exchange for arcane power. Still, most of the tales of pacts with Beelzebub are just that—stories with little basis in fact. In other words, many have claimed conjurers gain their powers from the devil, but few practitioners have agreed.

Finally, can such examples of African American folk spirituality justly be referred to as things of the past? To assume hoodoo, Voodoo, and conjure are dead is to make a grave mistake. Practitioners continue to operate across the nation, especially in cities with a large African American population. New spiritual supply shops, which cater to a hoodoo- and Voodoo-oriented clientele, open on a regular basis. As the presence of online hoodoo courses indicates, the number of both believers and professional practitioners appears to be on the rise. This trend is most evident in centers of tourism, most notably New Orleans, where references to Voodoo and African American magic are everywhere. Modern hoodoo doctors and Voodoo priests and priestesses know how to play off the stereotypes to improve their standard of living.

This book builds on these general themes and allows readers to develop a basis for understanding the varieties of African American folk magic and religion. Chapter 1 describes the practices of conjure and Voodoo and argues for their importance to black life and history. Chapter 2 examines the historical roots of the different varieties of black supernaturalism and analyzes the links between them. Chapter 3 consists of primary source documents accompanied by commentary. Chapter 4 investigates scholarly and popular viewpoints on hoodoo and Voodoo. Chapter 5 places African American supernaturalism in context by discussing its impact on other areas of American life.

The special features of *Hoodoo, Voodoo, and Conjure* complete the work and make it the best available reference on African American folk religion and magic available. A glossary defining the terminology unique to hoodoo and related black supernaturalism provides ready answers to many reference questions. For those seeking deeper knowledge, a lengthy bibliography is included, which divides both important and obscure sources into categories for easy reference. In addition to print sources, this handbook lists a wide range of Internet sources on all aspects of African American supernaturalism free for the perusal of the technologically savvy. A detailed index rounds out the work.

Conjure and Voodoo are broad topics. Books and articles about them have been appearing for well over a century. Scholarly and popular viewpoints have constantly fluctuated between condemnation and admiration for practitioners. This handbook will not be the final word on the topic. It should, however, be the first word on hoodoo and Voodoo for anyone who wants to delve deeper into the realm of African American spirituality.

WORKS CITED

Anderson, Jeffrey E. *Conjure in African American Society.* Baton Rouge: Louisiana State University Press, 2005.

Breslaw, Elaine G. "Tituba's Confession: The Multicultural Dimensions of the 1692 Salem Witch-Hunt." *Ethnohistory* 44 (1997): 535–556.

Chireau, Yvonne. *Black Magic: Religion and the African American Conjuring Tradition.* Berkeley: University of California Press, 2003.

Kulii, Elon Ali. "A Look at Hoodoo in Three Urban Areas of Indiana: Folklore and Change." Ph.D. diss., Indiana University, 1982.

Long, Carolyn Morrow. *Spiritual Merchants: Religion, Magic, and Commerce.* Knoxville: University of Tennessee Press, 2001.

"Magazine: Jackson Resorts to Voodoo." *MSNBC* Website. 2003. http://www.msnbc.com/news/880422.asp (March 11, 2003).

Pryse, Marjorie and Hortense J. Spillers, ed. *Conjuring: Black Women, Fiction, and Literary Tradition.* Bloomington: Indiana University Press, 1985.

Skeleton Key, The. Produced by Clayton Townsend. Directed by Iain Softley. 104 min. Brick Dust Productions LLC. DVD.

Yronwode, Catherine. *Lucky Mojo Curio Company* Website. 1995–2006. http://www.luckymojo.com.

One
Introduction

In contrast to the current fascination in popular culture with African American supernaturalism, it was for many years neglected by scholars. During the twentieth century few scholarly books examined hoodoo in any depth. By far the most important of these was Harry Middleton Hyatt's five-volume *Hoodoo-Conjuration-Witchcraft-Rootwork*. This impressive work, however, was simply a massive compilation of interviews with believers and practitioners, rendering it of limited value to general readers. To be sure, academics did not entirely ignore conjure. Several articles in the *Journal of American Folklore* and elsewhere treated hoodoo as something worthy of study. Likewise, many folkloric, historical, archaeological, medical, and psychological texts included sections about African American magic. Nevertheless, there was no attempt to synthesize the scattered material.

Voodoo, an African American religion once found in the Mississippi River Valley, received even less attention from serious researchers. The closest things to book-length scholarly texts were Zora Neale Hurston's 1931 article "Hoodoo in America" and Robert Tallant's *Voodoo in New Orleans*. Neither is a reliable source because of their authors' penchants for exaggeration and fabrication. The reasons for such neglect run the gamut from white prejudice to black embarrassment over what many continue to see as a negative aspect of African American culture.

Fortunately, since the turn of the twentieth-first century, the gap in the scholarship of hoodoo and Voodoo has shrunk. Since 2001, three full-length academic works have outlined the history of conjure. Other recent works have addressed specific aspects of hoodoo, most notably the lives of famous practitioners. This changing academic atmosphere is a consequence of the wider acceptance of conjure that is quietly permeating American society. Unfortunately, there remains a sharp divide between conjure and Voodoo scholarship and the general reader, who is more likely to encounter old fables of diabolic hoodoo or new myths depicting conjure as an early vehicle for civil rights. *Hoodoo, Voodoo, and Conjure: A Handbook* describes the practice, history, and study of conjure and Voodoo for interested nonscholars by combining original research with a synthesis of existing literature on the subject.

CONJURE

The Practice

Terminology

The practice of African American magic has a distinctive terminology. Most important are the multiple names by which it has been known. During the nineteenth century, *conjure* was the most prominent term. It was originally an English word that denoted the practice of calling up and controlling spirits. African Americans adopted other English terms to describe their supernatural practices. A few, such as *cunning* and *tricking,* were still in use during the first half of the twentieth century. The term *rootwork,* which remains popular along the Atlantic coast of the Lower South is likewise of European origin (Anderson, *Conjure,* ix–xii).

Other names for conjure have African roots. For instance, blacks from Georgia and South Carolina once commonly spoke of supernaturalism as *goofer* or *goopher,* a term probably of West Central African origin. *Mojo* and *jomo,* sometimes used to describe conjure, likewise have an African genesis and are today most popular in Mississippi and Tennessee. Scattered reports also speak of some African Americans calling their magical practices by terms like *obee* and *ober,* words akin to *obeah,* the Jamaican word for African-derived magic. These terms, regardless of their Old World origin, were partially supplanted in the early twentieth century by *hoodoo,* another African word that had long been popular in the Mississippi Valley but was rarely used outside of it until comparatively recent years (Chireau, *Black Magic,* 55, 182n36; Bell, "Pattern, Structure, and Logic," 483–486; Anderson, *Conjure,* ix-xii, 28).

Words describing practitioners of conjure generally derive from the work of supernaturalism itself. Thus practitioners of hoodoo are known as *conjure men, conjure women,* or *conjurers.* Titles like *rootworker, trick doctor, ober man, witch,* and *cunning woman* likewise reflect the magical services their bearers provide. *Two-headed* or *double-headed doctor* are some unusual designations for practitioners that do not directly refer to their professional expertise. According to most scholars, the terms refer to practitioners' possession of both natural and supernatural knowledge. It may also derive from the belief that children born with cauls are supernaturally gifted. Because cauls cover the heads of those born with them, it is possible that these were originally conceived of as the second "heads" of two-headed doctors (Bell, "Pattern, Structure, and Logic," 487; Anderson, "Two-headed Doctors").

Hoodoo also has unique words for magical items and actions. Many, however, have been restricted historically to specific regions of the country. For instance, in the New Orleans area, *zinzin, gris-gris,* and *wanga* were the names for different classes of charms. *Zinzin* referred only to positive charms, whereas *wanga* and sometimes *gris-gris* described the harmful variety. Around Memphis, Tennessee, female believers carried what they called *nation sacks.* These were bag charms worn next to the body, the contents of which could be changed depending on the sort of good luck or protection needed at the moment. Yet another term with a limited area of usage was *luck ball,* a Missouri word describing a magical ball that was usually enclosed in a small bag. Although these terms were once confined to small portions of the South, they may now be encountered well beyond their original range because of the rise of mail order and Internet-based hoodoo sales (Gwendolyn Hall, *Africans in Colonial Louisiana,* 163–164; Hyatt, *Hoodoo,* 620, 691–694, 744–888, 3293–3419; Mary Owen, *Old Rabbit*).

Other words were never confined to a small area. Perhaps the most common term for a conjure item is *hand,* something of a catch-all term for any sort of magical item used for good or ill purposes. Less widespread but still common is the word *mojo.* Mojos are usually bag charms designed for positive results, such as good fortune, money drawing, or protection. Unlike nation sacks, they are not limited to women, nor may their contents be removed and exchanged for others. A less common term describing a similar item is *toby.* The word *jack* designates a fortunetelling tool. Some terms describing evil hoodoo are *poison, trick,* and *fix.* Each of these, when used as a verb, means to curse a victim. *Poison* and *trick* can also be used as nouns when describing an item through which the curse was conveyed (Bell, "Pattern, Structure, and Logic," 482–488).

Paraphernalia

Conjurers use extremely varied materials. Traditionally, most of them came from the natural world of plants, animals, and minerals. Wonda Fontenot, a scholar of African American ethnomedicine recorded the use of 34 distinct plants used by hoodoo healers in three rural Louisiana parishes (137–139). Faith Mitchell, author of a similar work on Gullah herbal remedies found 56 plants in use among African American residents of South Carolina's Sea Islands. The most comprehensive treatment of the materials used by conjurers to appear so far is Catherine Yronwode's *Hoodoo Herb and Root Magic.* Yronwode's work lists and describes the often multiple uses of approximately 500 botanical, zoological, and mineralogical hoodoo curios. Despite their value as sources, none of these works are exhaustive in their treatment of conjure materials. Any study would be incomplete because under the right circumstances, virtually anything could become an item used in a hoodoo charm or spell.

Despite the scope of hoodoo's naturally occurring magical items, a few have gained special prominence. High John the Conqueror root is probably the most famous of all hoodoo charms. High John was in use by the late nineteenth century and probably before. As its name implies, it is a source of power and is almost always used for positive ends. Among its many uses are drawing money to its possessor, building personal power, and conquering enemies (Yronwode, *Hoodoo Herb and Root Magic,* 111–113). It is likely that a root carried by slaves to protect them from whipping was a version of High John (Douglass, 41–42, 47).

Less benevolent uses are assigned to black cat bones, which supposedly allow their possessors to become invisible, typically for criminal pursuits. Those wishing to find the right bone have to boil the cat alive at midnight until the flesh falls from the bones. According to some versions, the magical bone will be the one that comes to rest on top of the others. The possessor should then place it under his or her tongue in order to disappear (Yronwode, *Hoodoo Herb and Root Magic,* 49).

One of the most widely used hoodoo items was goopher dust, usually described as dirt taken from graves (Steiner, "Observations," 173–180). In some cases, graveyard dirt makes up only one of several ingredients to the dust. Compound goopher dust is usually a harmful agent and can be used to kill or otherwise harm enemies. In a pure form, however, graveyard dirt has numerous uses. For example, practitioners sometimes sprinkle it in the shoes of unwitting victims as part of spells designed to kill them. Just as common is the use of earth from a grave to attract a lover or to win success in gambling (Yronwode, *Hoodoo Herb and Root Magic,* 105–107, 109).

Other items have long been popular in conjure but have not reached the public consciousness as readily as High John the Conqueror, black cat bones, and goopher dust. Five finger grass, for instance, is an herb common in protection- and money-related charms. Adam and Eve root has long been popular in love charms. Puccoon root is a bringer of good luck, as are rabbits' feet. Those involved in legal problems use beef tongues to win court cases. Live frizzled chickens have strong protective power and can reportedly dig up and destroy hidden hoodoo curse packets. These items give a taste of the varied paraphernalia of conjure, but they represent only a small fraction of the naturally occurring items frequently found in hoodoo (Yronwode, *Hoodoo Herb and Root Magic,* 19–20, 52, 55, 95–96, 161; Robinson, interview by author).

In addition to naturally occurring materials, practitioners usually rely on a wide assortment of manmade items. The Bible is probably the most common human-produced conjure tool. Zora Neale Hurston went so far as to state that, "All hold that the Bible is the greatest conjure book in the world" ("Hoodoo in America," 414). Verses from it may be recited or written as parts of spells or during the manufacture of charms. The purpose of the magic need not serve the church. Neither must it be benevolent in character. Candles rival the Bible as the most common manufactured hoodoo items. These may be used in a variety of ways, ranging from finding a job to killing one's enemies. In addition, colognes and perfumes have been employed by conjurers for many years, who use them in love-drawing spells. The most popular of them has been Jockey Club, which has been used by practitioners since at least the early twentieth century. In parts of Louisiana, hoodoo healers carve staffs with animal motifs. These help their possessors walk as well as represent their spiritual powers. Even items as mundane as tinfoil can have magical uses. At least one Missouri conjurer was using it in his charms by the late nineteenth century (Table 1.1) (Long, *Spiritual Merchants*, 109; Hurston, "Hoodoo in America," 411–414; Fontenot, 117; Mary Owen, "Among the Voodoos," 232–233).

Since at least the late nineteenth century, manufacturers have produced some items solely for use in the conjure profession. Glass-encased candles with magical instructions printed on them are a prime example. Several brand-name hoodoo products are available by mail order or from spiritual supply shops across the country. Such products include bath salts, incense, powders, aerosol sprays, soaps, and a dizzying array of oils. In many cases, the manufactured items reference herbal or zoological curios of the same names. For example, numerous John the Conqueror oils and incenses are available, although they may have no more in common with the root than a name.

Not all of the accoutrements of hoodoo are physical. For instance, certain times, such as sunrise or midnight, are highly potent for particular spells. Places may be equally powerful. Locales with spiritual associations, such as graveyards or churches, are magically important. Crossroads are exceptionally significant to hoodoo, most notably as spots where folklore has aspiring practitioners go at midnight to sell their souls to the devil. On a smaller scale, household altars appear as sacred space for some hoodooists, especially in the region of the Mississippi River Valley (Hurston, "Hoodoo in America," 357–360, 390–391).

Sometimes, the working of hoodoo has been as simple as placing a John the Conqueror root in one's pocket for protection. Magical items, natural or manufactured, can certainly be used on their own, but far more often they are part of a complex charm or ritual. Prime examples of complex spiritual manufactures are mojo hands. One gambling mojo described in an interview conducted by Harry Middleton Hyatt required the maker to place High John the Conqueror root, an Adam and Eve root, a black lodestone, and violet incense powder on red flannel. The practitioner should then sew the flannel shut over the materials, sealing them inside. The possessor of the mojo was to feed it with Jockey Club Perfume whenever he or she went out to gamble (*Hoodoo*, 610).

A particularly complex charm was fashioned during the late nineteenth century by "King" Alexander, a Missouri hoodoo doctor. Alexander's charm, a

An example of the type of candle used in hoodoo
ceremonies. Author's personal collection.

type of luck ball, required a complex series of rituals that involved collecting
red clovers, tinfoil, and dust; using cotton and silk threads to tie knots around
these magical materials; praying; spitting whiskey on the charm; and sending the
charm's indwelling spirit into a nearby forest. It was important that the future
possessors of such charms continue to feed them with whiskey and wear them
under their right arms (Mary Owen, "Among the Voodoos," 232–233; Mary
Owen, *Old Rabbit*, 169–189).

Even something so apparently simple as burning a conjure candle can be more
complex than one might expect. One candle spell designed to bring back a wan-
dering lover requires that the practitioner obtain a "high-power" blue candle and
Jockey Club Perfume. To begin, one should write the lover's name on the candle
seven times. The next step is to roll the candle in the perfume. The spell is complete once the performer burns the candle for five minutes each at 6:00 A.M.,
12:00 P.M., and 6:00 P.M. (Hyatt, *Hoodoo*, 805).

Table 1.1: Common Materials Used in Conjure Spells and Charms

African American Name for Items	Common and Scientific Names for Items	Use in Conjure
Asafetida	*Ferula foetida*	Protection
Devil's shoe string	Common plantain (*Plantago major*), hobble bush (*Viburnum alnifolium*), or goat's rue (*Trephrosia virginiana*)	Various
Camphor	*Cinnamomum camphora*	Made into a purifying incense; also used for colds
Devil's Snuff Box	Puffball mushrooms (*Lycoperdon perlatum, pyriforme*, and others)	Various, used primarily in harmful ways
Pecune or puccoon root	Bloodroot (*Sanguinaria canadensis*) or hoary puccoon (*Lithospermum canescens*)	Good luck
Sassafras	*Sassafras albidum*	Medicinal uses when made into a tea and money-related uses
Red or Guinea pepper	*Capsicum annum*	Protection
Garlic	*Allium sativum*	Protection
Sarsaparilla	*Smilax officinalis, sarsaparilla* and related species	Various, including treatment of gonorrhea
Snake root	Sampson snakeroot (*Echinacea augustifolia, Psoralea pedunculata,* and others)	Various, including preventing snakebite
John the Conqueror, Conquer-John, or Conjure John	Various versions, including Solomon's seal (*Polygonatum biflorum*), Indian turnip (*Arum triphyllum*), St. John's wort (*Hypericum perforatum*), and jalap (*Ipomea jalapa* and *Convolvulus panduratus*)	Various uses, particularly to amplify the power of hands and for power
Chewing John the Conqueror	Galangal (*Alpinia officinarum and galangal*)	Protection
Adam and Eve root	*Aplectrum hyemale* and related species	Love and protection, primarily
Five finger grass	Cinquefoil (*Potentilla reptans, canadensis,* and related species)	Money-related luck, spiritual cleansing, and protection

Table 1.1: (continued)

African American Name for Items	Common and Scientific Names for Items	Use in Conjure
Nutmeg	*Myristica fragrans, Myristica moschata, Myristica officinalis*	Used for gambling
Mayapple	American mandrake (*Podophyllum peltatum*)	Used for making a purging tea, among other uses
Lodestones	Naturally magnetic stone	Protection and money drawing
Conjure stone	N/A	Gives or increases the power of conjure
Salt	N/A	Protection
Goopher Dust	Graveyard dirt	Various, including giving power to hands
Human bones, fingernails, hair, blood, and other parts or by-products	N/A	Various, including giving or heightening the power of conjure
Frizzly chickens	N/A	Protection from conjure
Rabbits' feet	N/A	Good luck
Parts of reptiles, amphibians, and insects	N/A	Numerous uses, but most commonly causing infestation of victims' bodies
Black cat bone	N/A	Invisibility
Eggs	N/A	Divination and other uses
Playing cards	N/A	Divination
Red brick dust	N/A	Protection and money drawing
Horseshoes	N/A	Protection
Candles	N/A	Used to please particular spirits or burned as part of spells
Silver money (usually dimes)	N/A	Protection from conjure
Needles and pins	N/A	Various, generally causing harm
Bibles	N/A	Various
Red flannel	N/A	Encloses charms, increasing their power

SOURCES: Anderson, *Conjure*, 69–70; Yronwode, *Hoodoo Herb and Root Magic*; Nickell; Crellin and Philpott; Mitchell; Fontenot, 137–139.

Compound charms need not be positive in nature. In the late 1920s, a Louisiana woman suffered from an unidentified illness. She had seen physicians and undergone an operation, but they had done her no good. When her father took her to a conjure woman for help, she told him he had come too late for her to cure his daughter. She was able, however, to tell the distraught father what had happened to his child. According to the hoodoo doctor, an evil conjure woman had taken one of her victim's menstrual clothes and put 12 brass pins and 12 eight-penny nails in it. The enemy had then buried the cloth. As the cloth rotted in its interment, the woman's organs developed holes, rapidly sending her to her own burial (Hyatt, *Hoodoo,* 311).

Patterns

Hoodoo's rituals and magical materials can be mind-bogglingly complex, but that does not necessarily mean that it is without method. Quite the contrary, scholars have long suggested that hoodoo has an underlying logic. At the heart of all magical practices are the principles of similarity and contagion. These apply as well to hoodoo as other magical systems.

Similarity refers to the concept that magic workers can manipulate objects or perform actions with characteristics similar to the desired result to bring it about. A spell that a 1930s interviewer entitled "To Drive Your Rival Out of the County" illustrates this principle. The conjurer stipulated that clients should measure the distance between his or her enemy's footprints with specially constructed measuring tools. Afterward, the client was to bury them where the rival would walk over them. Here, the enemy's old footprints represented walking, and the measuring of the distance between them was the means to ensure that the rival would continue to move until he or she left the county (Carmer, 218–219).

In contrast, the principle of contagion argues that objects once in contact continue to influence each other. Ideally, the materials used in this type of magic are portions of the intended victim's body or its by-products, including but not limited to feces, hair, and fingernail clippings. When these materials prove difficult or impossible to obtain, objects that have merely touched the body will do. For instance, to gain a woman's sexual favors, one could use "a string from her drawers" to make a powerful hand. In some cases, the items used need only to have been in metaphysical contact with the person to be conjured. Such is the case with "To Drive Your Rival Out of the County." The footsteps represented walking based on the principle of similarity, and the fact that they were the conjured person's tracks ensured that the spell would affect the intended victim. Sometimes, written names can substitute for physical contact, a practice that is most common in spells designed to influence court cases (Hyatt, *Hoodoo,* ii–iii, 417–418, 674; Herron, 117–118; Puckett, 183–187; Carmer, 218–222; Hurston, *Mules and Men,* 273–280).

Like any religious or magical system, however, hoodoo is unique. The most detailed investigation of the topic has been Michael Edward Bell's 1980 dissertation *Pattern, Structure, and Logic in Afro-American Hoodoo Performance.* Bell argues that although the surface features of conjurers' spells commonly differ in form and content, each is interpreted and formulated according to a shared deep structure of intended results, agents (materials), actions, spatial frameworks, and temporal frameworks. The basis of all hoodoo rests on five intended results: punishment, diagnosis and divination, curing and redressing, protection from hoodoo or evil forces, and good fortune. Each of these has a set number of possible agents, actions, and spatial and temporal frameworks to effect it. Nevertheless, conjurers have free reign in choosing their spells' subordinate features. For example, if a hoodoo doctor planned to banish someone from a home (a punishing act), he would use a "sender" (a type of agent used to cause movement), but the sender's specific material might range from red pepper to a banana peel. The former should drive the person out by its heat, and the latter's slickness could speed the victim along (Bell, "Pattern," 314–315).

Probably the most complex hoodoo spells have been those designed to cure cursed individuals. Traditionally, healing those who were thus afflicted took place in three steps: diagnosis, curing, and turning back. To begin with, a hoodoo doctor would use some form of divination to determine whether the ailing person had genuinely been cursed and what had happened. If so, the practitioner would often reveal who had initially laid the curse. For example, a typical diagnosis might be that the afflicted person had scorpions in his or her internal organs placed there when the victim had stepped over a buried charm secretly hidden by a specified enemy. Once diagnosed, the victim expected a cure, which the conjurer was usually willing to supply. In the case of buried charms, the cure would involve locating and removing the source of the ailment. The uncovered charm might be burned or otherwise ritually destroyed. In cases where live things inhabited the ailing person's body, the conjurer would remove them, usually by inducing the client to vomit. Once the curse was lifted, hoodoo doctors frequently turned the spell back onto the one who had originally cast it, eliminating any future recurrence and possibly providing the conjurer with an additional client (Bacon, 210–211; Anderson, *Conjure,* 102).

Practitioners

Historically, virtually anyone could be an amateur practitioner of conjure. For instance, the custom of wearing silver dimes on a string around the neck or ankle for protection against evil conjure had become widespread across the South by the early twentieth century. Moreover, those who choose to adopt this simple folk amulet need not have any great knowledge of hoodoo. The same could be said for people who carried a rabbit's foot for luck or a High John the Conqueror root for protection (Hyatt, *Hoodoo,* 484–493, 596–595, 632–634).

Professional hoodoo required a bit more than a simple understanding of charms. One's suitability as a conjurer was indicated by a variety of outward signs, the most common being unusual physical deformities such as persistently blood-shot eyes, misshapen jaws, and discolored skin. In all cases, those who desired to perform hoodoo spells or manufacture hands as a profession required specialized knowledge. Even today, for instance, obtaining a properly empowered rabbit's foot is not as simple as one might think. A St. Petersburg, Florida, informant of Harry Middleton Hyatt described the process for obtaining a foot that would be lucky in gambling. According to him, the search for the auspicious append-age should begin in a cemetery. The person in search of the foot was to begin by thrusting his or her hand as deeply into a grave of a known gambler as possible. The searcher did so to obtain graveyard dust from as close to the dead person's body as practicable. According to the informant, a rabbit would approach once the dirt was in hand. The possessor of the graveyard dirt must then kill the rab-bit, take its left hind foot, and tie both the dirt and foot in a rag. A mojo bag to

A Hodoo Doctor. This unusual title was applied by Samuel Taylor to a conjurer he met during the late nineteenth century. The object of the sketch was equally strange in appearance. His peg leg, tufted hair, and series of chains encircling his body marked him as someone out of the norm. The bizarre appearance was an attribute of many in his profession. Samuel C. Tay-lor, "A Hodoo Doctor, April 30, 1890," James S. Schoff Collection, William L. Clements Library, University of Michigan, Ann Arbor.

be carried in the pocket was the result (Puckett, *Folk Beliefs*, 200–204; Hyatt, *Hoodoo*, 633).

Complex lore, like that for getting a lucky rabbit's foot, could be passed down in oral tradition or learned from a specific friend or relative. Since the turn of the twentieth century, much knowledge has been available in how-to conjure books, which are easily ordered or purchased from local hoodoo shops. On the other hand, the average believer would likely suggest that the best source for specialized hoodoo expertise has long been a professional practitioner.

Many scholars and believers themselves divide hoodooists into a variety of types. The highly regarded folklorist Richard M. Dorson separated practitioners of African American supernaturalism, whom he referred to as "two-heads," into three categories: hoodoo doctors, healers, and fortunetellers. The first he described as those who cure magically induced ailments. Healers, in contrast, treat natural illnesses "through . . . secret arts." Fortunetellers see the future and locate lost items (Dorson, *Negro Folktales in Michigan*, 101). Practitioner Catherine Yronwode supports a similar tripartite division of conjurers into readers, healers, and rootworkers. In her understanding, readers diagnose spiritual needs. Healers then bring about personal healing, although usually not in the medical sense. Rootworkers perform magic of various sorts, both good and evil (Yronwode, interview by author).

Other kinds of practitioners less commonly addressed by folklorists are those who directly participate in the spiritual supplies industry. These include the manufacturing company owners and employees, as well as the proprietors of individual hoodoo shops and their employees. These practioners are rare in folkloric studies because many are nonbelievers who participate in the spiritual commerce for profit alone. It is quite possible, however, for a rural hoodoo doctor who gathers his or her materials from nature to feel just as a mercenary. Thus distinctions based on assumptions about the sincerity of traditional practitioners as compared to spiritual supply workers are invalid.

In fact, the business structure of modern hoodoo closely mimics the practice of traditional practitioners. For instance, manufacturing companies make the charms that would have once been the purview of those Yronwode calls healers and rootworkers. Shop employees, and to a lesser extent owners, fill the role of readers who determine the precise supplies their customers should purchase. Some shop owners or workers perform formal readings and even manufacture complex charms and perform difficult spells that were once the province of preindustrial hoodoo practitioners.

Although drawing distinctions between different sorts of practitioners can be handy for purposes of analysis, doing so too sharply can be misleading. Most of those whom Dorson would define as hoodoo doctors at least dabble in reading. Historically, hoodoo doctors have also practiced herbal medicine, rendering them

A portion of the spiritual supply section of a popular Memphis, Tennessee, shop.
Author's personal collection.

healers as well. Plenty of practitioners do specialize, but most at least occasionally venture outside of their area of expertise (Yronwode, interview by author).

Marketing has also created artificial categories that have little or no application to conjure in practice. Few people today refer to themselves as hoodoo doctors or conjurers because of the terms' strong magical connotations. Many African American Christians have qualms about associating themselves too strongly with conjure because of biblical injunctions against witchcraft. At the same time, whites have long—albeit erroneously—defined African American supernaturalism as an expression of backwardness or worse, a type of devil worship. Thus, practicing hoodoo could be problematic because doing so might buttress racist assumptions about African American "superstition." Many modern practitioners prefer to designate themselves by titles widely accepted among whites, such as *spiritual advisor, medium, psychic,* or *healer.* Doing so allows them to escape the sometimes negative connotations of older terminology while still attracting customers who desire services identical to those offered by their predecessors.

At the same time that many African Americans are moving away from older terminology, a growing number of whites and blacks are self-consciously identifying themselves as hoodoo doctors for cultural reasons. In particular, many African American intellectuals have come to see hoodoo as a link to their past. Thus adopting older terminology can be a source of self-assertion, a way of rejecting stereotypes. Whites, on the other hand, sometimes gravitate to conjure as a genuine folk magical system free from what Catherine Yronwode likes to call the "fluffy bunnyism" associated with Wicca and other New Age and Neopagan beliefs. In short, categories are fluid. Their validity rests on the period and region studied and the outlook of individual practitioners and believers (Anderson, *Conjure,* 18–24, 132–133).

VOODOO

The Spatial and Chronological Range of Voodoo

Conjure has been practiced across the United States, wherever significant numbers of African Americans have settled. The range of the creole religion known as Voodoo, however, has been far smaller. Voodoo has long been recognized as a fixture of New Orleans culture. Most popular authors assume that it was merely an import from St. Domingue—modern Haiti—brought to Louisiana by refugees fleeing revolution during the late eighteenth and early nineteenth centuries. There are indications, however, that Voodoo was practiced in Louisiana as early as the 1730s, when slaves were already performing large-scale rituals and Voodoo-specific terms like *gris-gris* were in use. Voodoo, however, did not acquire its fully developed form until the nineteenth century, after successive waves of slave imports and heavy immigration from St. Domingue altered the racial and ethnic makeup of New Orleans. By the late 1800s, Voodoo was a frequent subject in the city's press. Voodoo as a distinct religion probably survived into the early twentieth century, and some of its rituals continued to be practiced until at least the 1930s and perhaps beyond (Du Pratz, 253; Long, *Voudou Priestess,* 93; Porteous, 48; Dillon; Mary Owen, "Among the Voodoos"; Anderson, "Voodoo").

There is ample reason to believe that Voodoo was not confined to the Crescent City. Former slave William Wells Brown reported that he witnessed a Voodoo ceremony in St. Louis, Missouri, sometime around 1840 (*My Southern Home,* 68–69). Mary Alicia Owen similarly reported the existence of Voodoo in St. Joseph, Missouri. ("Among the Voodoos"; *Voodoo Tales*). Scattered references appear elsewhere as well. Voodoo likely existed in African American communities throughout the Mississippi River Valley, although sources describing it in places other than Louisiana are scant. The attention paid to the New Orleans version is a consequence of the many surviving sources that describe it, not because it was unique to the city.

The Religion

The Gods

Like any other religion, Voodoo had its own spiritual hierarchy. By the late nineteenth century, when Voodoo was making its most frequent appearances in the New Orleans newspapers, most blacks were Christians. Thus they believed in the Christian God, who held the highest position in the supernatural world. Moreover, unlike in the rest of the South, large numbers were Catholic, a legacy of the French and Spanish colonizers who had long held the region (Hall, *Africans in Colonial Louisiana*). What differentiated Voodoo from standard Catholicism was its many lesser deities or spirits. Table 1.2 lists some of those gods worshipped during the nineteenth century.

Generally, sources describe these deities in reference to ceremonies or magical performances but give limited clues about their nature and function. Blanc Dani, Papa Lébat, and Assonquer make the most frequent appearances in both nineteenth- and twentieth-century sources. The first two, in particular, figure prominently in large-scale rituals. As an accommodation to Catholicism, blacks equated

Table 1.2: The Gods of Mississippi Valley Voodoo

Name(s)	Function
Blanc Dani, Monsieur Danny, Voodoo Magnian; Grandfather Rattlesnake	Chief god, envisioned as a snake; god of discord; defeats enemies; may have merged with Grand Zombi
Papa Lébat, Liba, LaBas, Laba Limba	Trickster, doorkeeper, sometimes considered evil
Monsieur Assonquer, Onzancaire, On Sa Tier	God of good fortune
Grand Zombi	Important and perhaps chief god, whose name roughly translates as "Great God" or "Great Spirit;" may have merged with Blanc Dani
Jean Macouloumba, Colomba	Unknown
Maman You	Unknown
Yon Sue	Unknown
Monsieur Agoussou, Vert Agoussou	God of love
Vériquité	Multiple functions including causing illness
Dambarra Soutons	May be identical to Blanc Dani
Charlo	Child god
Monsieur d'Embarass	God of death; name may indicate a connection to Blanc Dani/Dambarra Soutons
Samunga	Called on when gathering mud among Missouri believers

SOURCES: Anderson, "Voodoo;" Dillon, "Voodoo," sec. "Marie the Mysterious," 3:1, 5:7, 9, 6:5A; sec. "St. John's Eve," 27; Cable, *The Grandissimes*, 99, 101, 135, 182, 184, 257, 272, 311, 447, 453-456, 468; Pitkin, 185–213, 260–292; Mary Owen, "Among the Voodoos," 238–242; Cable, "Creole Slave Songs," 807–828.

at least some of the spirits with Christian saints. For example, Blanc Dani was St. Michael the Archangel, Assonquer was St. Paul, and Papa Lébat was St. Peter. (Dillon, "Marie the Mysterious," 3:1, 5:7–9, 18A-18B, 20, 6:5A).

The spirits of the dead also figured prominently in Voodoo. In fact, considering that many believed the lesser deities and saints were the same, they can be understood as the exceptionally exalted dead. One need not be quite so prominent in life, however, to earn a place in Voodoo after death. A spell collected in the 1930s described making drink offerings to Marie Laveau by pouring milk

Artist E. W. Kemble's impression of Marie Laveau (seated) and her daughter, who supposedly took over her mother's Voodoo practice. George Washington Cable, "Creole Slave Songs," with illustrations by E. W. Kemble, *The Century Magazine* 31 (1886): p. 819. Courtesy of Cornell University Library, Making of America Digital Collection.

into holes in Congo Square, New Orleans. Doing so reportedly drew money to the one who performed the ritual. A man interviewed by Harry Middleton Hyatt named a German he called Dr. Crawford as an important spirit (Dillon, "Hoodoo Jambalaya," 64; Hyatt, *Hoodoo,* 1303).

The Ministers

Voodoo had its clergy, who presided over important rituals. Female ministers were more prominent in the New Orleans area than were men and were typically known as *queens.* Their primary responsibilities were to preside over ceremonies, most notably the annual St. John's Eve celebration (June 23) on the shores of Lake Pontchartrain. In addition, they usually told fortunes, prepared charms, and cast spells for paying clients, which is what earned them a living. By far the most famous queen was Marie Laveau of New Orleans, a free woman of color who was influential from antebellum times until her death in 1881. Her reputation was such that some assigned her the ability to cause storms and control white police and politicians. The queens sometimes had subordinates. For instance, there were drummers and other musicians at many ceremonies, and Laveau herself reportedly had a secretary named Zelina Ross (Dillon, "Marie the Great," 21–26, 33; "Marie the Mysterious," sec. "Congo Square," 3B; Long, *Voudou Priestess,* 151–154).

Male ceremonial leaders whose position roughly corresponded to that of the queens were far from unknown. Although they did not appear in St. John's Eve rituals, they officiated over a variety of other ceremonies, including initiations. Indeed, according to some practitioners, it was necessary that both sexes lead initiations and train future generations because women properly taught men and vice versa. The Missouri Voodooist calling himself "King" Alexander even adopted a royal title, although he was an exception to the general rule that confined such sobriquets to women. If possessing a title at all, male ministers were generally called *doctors.* In New Orleans, several men rose to considerable prominence, although perhaps the best known in his day was James Alexander. Another well-known hoodoo practitioner, Jean Montanée or Dr. John, may have also served as a ritual leader, although sources are inconclusive on the topic (Owen, "Among the Voodoos," 230–231; McKinney, 4; Dillon, "Famous Wangateurs," 4–15B, 19–21; Hearn, "Last of the Voudous").

Besides ministers there were Voodoo supernaturalists. Makers of charms were known as *wangateurs* if men and *wangateuses* if women. Both titles refer to their possessors' trade in wangas, a type of harmful charm. At the other extreme were those who dealt exclusively in the treating of ailments, who were called *traiteurs* and *traiteuses,* meaning "treaters." Others simply adopted titles, such as witch or conjurer, common outside of the Mississippi Valley (Dillon, "Famous Wangateurs," 1; Fontenot; Owen, "Among the Voodoos," 241)

The Ceremonies

The best-known and largest Voodoo ceremony was the annual St. John's Eve gathering. St. John's Eve had long been a celebratory occasion for whites, who held their own festivals. By the nineteenth century, African Americans in New Orleans had adopted it as both a time of celebration and of religious ritual (Long, *Voudou Priestess,* 119). An early ceremony, described as having occurred in 1825, occupied the grounds of an abandoned brickyard. Later ones generally took place on the shores of Lake Pontchartrain. The surviving records describe the events as including bonfires, music and dancing, feasting, animal sacrifices, ritual bathing, and apparent spirit possession. A queen would preside over the festivals. In fact, it is likely that the existence of queens was part of a much wider African diasporic tradition of conferring royal titles on those who presided over celebrations. If true, then the use of the word *queen* to describe female Voodoo ministers likely originated with the St. John's Eve festivities (Kiddy, 153–159; Marie Williams, 403–404; Dillon, "St. John's Eve").

Next to St. John's Eve, the most prominent Voodoo ceremonies were initiations, which were common throughout the Mississippi Valley. In Missouri, Mary Alicia Owen described a late nineteenth-century ceremony that was a form of self-initiation. It required preparation of a decoction of bark, rainwater, and whiskey to be drunk by the one desiring entrance into what practitioners called "the Circle." After doing so, the initiate was to isolate himself or herself from

A private Voodoo dance as depicted by a nineteenth-century artist. George Washington Cable, "Creole Slave Songs," with illustrations by E. W. Kemble, *The Century Magazine* 31 (1886): p. 816. Courtesy of Cornell University Library, Making of America Digital Collection.

society, fast, and watch for prophetic dreams that would guide him or her to an object that would confer power on its possessor. Afterward would follow a period of instruction by an established practitioner of the opposite sex ("Among the Voodoos," 230–231).

Initiations in the New Orleans area, called *openings,* required presiding ministers. References to initiations in the Crescent City were common from the mid-nineteenth century onward, but no full descriptions became available until a much later date. Zora Neale Hurston reported undergoing multiple initiations in both "Hoodoo in America" and *Mules and Men.* Although her descriptions are highly detailed, they are of dubious reliability (Anderson, *Conjure,* 197).

Apparently more reliable are accounts recorded by the Louisiana Writers' Project during the 1930s. According to one of the female practitioners who participated in the ceremony, its purpose was to feed the spirits that would work with the initiates. A man who called himself Nome Felix conducted the ceremony. He began by laying out an altar with food, a statue of St. Peter, and other items. Removal of shoes and other items of clothing followed. The rest of the ritual included prayers, trances, spinnings of the initiates by Felix, washings of the initiates' feet and heads, and presentations of various supernatural items, including candles. Once the complex ceremony was finished, Nome Felix pronounced his charges ready to practice hoodoo for themselves (Dillon, "Voodoo Openings," 25–28).

Numerous other ceremonies existed as well. Dances held in New Orleans' Congo Square during the early nineteenth century probably had religious aspects, for instance. Mary Alicia Owens wrote of multiple dances in her descriptions of Missouri Voodoo ("Among the Voodoos," 236–241). Charles Dudley Warner also described an example of a weekly ceremony he observed in New Orleans, which took place during the late nineteenth century. The most striking feature of the ceremony was when the officiating Voodoo doctor covered candles, fruit, candy, and other items with burning brandy and then distributed them to the participants. A ceremony known as a hoodoo rising was recorded during the 1930s. Although its precise purpose is unclear, it involved an offering to Marie Laveau, consisting of three knocks on her tomb and making a gift of flowers and 15 cents. Marie Laveau herself held ceremonies called rehearsals on Friday evenings. Finally, numerous rituals that involved laying out gifts for the spirits were called *parterres.* St. John's Eve rituals and openings usually incorporated *parterres* into the larger ceremonies (Warner, 64–74; Dillon, "Marie the Great," 55–56; "Marie the Mysterious," sec. "Seances," 5–8, Long, *Voudou Priestess,* 110).

Voodoo had conjure-like magic attached to it, although it was distinct from that in the rest of the South. For one, terms like *wanga, gris-gris,* and *zinzin* set it apart from hoodoo outside the Mississippi River Valley. More substantive differences also existed. For example, hoodoo practitioners in the Mississippi Valley called on gods, the spirits of the dead, and Catholic saints when performing magic, each of which was uncommon outside the region. Likewise, candles and altars had their start in Voodoo supernaturalism. The use of certain materials, like beef hearts, was also far more common in the region than in the rest of the South. Such practices were not entirely unknown outside of the home range of Voodoo, but they were exceptions to the rule outside the Mississippi River Valley. Not until Voodoo's reputation for powerful magic spread during the late nineteenth and early twentieth centuries did some of its rituals catch on elsewhere. Even then, they were uncommon until similar Afro-Caribbean faiths arrived in the United States and grew in prominence during the late twentieth century (McKinney, 304, 307–312; Hyatt, *Hoodoo*, 744–888).

African Creole Religions Outside the Mississippi River Valley

Doubtless, creolized African religions survived for a time outside the Mississippi River Valley, but few details of them have survived in historical records. Occasionally, there are tantalizing glimpses of what once was. Among the Geechees of the Georgia coast, the practices of placing offerings on the graves of the dead and of praying to river spirits continued to be practiced until at least the late nineteenth century. Likewise, festivals known as John Canoes or Jonkonnus were known in North Carolina, Virginia, and possibly farther south. These were times of masking, wearing of horned headdresses, singing, and parading, indicating that they may well have been at least partly religious in nature. Despite these clues, widespread acceptance of distinctive creole faiths apparently did not persist beyond the colonial era in most regions. Another possibility is that they did exist but simply never captured the public imagination as did New Orleans Voodoo (Georgia Writers' Project, 59, 113; Morgan, 594–595).

One exception to the apparent absence of African creole religions outside the Mississippi Valley was a faith confined to Florida, which observers called *Nañigo*. Nañigo flourished in cities with large populations of Afro-Cuban immigrants during the late nineteenth and early twentieth centuries, most notably Ybor City and Key West. It had gone into decline by the 1930s, however. In Cuba, *Ñáñigo* has negative connotations and refers to secret societies. Those who described the Floridian religion also used the term to denote clubs or societies, as well as the religion itself. It is quite possible, therefore, that the generally white observers who recorded details of the faith may not have used the name most popular among practitioners to describe it. At least one author reported that the word preferred by Afro-Cubans for their religious association was Carabali Apapa Abacua (Murphy, *Santería*, 32–33; Kennedy, "Ñañigo," 153; Hauptmann, 197–200; Cappick, 9, May 16, 1958).

Nañigo had a series of deities also known in Cuba, including but not limited to Abasi, the most powerful of the gods; Shangó, a deity of justice and

A turn-of-the-century depiction of a Missouri Voodoo dance.
Virginia Frazier Boyle, *Devil Tales*, with illustrations by A. B.
Frost (1900; reprint, Freeport: Books for Libraries Press, 1972),
facing p. 102.

thunder; and Las Jimaguas, twin spirits. Like Voodoo, Nañigo had elaborate
rituals, including parades and ceremonial dances, over which presided priests
and priestess, reportedly called *mamaloi* and *papaloi*, respectively. Sorcerers connected with the religion were known as *brujas*, the Spanish word for witches.
Like Voodoo, Nañigo was an initiatory faith, as indicated by the facts that its
Cuban counterparts, Santería and Palo Monte Mayombe, are as well and that
it involved religious associations. Unlike Mississippi Valley Voodoo, it did
not wholly die out. Instead, those elements that survived into the late 1950s

probably merged with the Santería practiced by newly arrived Cuban immigrants fleeing Fidel Castro's regime (Murphy, *Santería,* 32–33; Branson, 77; Kennedy, "Ñañigo," 153; Hauptmann, 197–200; Cappick, 9, 16 May 1958).

THE PLACE OF CONJURE AND VOODOO IN BLACK LIFE

Strength of Belief

One of the least studied features of an understudied topic is the strength of belief in hoodoo. All signs indicate that conjure has been a pervasive feature of black life since the days when Africans began the gradual process of evolution into African Americans. Some of the first references to conjure came from seventeenth-century Massachusetts, where apparent practitioners were sometimes accused of witchcraft. As early as 1656, an African American called Old Ham was accused of practicing diabolic magic, although he was far more likely to have been involved in one of the African belief systems that would later contribute to hoodoo. During the 1692 Salem witch scare, at least two people wrongly accused of Satanic witchcraft actually demonstrated some familiarity with what would later be called conjure (McMillan, 104; Breslaw, 535–556). Later, conjurers made frequent appearances in slave narratives and antebellum court cases. The most notable instance of the former was an encounter between the famed ex-slave and future abolitionist Frederick Douglass and a practitioner named Sandy Jenkins. Before he gained his freedom, Douglass had faced many cruel masters, but the worst was a man named Covey. To escape this brutality, Jenkins instructed him to carry a root in his pocket to prevent Covey from whipping him. Douglass was far from alone in his experience (Wyatt-Brown, 313, 315–316, 424–425; Fett, 84–108; Douglass, 41–42).

Much later, folklorists would attempt to assign percentages to the level of belief. Harry Middleton Hyatt attempted to do so while conducting research in the years before and during World War II. The lowest estimate given by one of his informants was 40 percent of African Americans. Other interviewees estimated in excess of 90 percent believed. These same informants universally argued in favor of a strong belief among whites as well. Some even maintained that more whites than African Americans believed. There have certainly been both white and black practitioners as well as clients (*Hoodoo,* ii–iii).

A few studies give more precise data. For example, a study conducted from 1913 to 1917 at the University of Oregon sought to determine the strength of what the researcher termed *superstition* among the student population. Its findings indicated that even among a highly-educated group of whites living in a state with a small African American population approximately 4 percent had believed in hoodoo curses at some point in their lives and that 3 percent continued to do so while enrolled at the university. Other features of hoodoo, including belief in prophetic dreams and various forms of fortunetelling were much higher in percentage of belief. Unfortunately, these are features shared with many other supernatural and religious systems, rendering their direct links to African American belief difficult to ascertain (Conklin, 90, 92).

Most assume that the strength of belief has declined in recent decades. The rising interest in the subject is one indication that both scholars and popular authors fear that it will soon disappear. On the other hand, there are some indications that belief might be on the rise. The same growth in scholarly and popular attention that demonstrates the feared loss of hoodoo also argues in favor of its continued relevance. Likewise, the growth of online hoodoo businesses suggests conjure is far from dying. Some of the best evidence about conjure's place in modern black life comes from the fields of medicine, psychology, and sociology. For example, sociologist Wilbur H. Watson studied the prevalence of herbal medicine in relation to other factors in the lives of elderly rural African Americans. To be sure, herbal medicine need not be related to the supernatural, but Watson's discovery of a strong correlation between the use of herbal medicines and religious faith indicate that it is in this population. He noted that among those who considered religion very important, 93 percent felt a need for herbal medicine. Only 1 percent of those who thought religion unimportant did so. Overall, Watson determined that belief in herbal medicine remained strongest among those with substandard educations, with moderately low incomes, and in poor health. The data are inconclusive on African American supernaturalism as a whole, but the study certainly indicates that at least the rootworking side of conjure remains strong among certain strata of society (Anderson, *Conjure*, 134–149; Watson, 53–66).

Social Power

Belief in the supernatural power of hoodoo has historically given conjurers social power in everyday life. In many cases, hoodoo practitioners have been among the most respected members of their communities as a consequence of their magical acumen. A few, like Marie Laveau and Dr. Buzzard of St. Helena Island, South Carolina, became nationally known figures in their own lifetimes. Those involved with African Diasporic religions like Voodoo and Nañigo also obtained the respect accorded to clergy. Their importance to the public rituals that were so integral to the two religions guaranteed both their visibility and social prominence. Regardless of the level of their fame, they have long been vitally important members of African American society.

Conjurers can promise their clients a wide range of services. In many cases, their practice consists of the sort of things commonly assigned to workers of magic: telling fortunes, casting love spells, laying curses, manufacturing good-luck charms, and the like. Hoodoo doctors have not dealt simply in broad terms, however. Their spells can be tailored to specific concerns. For example, a spell recorded in 1930s New Orleans described how to sell all of one's fish at fish fries. At least one modern practitioner claims the ability to help doctoral candidates write better dissertations (Hyatt, *Hoodoo,* 623; Deborah, interview by author).

As a form of practical spirituality that promised supernatural results, hoodoo could be a lucrative business for successful practitioners. During the nineteenth century, prices ranging from 25 cents charged by an antebellum fortuneteller to $50.00 by a postemancipation New Orleanian conjurer were reported. During the 1910s, Dr. Buzzard reportedly charged $4.01 to cure a bedridden woman. Around 1914, a conjure woman from Savannah, Georgia, called Aunt Sally, charged $5.00 to bring one client success in his gambling business. Some twentieth-century practitioners charged much higher prices for select spells and charms. During the Great Depression, researchers for the Louisiana Writers' Project recorded that one conjurer asked hundreds of dollars for some of her more difficult spells, including those designed to kill her clients' enemies (William Brown, *Narrative,* 91; Hearn, "Last of the Voudoos," 726–727; Hyatt, *Hoodoo,* 900, 907; Breaux and McKinney, 320–321).

It should come as no surprise that some conjure men and women became quite prosperous. For example, before the Civil War Marie Laveau occasionally owned slaves, an indication of at least moderate means (Long, *Voudou Priestess,* 72–78). Twentieth-century practitioners frequently achieved similar economic standing. According to author F. Roy Johnson, James Spurgeon Jordan of Como, North Carolina, became a wealthy man from his hoodoo practice. In fact, his income provided him the means to purchase additional businesses, further increasing his fortune.

In most cases, clients have turned to conjurers simply to obtain things difficult to acquire by normal means, but on occasion the need for magical services went much deeper. For the vast majority of American history, blacks have either been slaves or lived under openly discriminatory laws that defined them as biologically and socially inferior to whites. Moreover, the legacy of slavery was poverty, placing many of those things not already forbidden by law out of the reach of disproportionately poor African Americans.

Hoodoo provided a magical response to clients' racism and poverty. For example, conjurers taught slaves to secretly sprinkle magical powders around their masters to prevent whippings. From colonial days to the present rootworkers have provided medical services for a fraction of the price charged by physicians. Modern scholars likewise consider conjure a type of ethnopsychiatry, which helps distraught persons deal with mental stress and disorder by providing them with sympathetic listeners who promise supernatural remedies for their ills. Surely, African Americans living under slavery and segregation were in need of just such attention. One form of conjure distinct to the postemancipation era was designed to help clients obtain jobs, an ever-present need for poor African Americans. Hoodoo has even offered blacks hope for dealing with the very laws that were designed to keep them permanently subservient to whites. One way to prevent incarceration on either valid or trumped-up charges, for instance, was to place one's subpoena on a large piece of ice, put an inverted white candle burning from the bottom upon it, and sprinkle the whole with sugar. Doing so was designed to make the judge feel sympathy for the accused (Henry Bibb, 25–32; Watson, 53–66; Fontenot, 73–83; Hyatt, *Hoodoo,* 842).

Faith in magic has always been the bedrock of practitioners' temporal power, but hoodoo is not necessarily without more concrete sources of efficacy. Works addressing the medical and psychological aspects of hoodoo are numerous. For instance, scholar Wonda Fontenot researched the traditional rootworkers of Louisiana, called *treaters,* and determined that their practice is legitimate in part because they have a record of successes and preserve a valuable body of ethnomedical lore (134). Many other researchers have likewise argued that conjure can be beneficial to one's mental and physical health.

Of course, not all of conjure is designed for health, but a different purpose does not necessarily make it any less efficacious. For example, that curses can cause death has been well documented by anthropologists. Likewise, conjurers have long shown an aptitude for giving good advice while placing it in magical terms. Newbell Niles Puckett, an early twentieth-century researcher, recorded a spell in which a conjurer sold a woman a bottle of medicine to prevent her from fighting with her husband. According to Hyatt, the practitioner instructed his client to place some of the liquid in her mouth whenever her husband accosted her. She was not to swallow it until the quarrel was over, and once she did so, she was to immediately kiss him (Puckett, 209). At least one modern practitioner, Thomas "Pop" Williams, describes his primary duty as dispensing good advice. The rest of his practice rests entirely on the faith of his clients, he argues (Thomas Williams, interview by author). Whether desired results are accomplished by actual magic or by tangible means is far less important than that clients believe the supernatural has worked in their favor. Practitioners are far more likely to see satisfied customers again than those who go away disappointed.

Conjure and Voodoo are fascinating objects of study. Rather than being mere superstition, they are complex spiritual and business practices that require adepts to master a large body of folk belief. Those with the ability and desire to learn have proven able to become community leaders. Moreover, as will become clear in later chapters, hoodoo, Voodoo, and conjure have a history longer than that of the United States itself.

WORKS CITED

Anderson, Jeffrey E. *Conjure in African American Society.* Baton Rouge: Louisiana State University Press, 2005.

———. "Two-headed Doctors." *The Greenwood Encyclopedia of African American Folklore,* ed. Anand Prahlad. 3 vols. Westport: Greenwood, 2006.

———. "Voodoo." In *Encyclopedia of African American Religious Culture.* Anthony Pinn, ed. Santa Barbara, CA: ABC–CLIO, 2009.

Bell, Michael E. "Pattern, Structure, and Logic in Afro-American Hoodoo Performance." Ph.D. diss., Indiana University, 1980.

Bibb, Henry. *Narrative of the Life and Adventures of Henry Bibb, an American Slave.* 3rd ed. With an Introduction by Lucius C. Matlack. New York: Privately printed, 1850.

Brandon, George. *Santeria from Africa to the New World: The Dead Sell Memories.* Bloomington and Indianapolis: Indiana University Press, 1993.

Breaux, Hazel and Robert McKinney, Federal Writers Project. "Hoodoo Price List." In Robert Tallant Papers, 320–321. City Archives, New Orleans Public Library, New Orleans.

Breslaw, Elaine G. "Tituba's Confession: The Multicultural Dimensions of the 1692 Salem Witch-Hunt." *Ethnohistory* 44 (1997): 535–556.

Brown, William Wells. *My Southern Home: Or, the South and Its People.* A. G. Brown and Company, 1880; reprint, Upper Saddle River, NJ: The Gregg Press, 1968.

———. *Narrative of the Life of William Wells Brown, an American Slave.* London: Charles Gilpin, 1850.

Cable, George Washington. "Creole Slave Songs." With illustrations by E. W. Kemble. *The Century Magazine* 31 (1886): 807–828.

———. *The Grandissimes: A Story of Creole Life.* New York: Charles Scribner's Sons, 1891.

Cappick, Marie. *The Key West Story, 1818–1950.* Serialized in *The Coral Tribune,* May 2, 9, 16, 23; June 6, 1958.

Carmer, Carl. *Stars Fell on Alabama.* With an Introduction by J. Wayne Flynt. Tuscaloosa, AL and London: University of Alabama, 1985.

Conklin, Edmund S. "Superstitious Belief and Practice among College Students." *The American Journal of Psychology* 30 (1919): 83–102.

Deborah, pseudo. Interview by author. July 15, 2002. Bessemer, AL. Notes. Author's personal collection, Monroe, LA.

Dillon, Catherine. "Voodoo, 1937–1941." Louisiana Writers' Project, folders 118, 317, and 319. Federal Writers' Project, Cammie G. Henry Research Center, Watson Memorial Library, Northwestern State University, Natchitoches, LA.

Dorson, Richard M. *Negro Folktales in Michigan.* Cambridge: Harvard University Press, 1956.

Douglass, Frederick. *Narrative of the Life of Frederick Douglass.* With an introduction by William Lloyd Garrison, a letter from Wendell Phillips, and a new introductory note. New York: Dover, 1995.

Du Pratz, Le Page. *The History of Louisiana or of the Western Parts of Virginia and Carolina.* Translation. London: Becket and De Hondt, 1763.

Fett, Sharla. *Working Cures: Healing, Health, and Power on Southern Slave Plantations.* Chapel Hill: University of North Carolina Press, 2002.

Fontenot, Wonda L. *Secret Doctors: Ethnomedicine of African Americans.* Westport and London: Bergin & Garvey, 1994.

Georgia Writer's Project, Savannah Unit. *Drums and Shadows: Survival Studies among the Coastal Negroes.* With an Introduction by Charles Joyner and photographs by Muriel and Malcolm Bell, Jr. Athens and London: University of Georgia Press, 1986.

Hall, Gwendolyn Midlo. *Africans in Colonial Louisiana: The Development of Afro-Creole Culture in the Eighteenth Century.* Baton Rouge: Louisiana State University Press, 1992.

Hauptmann, O. H. "Spanish Folklore from Tampa Florida: (No. VII) Witchcraft." *Southern Folklore Quarterly* 3 (1939): 197–200.

Hearn, Lafcadio. "The Last of the Voudoos." *Harper's Weekly Magazine* 29 (1885): 726–727.

Herron, Leonora. "Conjuring and Conjure Doctors." *Southern Workman* 24 (1891): 117–118.

Hurston, Zora Neale. "Hoodoo in America." *Journal of American Folklore* 44 (1931): 317–417.

———. *Mules and Men.* In *Folklore, Memoirs, and other Writings,* selected and annotated Cheryl A. Wall. The Library of America. New York: Literary Classics of the United States, Inc., 1995.

Hyatt, Harry Middleton. *Hoodoo-Conjuration-Witchcraft-Rootwork.* 5 vols. Memoirs of the Alma Egan Hyatt Foundation. Hannibal: Western, 1970–1978.

Kennedy, Stetson. "Ñañigo in Florida." *Southern Folklore Quarterly* 4 (1940): 153–156.

———. *Palmetto Country.* 1942. Reprinted with a new afterword by the author and an appreciation by Woody Guthrie. Tallahassee: A & M University Press, 1989.

Kiddy, Elizabeth W. "Who Is the King of Congo? A New Look at African and Afro-Brazilian Kings in Brazil." In *Central Africans and Cultural Transformations in the American Diaspora,* ed. Linda M. Heywood, 153–182. Cambridge and New York: Cambridge University Press, 2002.

Long, Carolyn Morrow. *A New Orleans Voudou Priestess: The Legend and Reality of Marie Laveau.* Gainesville: University Press of Florida, 2006.

———. *Spiritual Merchants: Religion, Magic, and Commerce.* Knoxville: University of Tennessee Press, 2001.

McKinney, Robert, Federal Writers Project. "Popular Gris-gris among Present Day Hoodoo Queens." In Robert Tallant Papers, 302–317. City Archives, New Orleans Public Library, New Orleans.

McMillan, Timothy J. "Black Magic: Witchcraft, Race, and Resistance in Colonial New England." *Journal of Black Studies* 25 (1994): 99–117.

Mitchell, Faith. *Hoodoo Medicine: Gullah Herbal Remedies.* Columbia: Summerhouse Press, 1999.

Morgan, Philip D. *Slave Counterpoint: Black Culture in the Eighteenth-Century Chesapeake and Low Country.* Chapel Hill: University of North Carolina Press, 1998.

Murphy, Joseph M. *Santería: African Spirits in America.* With new Preface. Boston: Beacon Press, 1993.

Owen, Mary Alicia. "Among the Voodoos." In *The International Folk-lore Congress 1891: Papers and Transactions,* 230–248. London: David Nutt, 1892.

———. *Old Rabbit, the Voodoo and Other Sorcerers.* With an Introduction by Charles Godfrey Leland. With Illustrations by Juliette A. Owen and Louis Wain. London: T. Fisher Unwin, 1893; reprint, Whitefish, MT: Kessinger Publishing, 2003.

Pitkin, Helen. *An Angel by Brevet: A Story of Modern New Orleans.* Philadelphia and London: J. B. Lippincott Company, 1904.

Porteous, Laura L. "The Gri-gri Case." *Louisiana Historical Quarterly* 17 (1934): 48–63.

Puckett, Newbell Niles. *Folk Beliefs of the Southern Negro.* Patterson Smith Reprint Series in Criminology, Law Enforcement, and Social Problems, no. 22. Chapel Hill: University of North Carolina Press, 1926; reprint, Montclair: Patterson Smith, 1968.

Robinson, F. L. Interview by author. January 11, 2002. Micanopy, FL. Notes and audio recording. Author's personal collection, Monroe, LA.

Steiner, Roland. "Braziel Robinson Possessed of Two Spirits." *Journal of American Folk-Lore* 14 (1901): 226–228.

———. "Observations on the Practice of Conjuring in Georgia." *Journal of American Folk-Lore* 14 (1901): 173–180.

Tallant, Robert. *Voodoo in New Orleans.* New York: Macmillan, 1946; reprint, Gretna: Pelican, 1998.

Warner, Charles Dudley. *Studies in the South and West, with Comments on Canada.* New York: Harper & Brothers, 1889.

Watson, Wilburn H., ed. *Black Folk Medicine: The Therapeutic Significance of Faith and Trust.* New Brunswick and London: Transaction, 1984.

Williams, Thomas. Interview by author. October 25, 2001. Columbia, SC. Notes. Author's personal collection, Monroe, LA.

Wyatt-Brown, Bertram. *Southern Honor: Ethics and Behavior in the Old South.* New York and Oxford: Oxford University Press, 1982.

Yronwode, Catherine. *Hoodoo Herb and Root Magic: A Materia Magica of African-American Conjure and Traditional Formulary Giving the Spiritual Uses of Natural Herbs, Roots, Minerals, and Zoological Curios.* Forestville: Lucky Mojo Curio Company, 2002.

———. Interview by author. Telephone. January 15, 2001. Author's personal collection, Monroe, LA.

Two
Definitions and Classifications

One of the greatest problems in the study of African creole religions is determining just what one's sources are describing. The terminology of hoodoo and Voodoo is often unfamiliar to both scholars and laypersons (see Preface and Chapter 1). Moreover, casual observers frequently conflate different traditions. In keeping with the Western world's predilection for treating Africa as a single, monolithic unit, many wrongly understand Santería and other Afro-Caribbean faiths as mere subsets of a generalized Voodoo, profound religious and historical distinctions notwithstanding. More commonly, popular authors tend to confuse Mississippi Valley Voodoo with Haitian Vodou and West African Vodu. Even the terms and/ or their proper spelling remain disputed, with practitioners, scholars, and the general public often preferring different versions. For instance, what most Cuban and American believers call *Santería,* meaning "the way of the saints," is frequently called by the Yoruba term *Lucumí* by scholars and others wishing to emphasize its West African roots (Murphy, *Santería,* 2, 27; Brandon, 56). Similarly, although most whites call the black creole religion of the Mississippi Valley *Voodoo,* some practitioners prefer *Vodou* to emphasize its ties to Haiti. Many scholars use *Vodun* or *Voudou* to distance the religion from the negative connotations with which whites have invested the more popular *Voodoo.* The following discussion sorts through some of these conceptual problems by tracing the development of African American religion and supernaturalism and its nearest Afro-Latin relatives.

VODU AND OTHER AFRICAN TRADITIONAL RELIGIONS

African religions are many and varied. For centuries the North has been overwhelmingly Islamic. Sub-Saharan Africans have historically put their faith in various indigenous religions, collectively known as African Traditional Religions or African Philosophies. In some areas, such as Angola and Ethiopia, Christianity had become a prominent influence by the heyday of the Atlantic slave trade. Although monotheistic faiths of Asian origin have long been prominent in Africa, the foundation of black creole religions and supernaturalism was a blend of multiple African Traditional Religions. Africa, second largest of the continents, has a stunning array of traditional faiths, rendering any comprehensive treatment of them impossible. The following discussion addresses only those most directly linked to Voodoo, hoodoo, and conjure.

The African faith that scholars most commonly point to as *the* source of Haitian Vodou and Mississippi Valley Voodoo is Vodu, the traditional religion of the West African Ewe and the closely related Fon. Many West Africans, including the Ewe-Fon, have traditionally envisioned the universe as ruled by multiple tiers of gods and spirits. For the Ewe and Fon, Mawu or the spirit couple Mawu-Lisa are the all-powerful creator gods. Most believe them to be distant from their people, and thus they receive little in the way of worship (Rosenthal, *Ewe Voodoo,* 61; Thompson, *Flash of the Spirit,* 166, 167). Much more approachable are the lesser deities, called *voduwo* or *trowo* (singular *vodu* and *tro*). These gods have their own functions and personalities. For instance, Legba, whom the Fon adopted from the Yoruba, is a humorous and clownish but highly important trickster and spokesman for the gods. Dañh-gbi, the spirit of wisdom and earthly happiness, is a great benefactor of humankind, especially the Fon Kingdom of Dahomey. Numerous religious ceremonies, including initiations into various Vodu societies, invoke these and other lesser gods. One feature of Vodu worship that has never ceased to amaze outsiders is the phenomenon of worshippers' possession by such deities (Rosenthal, *Ewe Voodoo,* 1, 135–136; Opoku, 9–10, 14–18; Thompson, *Flash of the Spirit,* 165–167; Ellis, *The Ewe Speaking Peoples,* 56–63).

The spirits of the dead also have great importance in traditional faiths and receive offerings from their descendants, for whom they can bring good or ill. Sometimes, the dead become evil ghosts who seek to harm those who do not protect themselves by sacrificing fowl and suspending the dead birds above paths leading to dwellings. At the other extreme, prominent ancestors can rise into the ranks of lesser deities, as was the case with a legendary fifteenth-century Fon hero named Agasu, who became an important water god to later generations (Ellis, *The Ewe Speaking Peoples,* 83, 84, 101–116).

Below lesser deities and the ancestors are a wide range of additional spiritual beings and forces. One nineteenth-century observer recorded a vast array of local deities associated with particular bodies of water, hills, and other geographic features. Other such beings are the animistic spirits of animals or plants sacred to specific clans. The Ewe also believe that each person has his or her own indwelling spirit, to whom he or she offers sacrifices. Furthermore, Fon-Ewe supernaturalism relies heavily on amulets, which possess spiritual potency. Although these do not have spirits of their own, believers consider them to have powers emanating from deities (Ellis, *The Ewe Speaking Peoples,* 77–116).

Other West African peoples who unwillingly contributed immigrants to the New World had similar beliefs, although with numerous variations for each ethnicity. For instance, the Yoruba have a spiritual hierarchy that closely resembles that of the Fon and Ewe. A stress on *àshe,* a commanding power originating in the supreme being and residing in spiritually powerful animals, plants, objects, and people is one feature that sets the Yoruban religion apart from that of its neighbors. Another West African people, the Igbo, have a highly developed tradition of wisdom and supernaturalism known as *dibia,* which makes practitioners especially important in their society (Thompson, *Flash of the Spirit,* 5–9; Umeh, vol. 1, 1). Their importance is indicated by an Igbo proverb, "*Chukwu welu; Olu Dibia,*" which in English means "After God is dibia" (Umeh, Vol. 1, 2).

Religious societies operated throughout much of West Africa. Some examples are the modern Fon-Ewe *Gorovodu* and *Mama Tchamba* societies, which have recently received substantial treatment by anthropologist Judy Rosenthal. These have long been important orders that regulate not only the religious beliefs and rituals of members and their locales but also shape laws and otherwise order society (*Possession, Ecstasy, and Law in Ewe Voodoo,* 1). The Ewe and Fon are far from unique in their institutions. For example, the Krobo of modern Ghana have a sisterhood of their own in the Dipo Society. Farther west, Mande speakers created the male Poro and female Sande societies, which had spread to neighboring peoples by the nineteenth century. The Efik of the Niger River Delta have long had a leopard society, called the *Ekpe* or *Ngbe* Order (Gomez, 94–102; Olmos and Paravisini-Gebert, 87–88).

Traditional religionists from elsewhere in Africa crossed the Atlantic as well. Chief among them were slaves from West Central Africa, most notably from the Kingdom of the Kongo. Their traditional faith during the era of the heaviest slaving in the area shared much with the beliefs of West Africans. Most conspicuously, the Kongo religion had multiple gods. At the apex of the universe was Nzambi Mpungu, a supreme being, who roughly corresponded to the Ewe Mawu or Igbo Chukwu. On the other hand, the spirits of the dead held greater importance there than they typically garnered in West Africa. The ancestors, known as *Bakulu,* were next in importance to Nzambi Mpungu and were honored in numerous ceremonies. Below the *Bakulu* were three more classes of supernatural beings, all of whom had also once been living humans but had not achieved the status of honored ancestors. Souls could even reincarnate in living humans. This universal centrality of humanity is enshrined in the Kongo cosmogram, which in its simplest form resembles a plus symbol (+). This cosmogram symbolized a great many things to traditional Kongo believers, including the circulation of souls through the universe in the same way the points of the two lines can be understood as orbiting their point of intersection (MacGaffey, 63–89; Thompson, *Flash of the Spirit,* 108–116).

Similarly, supernaturalism was as important to the Kongo people as it was to West Africans. At the heart of much of their magic was the *nkisi* (plural *minkisi*), a type of charm. Each of them included magical materials, called *bilongo,* and a soul, called *mooyo.* One of the most popular materials that embodied these souls was graveyard dirt because of its direct connection to the dead. Such charms took a variety of forms, ranging from bags tied shut with string to cauldrons. Depending on the intentions of the maker, *minkisi* could serve either good or evil purposes (Thompson, *Flash of the Spirit,* 117–131).

Unlike many peoples, however, West Central Africans had early and persistent contact with Christianity. In 1491, the Kingdom of the Kongo officially adopted Catholicism and worked to convert surrounding peoples, although scholars continue to debate the pervasiveness of the new belief. The Kongo cosmogram acquired new meaning in light of the Christian cross, which it so strongly resembled, and religious objects often took on the protective roles of traditional *minkisi* charms. Problems between the Christian concept of the soul that enters either heaven or hell upon death and the Kongo idea that souls continued to circulate through the living world were generally ignored. All told, this syncretism in Africa was not terribly different from what would take place in the New World (Thornton, 71–90).

AFRO-LATIN CREOLE RELIGION AND SUPERNATURALISM

The slave trade ripped millions of Africans from their people, resettling them in lands far from their homes. This diaspora resulted in large black populations throughout much of the New World. Wherever Africans went, they carried their religious and magical traditions. In their new homes, blacks of diverse ethnic backgrounds faced daunting conditions: absence of traditional religious leaders, flora and fauna unknown in Africa, and systems of forced labor. In addition, they encountered Native Americans and Europeans, whose beliefs often radically differed from their own. The new environment and cultures they encountered required Africans to creatively reinterpret their faiths. The consequence was the rise of numerous creole beliefs—that is, religious and magical systems that arose in the New World out of African transplants. In all cases, blacks abandoned part of their own practices and adopted some belonging to those peoples they encountered, a process called syncretization. Modern Latin American nations have a variety of African creole religions, which differ by country or even by region within countries.

Vodou

Probably the best known of all creole faiths of the African Diaspora is Haitian Vodou. Generations of authors have made it famous by alleging ties with black magic, human sacrifice, and cannibalism. Although such writings grossly mis-characterize the faith, Vodou is certainly worthy of attention. It is a religion that has long influenced the lives of the citizens of the Western Hemisphere's second oldest independent nation (Métraux, 15, 16).

The origins of Vodou stretch back to the late seventeenth century, when French colonists began importing African slaves. In Haiti, conditions were so brutal that slaves felt compelled to resist—sometimes violently. An early rebel against white brutality was Makandal, who was a type of runaway slave known as a maroon. Transforming himself into a messianic figure, he gathered a band of followers. They used poison as a weapon of terror against whites until Makandal was captured in 1757 and burnt at the stake (Métraux, 25–57; Olmos and Paravisini-Gebert, 101–105).

A 1791 Vodou ceremony led by a priest named Boukman was reportedly the event that launched the Haitian Revolution, the only successful slave revolt in modern history. In 1803, the slave rebels established Haitian independence from France. The Catholic Church promptly withdrew its clergy, allowing Vodou to develop with comparatively little outside influence for decades. After the return of the clergy in 1860, the Haitian government sometimes embraced Vodou but generally frowned upon it, conducting large-scale campaigns to suppress it in 1896, 1913, and 1941. Nevertheless, Vodou survived alongside Catholicism as the religion of the average Haitian (Métraux, 25–57; Olmos and Paravisini-Gebert, 101–105).

The faith evolved into a complex blend of multiple African religions and Christianity. There is, for instance, a supreme god, named Bondyé, from the French *bon dieu,* meaning "good God" (Brown, *Mama Lola,* 4, 111). Bondyé takes the place of various African supreme beings, as well as the Christian God. Below Bondyé are the lwas or loas, a term evidently derived from the Yoruba word *l'awo,* meaning "mystery." These spirits or lesser deities are themselves di-vided into nations, based on their African origin. The most commonly called upon lwa are those of the Rada nation, which believers consider calm and gentle. The word *Rada* is a reference to their traditional point of origin, Arada in the Fon Kingdom of Dahomey. Next in importance to the Rada nation are the violent and hot-tempered Petwo lwa. They are especially revered as workers of magic. The origin of Petwo gods has yet to be determined with certainty, but tradition describes them as originating in Haiti under the oppression of slavery. Recent scholarship, however, has demonstrated that several Petwo spirits show markedly West Central African features and often have names with Kongo counterparts. Numerous other lwa nations exist, but they are less prominent and continue to decline in importance. They bear the names of a variety of African peoples and regions, including but not limited to the Ibo (Igbo), Nago (Yoruba), Siniga (Senegal), Congo, and Wangol (Angola) (Thompson, *Flash of the Spirit*, 166, 167; Heusch, 293–299; Geggs, 21–41; Métraux, 83–141, 324–330).

That these spirits typically have counterparts in Catholic saints is evidence of the influence of Christianity. For instance, Papa Legba, a Rada deity who opens communication between humans and other lwa, corresponds to St. Peter, keeper of the keys of heaven. Danbala, the Haitian version of the Fon serpent deity Dañh-gbi, is matched with St. Patrick, who traditionally appears with snakes at his feet in Catholic iconography. Some believers understand such saint/deity correspondences as meaning that the two are the same being, but others argue that they are separate entities with intertwined functions. Scholars have devoted considerable effort to unraveling the reason for the god-saint syncretism, and most have concluded that it initially developed as a way for slaves to continue traditional religious practices by disguising African deities behind a mask of Christianity. Blacks would understand that they were worshipping an African deity, although they might call it by a saint's name before whites. On the other hand, it is possible that the correspondences developed in the Catholic Kingdom of the Kongo, along the Christian-influenced West African coast, or simultaneously in both regions (Métraux, 324–330; Geggs, 21–41; Heusch, 290–299).

Haitian believers, like their African forebears, honor a variety of other spirits who do not quite reach the importance of deities. The spirits of the dead, for instance, are honored in elaborate funerary rites, which include ritual bathing of bodies, burial of the dead with the tools they used in life, and offerings of food. There is also a special reverence for the *Twins*, a divine pair, which has parallels in a vast array of African societies. Animistic beliefs are present as well. Each living thing as well as geographic features—even fields—have their own spirits. In addition, there is a general spirit of the earth that roughly corresponds to the Yoruba *àshe* (Métraux, 146–156, 243–265).

Vodou ritual resembles that of many African peoples. Numerous ceremonies of worship and initiation combine offerings, dance, ritual drumming to summon the lwa, and the drawing of sacred images, called *vèvè*, which likely originated as a fusion of Fon and Kongo originals. During these ceremonies, as in West Africa, the gods enter the bodies of their devotees through possession, communicating their wishes and advising supplicants on important matters. Although heads of families often preside over ceremonies honoring deceased kin, the primary religious specialists in Vodou are priests and priestesses, called *oungans* and *manbos,* respectively. The faithful conduct most of their public ceremonies in a temple, called an *ounfo* (Thompson, *Flash of the Spirit,* 188–191; Daniel, 1–12; Olmos and Paravisini-Gebert, 106–109; Murphy, *Working the Spirit,* 10–43).

Vodou is not a hierarchical religion, although it is certainly an organized one. Each ounfo operates independently. Its head oungan or manbo is an authoritative interpreter of the faith. In addition to the sense of community conveyed by participation in congregational ounfo rituals, Vodou is organized by a form of lineage based around a series of initiations into different levels of spiritual and ritual knowledge. Initiates owe respect to those who initiated them, much as a child should honor his or her parents. Secret societies also exist, providing yet another form of organization. The most famous of these is the Bizango society, although it is but one of many (Thompson, *Flash of the Spirit,* 188–191; Daniel, 1–12; Olmos and Paravisini-Gebert, 106–109, 124–130).

Supernaturalism is an important part of Haitians' beliefs. The world is familiar with zombies, for instance. The "zombie of the body" is by far the best known of multiple varieties that exist in Vodou belief. These are the living dead, reanimated by malevolent sorcerers to be used as servants. In the *Serpent and the Rainbow,* scholar Wade Davis argues that such zombies do exist, although as living people trapped in a drug-induced semiconscious state. Zombies of the body are rare, even in folk belief; much more common are "zombies of the soul," which are human souls captured by the living and used for a variety of tasks ranging from destroying harvests to checking children's homework. The African ethnic origin of the zombie concept has never been definitively proven, although beings of similar names and reputations are found among the Ewe and Mina of West Africa and the Kongo and related peoples of West Central Africa (Ackermann and Gauthier, 466–469, 474–484).

Haitian supernaturalism is not zombie-centric, however. Oungans and manbos are known for fashioning protective and luck-producing charms. They similarly administer herbal baths and make powders designed to heal illnesses, help clients obtain jobs, and otherwise better their situations. Just as important, priests usually engage in divination, most commonly by using cards. It is through such supernatural practices—all of which have African precedents, with the exception of card reading—that many oungans and manbos earn their livings. In opposition to Vodou's clergy are evil sorcerers called *bokors,* whose profession is to harm the enemies of paying clients. In addition to practicing zombification, many bokors can reputedly transform themselves into *loups-garous* (Haitian werewolves) and produce wangas, magical packets of West Central African origin used to harm enemies (Métraux, 266–322; Olmos and Paravisini-Gebert, 126, 127; Hall, *Africans in Colonial Louisiana,* 302).

Next to Vodou, Cuba's African creole religions are the best known. In Haiti, the traditional religions of various African peoples fused with Catholicism to form Vodou, with its many ethnic nations of deities. Cuba was different. There, distinct African faiths survived. Today, the two most prominent are Santería, also known as Lukumí or Regla de Ocho, and Palo Monte Mayombe. In addition, a male

One of New Orleans' best known modern Voodoo shops. Its products derive primarily from Haitian Vodou. Author's personal collection.

magical and religious society known as the Abakuá Society has survived as an entity largely independent of either faith.

Santería, the best known of these religions, is primarily Yoruba in origin. The Yoruba were and are a numerous West African people who in some ways resembled—and often fought with—their Fon and Ewe neighbors. In consequence, Santería resembles Vodou in its cosmology. At the head of the universe stands Olorun, an exalted and distant supreme being. Below Olorun are the orishas, equivalents of Vodou's lwas. In many cases, the kinship between orishas and lwas is evident. For example, Vodou's Legba is easily recognizable as the orisha Eleguá, whose similar name and almost identical functions demonstrates their common Yoruba heritage. In addition, as do Haitian lwas, Cuban orisha each have a corresponding saint. The term *Santería,* meaning "the way of the saints," reflects this fact (Olmos and Paravisini-Gebert, 24–60; Murphy, *Santería,* 2).

Despite their many commonalities, Vodou and Santería are not identical. One obvious distinction between them is the number of their deities. Haitians honor a vast array of spirits, made possible both by inter-African syncretism and the elevation of the honored dead to godheads. One author has collected the names of 232 different lwas in one far-from-exhaustive list. He went on to state that "scarcely one hundred pages would suffice to mention all the loas" (Rigaud, 51–58, quote from 58). In contrast, there are only 15 important orishas. Below the orishas are the ancestors, personal guardian spirits, and a variety of lesser spiritual beings. The survival of the clearly defined Yoruba concept of *àshe* under the name *aché* similarly sets Santería apart from Vodou. As in Africa, it remains an impersonal spiritual force that pervades the universe (Olmos and Paravisini-Gebert, 60–62; Brandon, 16, 76, 77; Murphy, *Santería,* 42–43).

As with African Traditional Faiths, Santería has its own series of initiations through which the faithful advance in spiritual knowledge and leadership. As believers progress through this process, they may also choose to enter the priesthood. Comparable to Vodou's oungans and manbos are the babalochas and iyalochas. Babalochas and iyalochas (roughly meaning "father of the saints" and "mother of the saints," respectively) are the "general practitioner" priests of Santería. There are also two major types of specialized priests. Oriaté priests, who are more highly trained than babalochas and iyalochas, preside over most initiations and possess detailed knowledge of almost all aspects of their faith, including ritual formulas still spoken in Yoruba. The second type of specialist is the babalao. Babalaos are the most respected of the Santería priesthood, largely because of their profound knowledge of divination. Priests of all stripes, however, have roles in Santería's worship rituals, which like Vodou, include music, dancing, and possession (Olmos and Paravisini-Gebert, 51, 52, 69–73; Murphy, *Santería,* 92, 93).

Supernaturalism is an important part of Santería, especially in the form of Yoruba-derived divination, one of the priests' primary duties. There are four important types of divination: direct messages from the deities during possession, the Obi, dilogún, and Ifá. Any believer can experience possession or practice Obi, the latter of which involves prayer, asking questions of the spirits, and casting four pieces of dried coconut shell onto a floor. The diviner then interprets the combination of upturned white and dark sides to communicate messages to clients. Dilogún divination, which is both more respected and complex, centers on the casting of 16 cowrie shells. It is the province of priests alone. The resulting patterns of shells with their mouths facing upward instructs the priest on the message to be communicated, as well as the actions required of the client. The most prestigious of all divining methods is Ifá, which is restricted to babalaos. It relies on a combination of two major tools, the ekuele chain and the palm nuts and divining table. As with Obi and dilogún divination, the key is casting the tools and interpreting patterns. In the case of Ifá, many thousands of combinations can result, each of which has its own instructions and folk stories attached. Babalaos must study for years to become adepts (Olmos and Paravisini-Gebert, 62–69).

A second Cuban faith, Palo Monte Mayombe, is of Kongo descent. It is quite prominent in Cuba but much less respected than Santería. As two American authors put it, "In contrast to Santería, which is predominantly used for good or neutral purposes, Palo Mayombe is primarily oriented toward malevolent sorcery" (Wetli and Martinez, 629). The ritual murders of 24 people by nominal practitioner Adolfo de Jesus Constanzo during the mid-to-late 1980s furthered this perception (Humes, ix–2). Palo is certainly less concerned with honoring deities than in controlling spirits of the dead for practical ends. Practitioners, referred to as *paleros,* keep the spirits they control in iron cauldrons, commonly called *ngangas,* a type of Kongo-style *nkisi.* To make their cauldrons, paleros place a combination of human body parts, all or portions of various plants and animals, alcohol, spices, graveyard dirt, and sticks (called *palos*) within the receptacle. The *nganga* is then buried, first in a graveyard and then in nature. Once the ritual is properly carried out, a spirit enters the cauldron and commands the spirits of the other items placed therein. It must serve its maker, however, carrying out his or her wishes for good or ill. Palo Monte Mayombe has its own deities, most notably the spirit Zarabanda, who hails from the Kongo, but believers often follow Santería as well (Olmos and Paravisini-Gebert, 78–82; Thompson, *Face of the Gods,* 60–63).

Cuba's Abakuá Society arose from the Efik, Efut, and Ejagham peoples who initially dwelt in the Cross River area of West Africa, whom the Spanish collectively referred to as Carabalí. In Africa, it was a male secret society dedicated to the jaguar. Members of the Abakuá Society are known as *Ñáñigos.* Although the society is not a full-fledged religion in its own right, membership in the society requires *Ñáñigos* to undergo initiation and to participate in ceremonies that typically include music and dancing. The society has long been known for its parades and public festivals, but it also serves as a source of practical assistance for members, to an extent resembling the mutual aid aspect of labor unions (Olmos and Paravisin-Gebert, 87–95; Thompson, *Flash of the Spirit,* 228, 229; Daniel, 135–137).

The folk religions of Cuba and Haiti are only a few of a wide array of African creole faiths. In Bahia Brazil, many practice a Yoruba-derived religion known as Candomblé. Jamaica has two magical systems, obeah for evil deeds and myal for beneficial acts. In fact, the existence of one or more systems of religion and/or magic is the rule rather than the exception for those regions of the New World in which Africans arrived in significant numbers. The faiths of Haiti and Cuba have proven far more important to the North American experience than religions from elsewhere, however, because of the frequent cultural interchanges between the United States and these island nations.

TRADITIONAL NORTH AMERICAN CREOLE RELIGION AND SUPERNATURALISM

Traditional Voodoo, hoodoo, and conjure, the practice of which was described in Chapter 1, have histories distinct but sometimes interacting with those of

Afro-Latin faiths. Based on historical distinctions, scholars have divided the creole beliefs of African Americans into two major cultural regions. Each region is based on the countries of origin of those whites who imported African slaves into them. One, called the Latin Cultural Zone, encompasses the Mississippi River Valley and the Gulf Coast from Florida to Texas. It may be subdivided into three subregions: the upper Mississippi Valley, the lower Mississippi Valley and western Gulf of Mexico, and the eastern Gulf of Mexico. The local versions of creole beliefs are distinguishable by characteristics shaped by unique ethnic mixes of white and black settlers and Native Americans. The Anglo Cultural Zone is the second major region and initially encompassed an area along the Atlantic coast stretching from northern Florida to Maryland and to a lesser extent the Northeast. Like the Latin Zone, it includes regional variations that can be designated the upper Atlantic and lower Atlantic, with North Carolina forming a borderland. The Anglo Zone, like the United States itself, spread westward over time, eventually mixing with the Latin culture in those areas near the Mississippi River and Gulf Coast (Long, *Spiritual Merchants,* 17, 71; Anderson, *Conjure,* 25–27).

The Latin Cultural Zone

The Latin Cultural Zone is so called because of its initial white settlers, the French and Spanish. By the early eighteenth century, the Spanish had been established in Florida and Texas for a century-and-a-half. Nevertheless, settlers were small in number throughout the colonial era, although the number of Hispanics in the region has risen dramatically since the early nineteenth century because of immigration, especially from Cuba into Florida, and Mexico into Texas. The French, who settled the Mississippi River Valley and portions of the Gulf Coast stretching from West Florida to Texas were likewise small in number, but the concentration of French settlers in New Orleans provided a locus of French culture unmatched by the Spanish.

Voodoo and Hoodoo

Voodoo is a religious faith unique to the Mississippi River Valley, although it was strongest near the river's mouth, especially in the city of New Orleans. The earliest evidence for the existence of Voodoo in Louisiana comes from a mid-eighteenth-century history of the then-French colony. Speaking of a time several years earlier, its author, Le Page du Pratz, recorded that slaves would gather on Sundays to "make a kind of a *Sabbath*" (Du Pratz, 271). He offers little more description, the racial assumptions of the day rendering white interest in the details of black culture unusual. Nevertheless, Du Pratz also wrote of the presence of gris-gris, magical bag charms, the name for which derives from the Mande language of the Senegambian region of extreme West Africa. Another type of charm, called zinzin, found in Louisiana by the nineteenth century, was likewise of Senegambian origin. Although little else is known about the early form of this African creole faith, some version was clearly in place during the early colonial era (Du Pratz, 255; Hall, *Africans in Colonial Louisiana,* 163).

The Senegambian influence on Voodoo remained strong throughout the colonial era and nineteenth century, but as time went by, other African peoples made their mark on Voodoo. Both linguistic and religious features point to the Bight of Benin region of West Africa as a major source of Voodoo beliefs. The Bight of Benin roughly corresponds to the coasts of modern-day Benin and its neighbors and includes the Ewe and closely-related Fon peoples. Among the features identifying the faith as heavily influenced by the Fon and Ewe is its name, *Voodoo,* which is the anglicized form of the West African *Vodu,* which means roughly "god" or "spirit" and is the name of the religion that honors them. Those deities worshipped by Voodoo adherents indicate the same regional origin. Blanc Dani, Vert Agoussou, Vériquité, Papa Lébat, and Assonquer are some of the prominent gods mentioned in sources from the nineteenth and early twentieth centuries. Of these, the first three came directly from the Fon and Ewe. Papa Lébat probably also arrived with slaves of Fon-Ewe heritage, although their Yoruba neighbors were probably the first to worship him. Assonquer, on the other hand, seems to be the direct descendant of the Yoruban Osanyin (Rosenthal, *Ewe Voodoo,* 1; Thompson, *Flash of the Spirit,* 66–67, 176–178; Anderson, "Voodoo," forthcoming).

Another African region to contribute to the cultural ferment of Voodoo was West Central Africa. The most evident contribution of this largely ignored group was the wanga, sometimes also known as a *ounga.* Wangas were originally harmful charms used by the Kongo people. By the late nineteenth and early twentieth century, wangas had become so strongly associated with Voodoo that priests, priestesses, and magic workers were known as *wangateurs* and *wangateuses,* referring to male and female purveyors of wangas, respectively. In addition, there is a possibility that a New Orleans-area spirit referred to as Unkus was a corruption of the Kongo word *nkisi,* meaning charm. Some modern Spiritual churches, which incorporate significant African elements, honor this same spirit under the name of Uncle with a bucket filled with sand into which are inserted three small American flags. It usually resides on an altar in the rear of the churches. The bucket and flags call to mind Palo *nganga* cauldrons, further suggesting the possibility of Kongo ties. That there are no mentions of either an Unkus or Uncle spirit before the twentieth century and because this spirit is now associated only with Spiritual churches, however, leaves its Kongo origins in some doubt (Hall, *Africans in Colonial Louisiana,* 302; Hyatt, *Hoodoo,* 1295–1309; Jacobs and Kaslow, 114–116).

Voodoo's blend of features from multiple African societies is a consequence of shifting slave importation patterns. The reason for Senegambian and Bight

Table 2.1: Sample of Unique Words Used in the Mississippi Valley and Their African Origins

Word	Meaning	African Place of Origin	African Meaning
Voodoo	Religion of some African Americans in the Mississippi Valley	Ewe-Fon	*vodu*—General name for lesser deities
hoodoo	Magic, originally conceived as a part of Voodoo	Ewe and/or Mina	In various forms "spirit work" or a specific Vodu ceremony, respectively
gris-gris	Bag charm identified with New Orleans	Mande	*gerregerys* or *gregorys*—Senegambia bag charm
zinzin	Charm of support or power	Mande	*zinzin*—charm for support or power
wanga	Harmful charm	Kongo	*wanga*—magical charm
Papa Lébat	Trickster and doorkeeper of the deities (corresponded to St. Peter)	Yoruba by way of Ewe-Fon	Legba—trickster and doorkeeper of the gods
Blanc Dani	Particularly powerful serpent deity (corresponded to St. Michael)	Ewe-Fon	Dañh-gbi, Da—python deity and chief earth god
Assonquer	Deity of good fortune (corresponded to St. Paul)	Yoruba	Osanyin—deity of herbalism

SOURCES: Long, *New Orleans Voudou Priestess*, 94; Rosenthal, e-mail to the author; Hall, *Africans in Colonial Louisiana*, 163, 302; Anderson, *Conjure*, 32–33, 58; Thompson, *Flash of the Spirit*, 166–167.

of Benin elements is simple. Between 1719 and 1743—the founding generation of Louisiana slavery—more than 29 percent of all slaves came from Ouidah (also known as Whydah) a port on the Bight of Benin. More than double that percentage (approximately 66%) hailed from Senegambia. During this earlier period, only one ship arrived from West Central Africa, rendering its inhabitants relatively unimportant to the early formation of Voodoo (Hall, *Africans in Colonial Louisiana,* 60).

The situation reversed during the late eighteenth century during the Spanish administration of Louisiana, when slave cargos were heavily from West Central Africa. Within these shipments, slaves of Kongo origin formed by far the largest ethnicity. One might reasonably have expected the late dominance of West Central Africans to have erased many of Voodoo's West African features. It did not, in part because of the late eighteenth- and early nineteenth-century influx of approximately 15,000 Haitian immigrants who brought Vodou with them. Vodou's Fon-Ewe features helped bolster the existing West African character of early Voodoo. After the U.S. acquisition of the Louisiana Territory, the influence of specific ethnicities declined in the face of in-migration from the Anglo Cultural Zone (Hall, *Africans in Colonial Louisiana*, 276–315; Gomez, 150–153; Dessens, 11–45).

Lower Mississippi Valley Voodoo was merely the best known form of the religion. It also existed along the upper Mississippi River and its tributaries. For example, Dick Perry, author of a popular history of Cincinnati, Ohio, wrote that in 1849 the city's African American population performed ceremonies along the public landing to drive off a cholera epidemic. According to him, the ceremony involved chanting, producing rhythm by beating sticks on the ground, and prayer (Perry, 37). Similarly, in an 1891 report to the International Folk-Lore Congress, Mary Alicia Owen attested that Voodoo was still practiced in northern Missouri during the 1890s. Like New Orleans Voodoo, the Missouri version required a form of initiation and involved ritual dances and occasional animal sacrifice. Although the name of but a single deity, Samunga, survived into the late nineteenth century, his presence hints at a once-broader pantheon. Moreover, this collection of deities almost certainly differed from that of the Louisiana area, where Samunga appears to have been absent. There were also etymological differences between the areas. For instance, King Alexander used the word *obeah* to refer to practitioners from farther south while referring to himself as a *Voodoo*. Owen reported that laypersons referred to all practitioners as *Voodoos* and their doings as *noodoos*. The remaining data on Voodoo in the upper Mississippi Valley is sparse, but the extant material indicates a distinctive local variety (Owen, "Among the Voodoos," 241).

Hoodoo, according to modern usage, is a form of African American folk magic that operates independent of the gods, communal ceremonies, and other religious trappings of Voodoo. Most scholars draw no distinction between conjure and hoodoo. Indeed, since the early twentieth century, the two have been synonymous. Historically, however, they appear to have developed along distinctly different paths. The English word *conjure* was in use during colonial times along the Atlantic Coast but was unknown in the French- and later Spanish-ruled Mississippi River Valley. *Hoodoo,* probably already in use before the nineteenth century, seems to have initially appeared in print during the first half of the 1860s in reference to practitioners from Memphis, Tennessee. The term's use increased throughout the late nineteenth and early twentieth centuries, usually but not exclusively in connection with the Mississippi River Valley. It was not until the early decades of the twentieth century that African Americans adopted *hoodoo* to refer to magical practices outside the Latin Cultural Zone. The reason for the shift likely stemmed from Louisiana hoodoo's reputation for success and the rise of blues music—itself centered on the Mississippi—which makes frequent references to supernaturalism as *hoodoo.* In short, the Latin Zone appears to have been the home of a distinctive brand of magic that later blended with non-Latin conjure to create modern African American supernaturalism (Randolph, 17–21; Yronwode, *Southern Spirits,* http://www.southern-spirits.com/anon-voudooism-in-memphis.html; Anderson, *Conjure,* 28, 195).

There can be little doubt that hoodoo and Voodoo were not separated before the late nineteenth century. During the 1880s, prominent author George Washington Cable noted that what whites referred to as *Voodoo,* African Americans called *hoodoo* (Cable, "Creole Slave Songs," 815). Likewise, during the same era, author Thaddeus Norris used the latter term to speak of what is usually now known as New Orleans Voodoo (Norris, 92–93). Initially, *hoodoo* referred to a segment or segments of the West African *Vodu* faith. One likely source for the word as used in the lower Mississippi Valley are the Ewe words *hu* and *do* or *edo.* When used together, they can mean spirit work, among other things. Another possibility is the Mina *hudu* ritual, which means "eating of blood." The translation literally refers to the ceremonial consumption of kola nuts that have been covered with the blood of sacrificial animals and/or sauces made from their blood and figuratively to the spiritual forces ingested by doing so (Rosenthal, e-mail to the author). That many of the words associated with Louisiana Voodoo and hoodoo have origins in Senegambia and the Bight of Benin supports this interpretation of hoodoo. At the same time, because hoodoo's aims became more and more magical in nature as it grew increasingly distinct from its religious origins, it certainly adopted beliefs from other parts of Africa. After all, those seeking primarily practical results need not stay true to a particular ethnic or religious heritage.

Despite the interactions of various African cultures that occurred in both cultural regions, historical hoodoo differed from conjure. For instance, the common use of beef hearts in the lower Mississippi Valley was rare outside of the area. Similarly, calling on deities other than the Christian God was virtually unknown by the nineteenth century outside of the Latin Cultural Zone. Doing so was common in the lower Mississippi Valley, eastern Gulf Coast, and to a lesser extent the upper Mississippi Valley. At the same time, French and Spanish influence led to the incorporation of saint images, candles, and other Catholic paraphernalia into the Latin Zone's supernaturalism, features that were largely absent from the practices of the Anglo Zone (Long, *Spiritual Merchants,* 56; Anderson, *Conjure,* 94; Cable, *Grandissimes,* 100–101; Owen, "Among the Voodoos," 241–242).

Spiritual Churches

Apparent descendants of nineteenth-century Voodoo and hoodoo are the modern Spiritual churches. Their exact origin is obscure, but they seem to have arisen in the early twentieth century in various parts of the United States. Hans

A small New Orleans Spiritual Church before Hurricane Katrina. Author's personal collection.

Baer, author of *The Black Spiritual Movement,* identified Chicago, New Orleans, New York, Detroit, and Kansas City as major centers of early Spiritual church activity. Basing his interpretation on documentary sources that trace the founding of early Spiritual churches to the first two decades of the twentieth century, Baer concluded that the Great Migration of rural southern blacks to the urban North led to the rise of this new belief system. His interpretation raises questions about just where the new beliefs came from. Quite possibly there were already prototypes for the Spiritual churches operating in the South. At any rate, all scholars agree that the Spiritual churches underwent significant development in the context of New Orleans Voodoo and hoodoo (Baer, *Spiritual Church Movement,* 17–24; Jacobs and Kaslow, 30–48).

According to many accounts, the first Spiritual churches in New Orleans were founded by Leafy Anderson, who supposedly began the first congregation there sometime around 1920. Anderson, however, appears to have originally considered herself a Spiritualist. Spiritualism, a religion based around contacting spirits of the dead, was founded in 1848 in New York and quickly gained considerable popularity throughout the country, including New Orleans. Its services centered on calm séances in darkened rooms, during which spirits, usually of departed relatives, communicated messages to the living. In keeping with her understanding of Spiritualism, Anderson reportedly denied any connection to either Voodoo or hoodoo, and later observers of her congregations support this interpretation (Jacobs and Kaslow, 30–48; Weisberg, 1–8).

Whatever Anderson's vision may have been, modern Spiritual churches clearly bear the marks of African American creole religions and supernaturalism. The most obvious difference between Spiritualist and Spiritual churches is the nature of their meetings. New Orleans's Spiritual church services are anything but sedate séances. One scholar of African American religion and supernaturalism reported on a 2001 service that involved singing, dancing, and a cleansing ritual during which believers stood on a folded cloth and were repeatedly struck by flowers that had been dipped in salt water. Because of the fragmentary nature of historical records addressing African American creole beliefs in New Orleans, the ceremony cannot be definitively traced to a particular Voodoo ceremony. Still, such exuberance is in keeping with Voodoo, not Spiritualism (Anderson, *Conjure,* 156–157).

Today, most Spiritual people consider themselves Christians, yet they also believe in a wide array of spirits in addition to the Trinity. These include angels and the spirits of the dead. Native American spirits are particularly prominent. In recent years, Jason Berry and other scholars have noted many New Orleans congregations' devotion to Black Hawk, apparently the spirit of an early nineteenth-century leader of Sauk and Fox resistance to the westward movement of whites. Although American Indian spirits figured prominently in antebellum white Spiritualism as well, Black Hawk's unique importance is more likely a legacy of African Americans' identification with him as a fellow sufferer of oppression and of Leafy Anderson's personal emphasis on him. Another feature linking these spirits more strongly to the African American experience than to Spiritualism is the propensity for spirits to possess congregants. Such behavior was typical for Haitian Vodou, Louisiana Voodoo, and many African Traditional Religions. Spiritualists, on the other hand, generally required mediums to convey messages from the dead, although spirits did occupy their bodies on occasion. Just as important, possession in both nineteenth-century Voodoo and modern Spiritual churches can be recognized by one or more of the following symptoms: trance, seizure, prolonged dancing, writhing, sudden unconsciousness, and the making of strange sounds. Such striking indicators of possession have never been prominent in Spiritualism (Anderson, *Conjure,* 73–74; Cox, 189–232; Jacobs and Kaslow, 35–36, 129–147).

In addition to their links to Voodoo, Spiritual churches are strongly tied to supernaturalism. Although most Spiritual people deny any links to hoodoo, they do so on the understanding that it is evil. Their work, they maintain, is good. Outside of the moral dimension, however, hoodoo and Spiritual supernaturalism differ little. For instance, one observer recorded that during a service, church leaders recommended lacing children's bathwater with a specially prepared formula that would make them grow to be good people. David Winslow, reporting on a Spiritual church leader in Philadelphia, stated that the man also operated a shop selling magical goods. Many of the items he carried, including graveyard dirt, incense, and books on Jewish magic, had long been favorites among conjurers. Author Rod Davis noted the same link between Spiritual churches and hoodoo establishments in New Orleans (Anderson, *Conjure,* 122, 142, 156, 157; Winslow, 59–80; Davis, *American Voudou,* 39–41).

The altar of a New Orleans Spiritual Church. Note the blend of Catholic, Native American, and African elements. Of particular interest is the *nganga*-style bucket containing a small flag and Indian bust, in the lower right-hand corner. Author's personal collection.

Ñañigo

This little-known religion of the western Gulf Coast flourished in Tampa and other parts of Florida during the late nineteenth century but quickly faded early in the next century. It was the North American parallel of Cuban folk religions. In fact, based on the small Hispanic population in Florida before Cuban immigration during the nineteenth century, it is likely that Ñañigo derived from the predecessors of modern Santería, Palo Monte Mayombe, and the Abakuá Society. The term for the religion was approximately the same as the modern Cuban word for members of the Abakuá Society, *Ñáñigos*. It also went by the name *Carabali Apapa Abacua,* meaning roughly "Society of the Old Efik," clearly identifying its African regional origin as the same as that of the Cuban Abakuá Society. At the same time, believers worshipped deities of Yoruba heritage, including Elegba and Yemaya, who were also prominent in Cuban Santería. The names for the priests were *papaloi* and *mamaloi,* respectively. These likewise have descended from a Yoruba original, *babalawo,* which translates "father of mysteries" and refers to a type of diviner/herbalist. Santería's babalao diviners are the closest Cuban parallel. In addition, that believers called magical practitioners *brujas,* meaning "witches," suggests a possibility of West Central African influence. In Cuba and the United States, many modern practitioners of Santería consider Palo Monte Mayombe a form of witchcraft because of its capture and manipulation of the spirits of the dead, a clear parallel to the *papaloi/mamaloi-bruja* distinction present in nineteenth-century Ñañigo (Anderson, *Conjure,* 45, 92–93; Olmos and Paravisini-Gebert, 78–80, 87–93, 215; Lopez, 2–3; Boggs, 1–12; Kennedy, "Ñañigo in Florida," 153–156; Thompson, *Flash of the Spirit,* 166; Wetli and Martinez, 629).

One of the chief differences between the situation in Cuba and Florida is that observers discerned no distinctions between faiths of Yoruba and Kongo origin. Perhaps these largely white authors lacked the requisite knowledge to understand such distinctions. On the other hand, the Cuban immigrant population that introduced these faiths may have voluntarily allowed them to merge. After all, they were a small minority in an overwhelmingly white society that lumped them into a single category alongside other "nonwhites." In such circumstances, religious solidarity could have proven very useful.

The Anglo Cultural Zone

Outside of the Mississippi Valley, a different form of African American magic predominated. *Voodoo* and *hoodoo* were terms rarely employed before the late nineteenth century, at which point their usage gradually spread across the South alongside the fame of New Orleans's practitioners. *Conjure* was the preferred word in the Anglo Cultural Zone. In the upper Atlantic subregion, it was also known as *cunning,* like *conjure,* an old English term for magic. Believers referred to practitioners as *cunning doctors, trick doctors, high men* and *women,* and *witches.* On rare occasions, they were even known as *pow-wow* doctors, from a German magical tradition of the same name. The presence of so many English terms reflects the long history of slavery in the region compared to elsewhere. For instance, Virginia was importing slaves for a century or more before the first shipments reached places like Louisiana and Georgia. The greater duration of slavery in the northern Atlantic naturally led to greater acculturation for slaves. Nevertheless, African words were not entirely unknown. *Ubia, ubi, obi, obia,* or *ober,* synonyms for conjure, were most likely of Igbo origin, although many other African peoples used similar words. The word *gombre* was another word for African American supernaturalism of probable African origin (Anderson, *Conjure,* 54, 57–58; Morgan, 612–621; Hyatt, *Hoodoo,* 11, 17, 275, 278, 280–281, 284, 308, 310, 314, 336, 337; S., 28; Puckett, 19).

In the lower Atlantic subregion, the terminology of conjure reflected the comparatively late arrival of its black population, which continued to be legally imported directly from Africa as late as 1808. Among them, peoples of West Central Africa were the most plentiful. The word *conjure* was widely used in South Carolina and Georgia, but other English terms for the practice were rare. The variations of *ubia* were known in South Carolina, as they were in Virginia. More popular was *goopher,* which referred to conjure in general and magic involving the spirits of the dead in particular. It likely derived from the Kongo word, *kufwa*, meaning "to die." An alternative interpretation is that the word came from the Mande term *gafa*, which translates as "spirit" or "idol." *Mojo* or *jomo*, words for bag charms popular throughout the lower South, was of possible Kongo origin, although the paucity of references to it in early documents has made it difficult to determine whether it spread from the Latin or Anglo zones. Several more specific terms survived in the isolated Sea Islands, where Gullahs and Geechees preserved much of their African languages long after those in constant contact with whites had extensively acculturated (Morgan, 620–622; Gomez, 150; Anderson, *Conjure*, 28; Chambers, 52).

Besides terminology, there were other important distinctions, most notably the separation of African American supernaturalism from African religions. Some elements of African faiths did survive. For instance, John Canoe or Jonkonnu Festivals involved drumming, dancing, parading, masking, and ritual attire, doubtless of African religious origin. In Georgia, African Americans undergoing baptism into Christianity frequently prayed to rivers, requesting that the bodies of water cleanse them from sin. This practice reflected the belief in spirits called *simbis*, who inhabited sources of fresh water and were derived from West Central African beings of the same name and habitation (Morgan, 594–595, 599; Georgia Writers' Project, 113, 125, 131; Brown, 312–313).

By the middle of the nineteenth century, African religions had largely disappeared outside the Mississippi River Valley. By the close of the Second Great Awakening, many blacks had converted to Christianity. Moreover, because of tight restrictions on gatherings and other activities, few Anglo Zone slaves had been able to openly practice traditional African faiths, with their associated music, dancing, animal sacrifices, and spirit possession. In contrast to the Catholicism of the Latin Zone, British Protestantism did not have the saints to mask continued devotion to the old gods. In addition, because the Kingdom of the Kongo, an at least nominally Christian nation, supplied so many of the slaves to the lower Atlantic, it is likely that many had abandoned traditional faiths long before reaching the United States (Anderson, *Conjure*, 31–32, 34; Thornton, 83–90).

European elements filled the gaps left as African religion declined in the Anglo Cultural Zone. Bibles, for instance, became powerful conjure texts. A common use was divination. Another was the reading or reciting of psalms during charm preparation. Lucky horseshoes, a good-luck charm of European origin, had likewise entered conjure by the late nineteenth century. Five finger grass, a money-drawing and protective agent in conjure, found its way from European folklore, where it served as a guard against witches. During the late nineteenth and early twentieth centuries, the spread of do-it-yourself hoodoo books, such as Henri Gamache's *Master Book of Candle Burning*, and a growing popular impression that Louisiana hoodoo was highly effective introduced Catholic religious paraphernalia to the Anglo Cultural Zone. Some examples include candles and altars, long popular in Voodoo and the Spiritual churches but comparatively unimportant until recently outside the Mississippi Valley (Yronwode, *Hoodoo Herb and Root Magic,* "Five-Finger Grass"; Anderson, *Conjure,* 51–62, 69–70).

THE SPIRITUAL SUPPLY INDUSTRY

In the past, hoodoo and conjure were the provinces of skilled practitioners or Voodoo priests. Sometime during the nineteenth century, African Americans whose primary profession was the working of magic began to fade in importance. They were replaced by a new institution, known as either the hoodoo shop or spiritual supply store. Alongside old-fashioned items like High John the Conqueror, five finger grass, and candles, these stores began to sell manufactured magical supplies that bore little resemblance to their traditional forebears. Oils, incenses, and eventually aerosol sprays gained popularity and fill much of the shelf space in modern stores. Names like John the Conqueror Oil proclaim their historical ties to magical herbalism, even though their synthetic ingredients often show nothing of the sort. Few owners of such shops spend much time fashioning charms. On the contrary, they are managers of businesses whose chief duty is to supply customer demand for their products. In most cases, employees determine the needs of customers and recommend specific products to achieve the desired results (Long, *Spiritual Merchants,* 99–126; Anderson, *Conjure,* 112–133).

To a significant extent, the development of the spiritual supplies industry simply reflected the general late nineteenth-century growth of big business, but

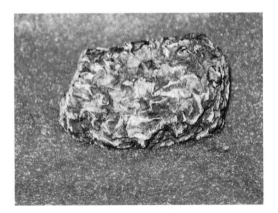

Jalap, the version of High John the Conqueror root most common today. It is unlikely that nineteenth-century hoodoo practitioners used jalap. Author's personal collection.

there were hoodoo-specific peculiarities. Most prominent was the link between spiritual supplies and medicine. For instance, many of the earliest spiritual supply shops developed out of pharmacies. Nineteenth- and early twentieth-century drugstores were where many African Americans purchased herbal products for both medical and magical uses. At some point, probably before the Civil War in New Orleans, some pharmacists recognized that there was a market for hoodoo supplies. A few hoodoo pharmacies eventually gave up the medical side of their business altogether, finding conjure more profitable. Others businesses eventually followed the lead of pharmacies and opened spiritual supply shops that catered only to those seeking magical products. By the early twentieth century, most major cities had hoodoo shops, and advertisements for them appeared in black-oriented periodicals. In response to demand, entrepreneurs opened hoodoo-oriented companies to mass produce spiritual supplies. Many shops and manufacturers even carried on a brisk mail-order business. Today, some have also turned to the Internet for their trade (Anderson, *Conjure,* 115–123; Long, 127–219; Yronwode, interview by author).

The interaction between patent medicines and conjure was another example of the interaction between conjure and medicine. Patent medicines are best defined as nostrums produced and sold for profit by their proprietors. Until the early twentieth century, they were extremely popular, albeit equally varied in efficacy. Manufactured hoodoo took many cues from the patent medicine industry. Most obviously, spiritual goods suppliers' use of newspapers for marketing was identical to the advertising strategy of patent medicine owners. In fact, many dealers in hoodoo goods also sold patent medicines. Moreover, the bottled oils that are so much a part of modern hoodoo strongly resemble patent medicines and may have been partially inspired by them. Like conjure oils that promised love, luck, and victory over enemies, patent medicine made extravagant claims. Some proprietors even claimed that God communicated formulas to them, a practice well attested among hoodoo practitioners. The proprietors of both patent medicines and spiritual supplies touted their products' ability to grant their customers' desires, the most noticeable difference being that hoodoo goods might just as easily promise the death of enemies as the health of customers. In most cases, neither group had much evidence to support its claims. Restrictions placed on the manufacture of patent medicines by the Pure, Food, Drug, and Cosmetics Act of 1938 and similar laws made it equally difficult for hoodoo practitioners to legally make and sell their products (Hyatt, *Hoodoo-Conjuration-Witchcraft-Rootwork,* 1097–1114, 1158–71, 4514; Young, *Toadstool Millionaires,* 144–244; Young, *American Self-Dosage Medicines,* 1–31; Anderson, *Conjure,* 126).

The rise of manufactured hoodoo affected African American supernaturalism in profound ways. For one, it introduced a business owner-consumer association

A common feature of twentieth-century hoodoo, the mail-order catalog, this one from a California-based company. Courtesy of Catherine Yronwode. All rights reserved.

in place of the traditional conjure doctor-client relationship. It also helped to create greater uniformity in the practice of hoodoo, erasing many of the regional distinctions that had once set Anglo Zone conjure apart from Latin Zone hoodoo. On the downside, it aided the larger process by which Americans of all backgrounds became ever more separate from the natural world. More specifically, it detached African Americans from many of the herbal and animal curios and magical concepts that their ancestors had brought from Africa. Moreover, the greater visibility created by large-scale businesses and advertising made it easier for state and national governments to suppress such "superstitions" by prosecuting practitioners for mail fraud, practicing medicine without a license, and other alleged crimes (Anderson, *Conjure,* 149; Long, *Spiritual Merchants,* 131–139, 145).

HOODOO, CONJURE, AND VOODOO
IN THE POSTMODERN NEW AGE

Today, spiritual supply shops and traditional practitioners carry on their business, even as hoodoo continues to evolve. Recent intellectual trends have done much to transform conjure from a shunned aspect of African American life into an oft-accepted form of supernaturalism in which anyone can participate. The rise of the postmodern movement among artists and intellectuals has helped undermine old ideas about conjure and Voodoo. At the center of postmodern thinking is the idea that all moral authority is subjective and can be defined only by the individual. Such thinking has worked alongside a growing appreciation of African American heritage to significantly expand attention to the place of supernaturalism and creole religions in black life. An increasing volume of artworks and literature celebrating them reflect this new outlook. Likewise, many African American women view the practice of conjure as a way to connect with their African past and a long tradition of powerful female hoodoo practitioners. No longer can Voodoo simply be defined as diabolic by those hostile to it, at least not without challenge (Harvey, *Condition of Postmodernity,* 43; Anderson, *Conjure,* 18–21, 140–149; Yronwode, interview by author; Savage, interview by author).

Among scholars and other consumers of high culture, the effects of postmodernism are readily apparent, but to most practitioners and believers, they are not so obvious. To them, the New Age and neopagan movements have been far more important. The closely related movements, in fact, can be understood as popular culture's version of postmodernism. Most notably, both postmodernists and New Agers/neopagans reject traditional sources of authority and maintain that individual experience and belief should guide one's outlook. New Age adherents and neopagans, who are largely affluent whites, tend to create personal collages of beliefs from different cultures and peoples rather than adopting Christianity or whatever else is normative for others of their background (Kylc, 10–11, 27–39, 49–53, 57–74; Heelas, 106–132; Baker, *New Consciousness,* 15–16; Faber, 1–16).

This approach to spirituality has led many whites to incorporate elements of hoodoo into their personal beliefs and practice. Some have gone so far as to pursue serious study of conjure as evidenced by the hundreds of students who take Catherine Yronwode's Hoodoo Rootwork Correspondence Course each year. One consequence of the partial breakdown of taboos against white participation is that hoodoo is becoming increasingly multicultural. The growing diversity of practitioners and believers is further accelerating the acceptance of conjure as something other than evil. At the same time, New Age/neopagan attention threatens to detach conjure from its African American roots and render it just another ingredient in the American religious/supernatural melting pot (Anderson, *Conjure,* 140–149).

Conjure, hoodoo, and Voodoo have undergone enormous change since the first African slaves brought their traditional beliefs to the New World. Not since the early twentieth century has an indigenous African creole religion been widely practiced in the United States. Even traditional practitioners who gather their magical materials from the natural world are increasingly hard to find. That modern conjurers are almost as likely to be white as black would have shocked nineteenth-century observers more than words can easily express. It will come as no surprise that a heritage of such change should provide fertile ground for debate among artists, authors, scholars, and the general public.

WORKS CITED

Ackermann, Hans-W. and Jeanine Gauthier. "The Ways and Nature of the Zombi." *Journal of American Folklore* 104 (1991): 466–494.

Anderson, Jeffrey E. *Conjure in African American Society.* Baton Rouge: Louisiana State University Press, 2005.

———. "Voodoo." In *Encyclopedia of African American Religious Culture.* Anthony Pinn, ed. Santa Barbara, CA: ABC–CLIO, 2009.

Baer, Hans A. *The Black Spiritual Movement: A Religious Response to Racism.* 2nd ed. Knoxville: University of Tennessee Press, 2001.

Baker, Melody. *A New Consciousness: The True Spirit of the New Age.* Duluth: New Thought, 1991.

Berry, Jason. *The Spirit of Black Hawk: A Mystery of Africans and Indians.* Jackson: University Press of Mississippi, 1995.

Boggs, Ralph Steele. "Spanish Folklore from Tampa Florida." *Southern Folklore Quarterly* 1 (1937): 1–12.

Brandon, George. *Santeria from Africa to the New World: The Dead Sell Memories.* Bloomington and Indianapolis: Indiana University Press, 1993.

Brown, Karen McCarthy. *Mama Lola: A Vodou Priestess in Brooklyn.* Updated and expanded. Berkeley: University of California Press, 2001.

Brown, Ras Michael. "'Walk in the Feenda': West-Central Africans and the Forest in the South Carolina—Georgia Lowcountry." In *Central Africans and Cultural Transformations in the American Diaspora,* ed. Linda M. Heywood, 289–317. Cambridge and New York: Cambridge University Press, 2002.

Cable, George Washington. "Creole Slave Songs." With illustrations by E. W. Kemble. *The Century Magazine* 31 (1886): 807–828.

———. *The Grandissimes: A Story of Creole Life.* New York: Charles Scribner's Sons, 1891.

Chambers, Douglas B. *Murder at Montpelier: Igbo Africans in Virginia.* Jackson: University Press of Mississippi, 2005.

Cox, Robert S. *Body and Soul: A Sympathetic History of American Spiritualism.* Charlottesville: University of Virginia Press, 2003.

Daniel, Yvonne. *Dancing Wisdom: Embodied Knowledge in Haitian Vodou, Cuban Yoruba, and Bahian Candomblé.* Urbana: University of Illinois Press, 2005.

Davis, Rod. *American Voudou: Journey into a Hidden World.* Denton: University of North Texas Press, 1999.

Davis, Wade. *The Serpent and the Rainbow: A Harvard Scientist's Astonishing Journey into the Secret Societies of Haitian Voodoo, Zombis, and Magic.* New York: Simon and Schuster, 1986.

Dessens, Nathalie. *From Saint-Domingue to New Orleans: Migration and Influences.* Gainesville: University Press of Florida, 2007.

Du Pratz, Le Page. *The History of Louisiana or of the Western Parts of Virginia and Carolina.* Two vols. Translation. London: Becket and De Hondt, 1763.

Ellis, A. B. *The Ewe-Speaking Peoples of the Slave Coast of West Africa: Their Religion, Manners, Customs, Laws, Languages, &c.* London: Chapman and Hall, 1890.

Faber, Mel D. *New Age Thinking: A Psychoanalytic Critique.* Religion and Beliefs Series, no. 5. University of Ottawa Press, 1996.

Farrow, Stephen S. *Faith, Fancies and Fetich, Or Yoruba Paganism: Being an Account of the Religious Beliefs of the West African Blacks, Particularly of the Yoruba Tribes of Southern Nigeria.* Society for Promoting Christian Knowledge, 1926; reprint Athelia Henrietta Press, 1996.

Gamache, Henri. *The Master Book of Candle Burning.* Revised ed. Plainview: Original, 1998.

Geggus, David. "Haitian Voodoo in the Eighteenth Century: Language, Culture, Resistance." *Jahrbuch für Geschichte von Staat, Wirtschaft und Gesellschaft Lateinamerikas* 28 (1991): 21–51.

Georgia Writers' Project, Savannah Unit. *Drums and Shadows: Survival Studies among the Coastal Negroes.* With an Introduction by Charles Joyner and photographs by Muriel and Malcolm Bell, Jr. Athens: University of Georgia Press, 1986.

Gomez, Michael A. *Exchanging Our Country Marks: The Transformation of African Identities in the Colonial and Antebellum South.* Chapel Hill and London: University of North Carolina Press, 1998.

Hall, Gwendolyn Midlo. *Africans in Colonial Louisiana: The Development of Afro-Creole Culture in the Eighteenth Century.* Baton Rouge: Louisiana State University Press, 1992.

Harvey, David. *The Condition of Postmodernity: An Enquiry into the Origins of Cultural Change.* Cambridge and Oxford: Blackwell, 1990.

Heelas, Paul. *The New Age Movement: The Celebration of the Self and the Sacralization of Modernity.* Oxford and Cambridge: Blackwell, 1996.

Heusch, Luc de. "Kongo in Haiti." *Man,* New Series, 24 (1989): 290–303.

Humes, Edward. *Buried Secrets: A True Story of Murder, Black Magic, and Drug-Running on the U.S Border.* New York: Penguin, 1991.

Hyatt, Harry Middleton. *Hoodoo-Conjuration-Witchcraft-Rootwork.* 5 vols. Memoirs of the Alma Egan Hyatt Foundation. Hannibal: Western, 1970–1978.

Jacobs, Claude F. and Andrew J. Kaslow. *The Spiritual Churches of New Orleans: Origins, Beliefs, and Rituals of an African-American Religion.* Knoxville: University of Tennessee Press, 1991.

Kennedy, Stetson. "Ñañigo in Florida." *Southern Folklore Quarterly* 4 (1940): 153–156.

Long, Carolyn Morrow. *Spiritual Merchants: Religion, Magic, and Commerce.* Knoxville: University of Tennessee Press, 2001.

Kyle, Richard. *The New Age Movement in American Culture.* Lanham, New York, and London: University Press of America, Inc., 1995.

Lopez, A. L. "Nanigo Dance: Superstitions and Customs of Cuban Negroes in Tampa." In "Tampa." Tampa: Federal Writers Project, [1938]. P. K. Yonge Library of Florida History, Department of Special and Area Studies Collection, George A. Smathers Libraries, University of Florida, Gainesville.

MacGaffey, Wyatt. *Religion and Society in Central Africa: The BaKongo of Central Zaire.* Chicago and London: The University of Chicago Press, 1986.

Métraux, Alfred. *Voodoo in Haiti.* Translated by Hugo Charteris and with an Introduction by Sidney W. Mintz. New York: Schocken, 1972.

Morgan, Philip D. *Slave Counterpoint: Black Culture in the Eighteenth-Century Chesapeake and Low Country.* Chapel Hill: University of North Carolina Press, 1998.

Murphy, Joseph M. *Santería: African Spirits in America.* With new Preface. Boston: Beacon Press, 1993.

———. *Working the Spirit: Ceremonies of the African Diaspora.* Boston: Beacon Press, 1994.

Norris, Thaddeus. "Negro Superstitions." *Lippincott's Monthly Magazine* 6 (1870): 90–95.

Olmos, Margarite Fernández and Lizbeth Paravisini-Gebert. *Creole Religions of the Caribbean: An Introduction from Vodou and Santería to Obeah and Espiritismo.* New York University Press, 2003.

Opoku, Kofi Asare. *West African Traditional Religion.* Accra, London, et al: FEP International Private Limited, 1978.

Owen, Mary Alicia. "Among the Voodoos." In *The International Folk-lore Congress 1891: Papers and Transactions,* 230–248. London: David Nutt, 1892.

Perry, Richard S. *Vas You Ever in Zinzinnati?: A Personal Portrait of Cincinnati.* Garden City: Doubleday, 1966.

Puckett, Newbell Niles. *Folk Beliefs of the Southern Negro.* Patterson Smith Reprint Series in Criminology, Law Enforcement, and Social Problems, no. 22. Chapel Hill: University of North Carolina Press, 1926; reprint, Montclair: Patterson Smith, 1968.

Randolph, Beverly Paschal. *Seership! The Magnetic Mirror.* Toledo, OH: K. C. Randolph, 1896.

Rigaud, Milo. *Secrets of Voodoo.* Translated by Robert B. Cross. New York: Arco, 1969; reprint, San Francisco: City Lights, 1985.

Rosenthal, Judy. *Possession, Ecstasy, and Law in Ewe Voodoo.* Charlottesville and London: University Press of Virginia, 1998.

———. "Re: A question on Ewe beliefs" and "More on Ewe words." E-mails to the author. August 10, 2006.

S. In "Letters from Hampton Graduates." *Southern Workman* 7 (1878): 28.

Savage, Phoenix. Interview by author. July 28, 2002, phone call between Birmingham, AL and Nashville, TN. Notes. Personal collection, Monroe, LA.

Thompson, Robert Farris. *Face of the Gods: Art and Altars of Africa and the African Americas.* New York: The Museum of African Art, 1993.

————. *Flash of the Spirit: African and Afro-American Art and Philosophy.* New York: Random House, 1983.

Thornton, John K. "Religious and Ceremonial Life in the Kongo and Mbundu Areas, 1500–1700." In *Central Africans and Cultural Transformations in the American Diaspora,* ed. Linda M. Heywood, 71–90. Cambridge and New York: Cambridge University Press, 2002.

Umeh, John Anenechukwu. *After God is Dibia: Igbo Cosmology, Divination and Sacred Science in Nigeria.* 2 vols. London: Karnak House, 1997, 1999.

Weisberg, Barbara. *Talking to the Dead: Kate and Maggie Fox and the Rise of Spiritualism.* New York: HarperCollins, 2004.

Wetli, Charles V. and Rafael Martinez. "Brujeria: Manifestations of Palo Mayombe in South Florida." *Journal of the Florida Medical Association* 70 (1983): 629–634.

Winslow, David J. "Bishop E. E. Everett and Some Aspects of Occultism and Folk Religion in Negro Philadelphia." *Keystone Folklore Quarterly* 14 (1969): 59–80.

Young, James Harvey. *American Self-Dosage Medicines: An Historical Perspective.* Lawrence: Coronado Press, 1974.

————. *The Toadstool Millionaires: A Social History of Patent Medicines in America before Federal Regulation.* Princeton: Princeton University Press, 1961.

Yronwode, Catherine. *Hoodoo Herb and Root Magic: A Materia Magica of African-American Conjure and Traditional Formulary Giving the Spiritual Uses of Natural Herbs, Roots, Minerals, and Zoological Curios.* Forestville: Lucky Mojo Curio Company, 2002.

————. Interview by author. January 15, 2001, phone call between Gainesville, FL and Forestville, CA. Notes. Personal collection, Monroe, LA.

————. *Southern Spirits: Ghostly Voices from Dixie Land.* 2004. http://www.southern-spirits.com/ (September 23, 2007).

Three
Examples and Texts

HOODOO AS THREAT

A Fictional Encounter with an Evil Trick Doctor from Red Rock

As the travellers drove along they passed a small house, just off the road, hardly more than a double cabin, but it was set back amid fruit-trees, sheltered by one great oak, and there was an air of quietude and peace about it which went to Ruth's soul. A lady in black, with a white cap on her gray hair, and a white kerchief on her shoulders, was sitting out on the little veranda, knitting, and Ruth was sure that as they drove by she bowed to them.

The sense of peace was still on the girl when they came on a country store, at a fork in the road a mile below. There was a well, off to one side, and a small group of negroes stood around it, two or three of them with muskets in their hands, and one with a hare hung at his waist. Another, who stood with his back to the road and had a twisted stick in his hand, and an old army haversack over his shoulder, was, at the moment the wagon drew up, talking loudly and with vehement gesticulation; and, as Major Welch stopped to ask a question, Ruth caught the end of what this man was saying:

"I'm jest as good as any white man, and I'm goin' to show 'em so. I'm goin' to marry a white 'ooman and meck white folks wait on me. When I puts my mark agin a man he's gone, whether he's a man or a 'ooman, and I'se done set it now in a gum-tree."

His hearers were manifestly much impressed by him. An exclamation of approval went round among them.

The little wagon stopping attracted attention, and the speaker turned, and then, quickly, as if to make amends for his loud speech, pulled off his hat and came toward the vehicle with a curious, cringing motion.

"My master; my mistis," he said, bowing lower with each step until his knee almost touched the ground. He was a somewhat strongly built, dark mulatto, perhaps a little past middle age and of medium height, and, as he came up to the vehicle, Ruth thought she had never seen so grotesque a figure, and she took in by an instinct that this was the trick-doctor of whom Dr. Gary had spoken. His chin stuck so far forward that the lower teeth were much outside of the upper, or, at least, the lower jaw was; for the teeth looked as though they had been ground down, and his gums, as he grinned, showed as blue on the edges as if he had painted them. His nose was so short and the upper part of his face receded so much that the nostrils were unusually wide, and gave an appearance of a black circle in his yellow countenance. His forehead was so low that he had evidently shaved a band across it, and the band ran around over the top of his flat head, leaving a tuft of coarse hair right in the middle, and on either side of it were certain lines which looked as if they had been tattooed. Immediately under these were a pair of little furtive eyes which looked in quite different directions, and yet moved so quickly at times that it almost seemed as if they were both focussed on the same object. Large brass earrings were in his ears, and about his throat was a necklace of blue and white beads.

Major Welch, having asked his question, drove on, the mulatto bowing low at each step as he backed away with that curious motion toward his companions by the well; and Ruth, who had been sitting very close to her father, fascinated by the negro's gaze and strange appearance, could hardly wait to get out of hearing before she whispered: "Oh, father, did you ever see such a repulsive-looking creature in all your life?"

The Major admitted that he was an ugly fellow, and then, as a loud guffaw came to them from the rear, added, with that reasonable sense of justice which men possess and are pleased to call wisdom, that he seemed to be very civil and was, no doubt, a harmless good-natured creature.

"I don't know," said Ruth, doubtfully. "I only hope I shall never set eyes on him again. I should die if I were to meet him alone."

Source: Thomas Nelson Page, *Red Rock: A Chronicle of Reconstruction* (New York: Charles Scribner's Sons, 1898), 291–293.

Commentary

This selection illustrates the low opinion white southerners historically held of both conjure and African Americans. Here Thomas Nelson Page, a late nineteenth-century author of the moonlight-and-magnolias school of southern literature, introduces a villain in the course of a novel about Reconstruction. As implied by the author's grotesque description of the trick doctor named Moses and the reaction of Ruth, a white immigrant to the South, the conjurer appears distinctly threatening. Ruth's misgivings are proven accurate later in the tale when Moses waylays her and attempts to lead her into the forest. His clear intent is rape. Depictions like these helped whites justify consigning African Americans to second-class citizenship.

HOODOO AS CHARLATANRY

Two Accounts from Former Slaves

Us had a ol' quack herb doctor on de place. Some bad boys went up to his house one night an' poured a whole lot of de medicine down him. An honey, dat ol' man died de next day.

> *Source:* Cornelia Robinson, "De Yankees Wuz a Harricane," interview by Preston Klein (Opelika, AL), 1937, in George P. Rawick, ed., *The American Slave: A Composite Autobiography* (Westport: Greenwood, 1972–78), 6, pt. 1:331.

I keeps a flour sifter an' a fork by my bed to keep de witches f'um ridin' me. How come I knows dey rides me? Honey, I bees so tired In de mawnin' I kin scarcely git outten my bed, an' its all on account of dem witches ridin' me, so I putt de sifter dere to cotch 'em. Sometimes I wears dis dime wid de hole in it aroun' my ankle to keep off de conjure, but since Monroe King tuk an' died us ain't had much conjerin' 'roun' here. You know dat ole nigger would putt a conjure on somebody for jus' a little sum of money. He sold conjure bags to keep de sickness away. He could conjure de grass an' de birds, an' anything he wanted to. De niggers 'roun' useta give him chickens an' things so's he wouldn't conjure 'em, but its a funny thing mistis, I ain't never understood it, he got tuk off to jail for stealin' a mule, an' us niggers waited 'roun' many a day for him to conjure hisself out, but he never did. I guess he jus' didn't have quite enough conjurin' material to git hisself th'ough dat stone wall. I ain't never understood it, dough.

> *Source:* Silvia Witherspoon, "Foot Gets Tired from Choppin' Cotton," interview by Susie R. O'Brien and John Morgan Smith (AL), June 25, 1937, in George P. Rawick, ed., *The American Slave: A Composite Autobiography* (Westport: Greenwood, 1972–78), 6, pt. 1:431.

Commentary

Most slaves may have believed in conjure, but some certainly had their doubts. Whites frequently used blacks' supposedly primitive belief in conjure to buttress their own feelings of superiority. As these examples demonstrate, blacks—even slaves—could be just as discerning as whites. Belief in the powers of a particular practitioner rested on his or her success, not mere faith in the universal efficacy of magic. The preceding examples come from testimony recorded in Alabama during the 1930s by Federal Writers' Project workers. The project was one of the many New Deal programs created by the government during the Great Depression to provide work relief for those who would otherwise be unemployed. The project recorded an impressive amount of information on African American folk beliefs before wartime prosperity persuaded the government that the New Deal was no longer necessary. The original spelling and syntax have been retained throughout. It says as much about the white interviewers as it does the black subjects.

VOODOO/HOODOO AS SUPERSTITION

"The Voodoos"

The dance and song entered into the negro worship. That worship was as dark and horrid as bestialized savagery could make the adoration of serpents. So revolting was it, and so morally hideous, that even in the West Indian French possessions a hundred years ago, with the slave-trade in full blast and the West Indian planter and slave what they were, the orgies of the Voodoos were forbidden. Yet both there and in Louisiana they were practiced.

The Aradas, St. Méry tells us, introduced them. They brought them from their homes beyond the Slave Coast, one of the most dreadfully benighted regions of all Africa. He makes the word Vaudaux. In Louisiana it is written Voudou and Voodoo, and is often changed on the negro's lips to Hoodoo. It is the name of an imaginary being of vast supernatural powers residing in the form of a harmless snake. This spiritual influence or potentate is the recognized antagonist and opposite of Obi, the great African manitou or deity, or him whom the Congoes vaguely generalize as Zombi. In Louisiana, as I have been told by that learned Creole scholar the late Alexander Dimitry, Voodoo bore as a title of greater solemnity the additional name of Maignan, and that even in the Calinda dance, which he had witnessed innumerable times, was sometimes heard, at the height of its frenzy, the invocation—

"Aie! Aie!
Voodoo Magnan!"

The worship of Voodoo is paid to a snake kept in a box. The worshipers are not merely a sect, but in some rude, savage way also an order. A man and woman chosen from their own number to be the oracles of the serpent deity are called the king and queen. The queen is the more important of the two, and even in the present dilapidated state of the worship in Louisiana, where the king's office has almost or quite disappeared, the queen is still a person of great note.

She reigns as long as she continues to live. She comes to power not by inheritance, but by election or its barbarous equivalent. Chosen for such qualities as would give her a natural supremacy, personal attractions among the rest, and ruling over superstitious fears and desires of every fierce and ignoble sort, she wields no trivial influence. I once saw, in her extreme old age, the famed Marie Laveau. Her dwelling was in the quadroon quarter of New Orleans but a step or two from Congo Square, a small adobe cabin just off the sidewalk, scarcely higher than its close board fence, whose batten gate yielded to the touch and revealed the crazy doors and windows spread wide to the warm air, and one or two tawny faces within, whose expression was divided between a pretense of contemptuous inattention and a frowning resentment of the intrusion. In the center of a small room whose ancient cypress floor was worn with scrubbing and sprinkled with crumbs of soft brick—a Creole affectation of superior cleanliness—sat, quaking with feebleness in an ill-looking old rocking-chair, her body bowed, and her wild, gray witch's tresses hanging about her shriveled, yellow neck, the queen of the Voodoos. Three generations of her children were within the faint beckon of her helpless waggling wrist and fingers. They said she was over a hundred years old, and there was nothing to cast doubt upon the statement. She had shrunken away from her skin; it was like a turtles. Yet withal one could hardly help but see that the face, now so withered, had once been handsome and commanding. There was still a faint shadow of departed beauty on the forehead, the spark of an old fire in the sunken, glistening eyes, and a vestige of imperiousness in the fine, slightly aquiline nose, and even about her silent, woe-begone mouth. Her grandson stood by, an uninteresting quadroon between forty and fifty years old, looking strong, empty-minded, and trivial enough; but his mother, her daughter, was also present, a woman of some seventy years, and a most striking and majestic figure. In features, stature, and bearing she was regal. One had but to look on her, impute her brilliancies—too untamable and severe to be called charms or graces—to her mother, and remember what New Orleans was long years ago, to understand how the name of Marie Laveau should have driven itself inextricably into the traditions of the town and the times. Had this visit been postponed a few months it would have been too late. Marie Laveau is dead; Malvina Latour is queen. As she appeared presiding over a Voodoo ceremony on the night of the 23d of June, 1884, she is described as a bright mulattress of about forty-eight, of "extremely handsome figure," dignified bearing, and a face indicative of a comparatively high order of intelligence. She wore a neat blue, white-dotted calico gown, and a "brilliant *tignon* (turban) gracefully tied."

It is pleasant to say that this worship, in Louisiana, at least, and in comparison with what it once was, has grown to be a rather trivial affair. The practice of its midnight forest rites seemed to sink into inanition along with Marie Laveau, It long ago diminished in frequency to once a year, the chosen night always being the Eve of St. John, For several years past even these annual celebrations have been suspended; but in the summer of 1884 they were—let it be hoped, only for the once—resumed.

When the queen decides that such a celebration shall take place, she appoints a night for the gathering, and some remote, secluded spot in the forest for the rendezvous. Thither all the worshipers are summoned. St. Méry, careless of the power of the scene, draws in practical, unimaginative lines the picture of such a gathering in St. Domingo, in the times when the "*veritable Vaudaux*" had lost but little of the primitive African character. The worshipers are met, decked with kerchiefs more or less numerous, red being everywhere the predominating color. The king, abundantly adorned with them, wears one of pure red about his forehead as a diadem. A blue ornamental cord completes his insignia. The queen, in simple dress and wearing a red cord and a heavily decorated belt, is beside him near a rude altar. The silence of midnight is overhead, the gigantic forms and shadows and still, dank airs of the tropical forest close in around, and on the altar, in a small box ornamented with little tinkling bells, lies, unseen, the living serpent. The worshipers have begun their devotions to it by presenting themselves before it in a body, and uttering professions of their fidelity and belief in its power. They cease, and now the royal pair, in tones of parental authority and protection, are extolling the great privilege of being a devotee, and inviting the faithful to consult the oracle. The crowd makes room, and a single petitioner draws near. He is the senior member of the order. His prayer is made. The king becomes deeply agitated by the presence within him of the spirit invoked. Suddenly he takes the box from the altar and sets it on the ground. The queen steps upon it and with convulsive movements utters the answers of the deity beneath her feet. Another and another suppliant, approaching in the order of seniority, present, singly, their petitions, and humbly or exultingly, according to the nature of the responses, which hangs on the fierce caprice of the priestess, accept these utterances and make way for the next, with his prayer of fear or covetousness, love, jealousy, petty spite or deadly malice. At length the last petitioner is answered. Now a circle is formed, the caged snake is restored to the altar, and the humble and multifarious oblations of the worshipers are received, to be devoted not only to the trivial expenses of this worship, but also to the relief of members of the order whose distresses call for such aid. Again the royal ones are speaking, issuing orders for execution in the future, orders that have not always in view, mildly says St. Méry, good order and public tranquillity. Presently the ceremonies become more forbidding. They are taking a horrid oath, smearing their lips with the blood of some slaughtered animal, and swearing to suffer death rather than disclose any secret of the order, and to inflict death on any who may commit such treason. Now a new applicant for membership steps into their circle, there are a few trivial formalities, and the Voodoo dance begins. The postulant dances frantically in the middle of the ring, only pausing from time to time to receive heavy alcoholic draughts in great haste and return more wildly to his leapings and writhings until he falls in convulsions. He is lifted, restored, and presently conducted to the altar, takes his oath, and by a ceremonial stroke from one of the sovereigns is admitted a full participant in the privileges and obligations of the devilish freemasonry. But the dance goes on about the snake. The contortions of the upper part of the body, especially of the neck and shoulders, are such as threaten to dislocate them. The queen shakes the box and tinkles its bells, the rum-bottle gurgles, the chant alternates between king and chorus—

"Eh! eh! Bomba, hone! Hone!
Canga bafio tay,
Canga moon day lay,
Canga do keelah,
Canga li——"

There are swoonings and ravings, nervous tremblings beyond control, incessant writhings and turnings, tearing of garments, even biting of the flesh—every imaginable invention of the devil. . . .

To what extent the Voodoo worship still obtains here would be difficult to say with certainty. The affair of June, 1884, as described by Messrs. Augustin and Whitney, eyewitnesses, was an orgy already grown horrid enough when they turned their backs upon it. It took place at a wild and lonely spot where the dismal cypress swamp behind New Orleans meets the waters of Lake Pontchartrain in a wilderness of cypress stumps and

PLANTER AND VOODOO CHARM.

A planter confronting a group of slaves with a charm. Note the white man's disdain for it, which sharply contrasts with the concern evident in the African Americans' faces. George Washington Cable, "Creole Slave Songs," with illustrations by E. W. Kemble, *The Century Magazine* 31 (1886): p. 821. Courtesy of Cornell University Library, Making of America Digital Collection.

rushes. It would be hard to find in nature a more painfully desolate region. Here in a fisherman's cabin sat the Voodoo worshipers cross-legged on the floor about an Indian basket of herbs and some beans, some bits of bone, some oddly wrought bunches of feathers, and some saucers of small cakes. The queen presided, sitting on the only chair in the room. There was no king, no snake—at least none visible to the onlookers. Two drummers beat with their thumbs on gourds covered with sheepskin, and a white-wooled old man scraped that hideous combination of banjo and violin, whose head is covered with rattlesnake skin, and of which the Chinese are the makers and masters. There was singing"—"*M'allé couri dans désér*" ("I am going into the wilderness"), a chant and refrain not worth the room they would take—and there was frenzy and a circling march, wild shouts, delirious gesticulations and posturings, drinking, and amongst other frightful nonsense the old trick of making fire blaze from the mouth by spraying alcohol from it upon the flame of a candle.

   But whatever may be the quantity of the Voodoo *worship* left in Louisiana, its superstitions are many and are everywhere. Its charms are resorted to by the malicious, the jealous, the revengeful, or the avaricious, or held in terror, not by the timorous only, but by the strong, the courageous, the desperate. To find under his mattress an acorn hollowed out, stuffed with the hair of some dead person, pierced with four holes on four sides, and two small chicken feathers drawn through them so as to cross inside the acorn; or to discover on his door-sill at daybreak a little box containing a dough or waxen heart stuck full of pins; or to hear that his avowed foe or rival has been pouring cheap champagne in the four corners of Congo Square at midnight, when there was no moon, will strike more abject fear into the heart of many a stalwart negro or melancholy quadroon than to face a leveled revolver. And it is not only the colored man that holds to these practices and fears. Many a white Creole gives them full credence. What wonder, when African Creoles were the nurses of so nearly all of them? Many shrewd men and women, generally colored persons, drive a trade in these charms and in oracular directions for their use or evasion; many a Creole—white as well as other tints—female, too, as well as male—will pay a Voodoo "*monteure*" to "make a work," i.e. to weave a spell, for the prospering of some scheme or wish too ignoble to be prayed for at any shrine inside the church. These milder incantations are performed within the witch's or wizard's own house, and are made up, for the most part, of a little pound cake, some lighted candle ends, a little syrup of sugar-cane, pins, knitting-needles, and a trifle of anisette. But fear naught; an Obi charm will enable you to smile defiance against all such mischief; or if you will but consent to be a magician, it is they, the Voodoos, one and all, who will hold you in absolute terror. Or, easier, a frizzly chicken! If you have on your premises a frizzly chicken, you can lie down and laugh—it is a checkmate!

A planter once found a Voodoo charm, or *ouanga* (wongah); this time it was a bit of cotton cloth folded about three cow-peas and some breast feathers of a barn-yard fowl, and covered with a tight wrapping of thread. When he proposed to take it to New Orleans his slaves were full of consternation. "Marse Ed, ef ye go on d'boat wid dat-ah, de boat'll sink wi' yer. Fore d'Lord, it will!" For some reason it did not.

Source: George Washington Cable, "Creole Slave Songs," with illustrations by E. W. Kemble, *The Century Magazine* 31 (1886): 815, 817–821. Cable's source: Médéric Louis-Élie Moreau de Saint-Méry. One footnote was eliminated.

Commentary

Cable's journalistic article is one of the best-known descriptions of a Voodoo ceremony. Moreover, it contains one of the earliest uses of the word *hoodoo,* which the author equates with *Voodoo.* Cable relied on an eighteenth-century description of Haitian Vodou by Médéric Louis-Élie Moreau de Saint-Méry as his basis for understanding late nineteenth-century New Orleans Voodoo, a practice continued by many who came after him. For Cable, African American beliefs were curious—and in the case of Voodoo, repulsive—superstitions. Although he found Voodoo ceremonies and charms interesting enough to write about, he remains dismissive throughout this selection. Notably lacking, however, is the overtly threatening characterization of Thomas Nelson Page's Moses. In fact, Cable closes by describing believers and practitioners as laughable.

HOODOO AS FOLKLORE

"Conjuring and Conjure-Doctors"

The following paper read at the April meeting of the Hampton Folk-Lore Society, was compiled from a series of essays on Conjure-Doctors written in 1878 by students at Hampton, some of which were then published in *Southern Workman*.

The Negro's belief in conjuration and magic is very probably a relic of African days, though strange and incongruous growths rising from association with the white race, added to and distorted it from time to time, till it became a curious conglomerate of fetishism, divination, quackery, incantation and demonology.

Overt and natural means of obtaining justice being forbidden the Negro, was it surprising that, brought up in ignorance, and trained in superstition, he should invoke secret and supernatural powers to redress his wrongs and afford him vengeance on those of his fellows whom envy, jealousy or anger prompted him to injure?

The agent of this vengeance was usually the Conjure Doctor. This individual might be a man or a woman, white or colored, but was found in every large Negro community, where though held in fear and horror, his supernatural powers were still implicitly believed in. The source of these powers is but ill defined. One authority says: "I have always heard that those doctors sold themselves to the Devil before they were given this power." Another, in speaking of a certain old woman who was a conjure doctor, says: "She said she had a special revelation from God, as do all the conjure doctors I have ever heard of." One rather noted conjure doctor described by several of our writers, claimed his power in virtue of being the "seventh son of a seventh son," and having been "born with seven cauls over his face." It is said by some, however, that women who conjure sometimes give instruction in the art, and that if a conjure doctor is asked where he got his teaching, he will tell you of some old person who has been dead for years as having been his teacher.

The conjure doctor's business was of two kinds: to conjure, or "trick," a person, and to cure persons already "conjured." They were appealed to upon the least pretext to exert their powers in the former way. Jealousy or envy of a more fortunate neighbor or associate was a frequent cause for appealing to the conjure doctor, who would be requested to "trick" the object of ill feeling. A quarrel between the two neighbors, even over the merest trifle, would result in a visit to the conjure doctor and the subsequent illness, or death perhaps, of one of the parties. Love affairs gave plenty of employment to the conjure doctors, as they were believed to be able to "work their roots" so to make one person return another's affection, and, if the affair resulted unhappily, the slighted party sought revenge in having the other "tricked" so that no rival should be more successful.

In slavery times, there are frequent records of the conjure doctor's being appealed to save the slave from punishment, to enable him to escape the "patrollers" or, in the case of a runaway, to enable him to return home without suffering from his master's anger.

In all these cases there was the most implicit faith in the conjure doctor's power. Disliked and feared as these men and women were, gruesome as were the beliefs about them, the confidence in their abilities was unbounded; and deliberate open impostors as most of them evidently were, they were nevertheless able to wring from their victims the money they could so little spare from the needs of everyday life.

Some curious things are told of the personal appearance of these doctors. Almost all agree that they are usually tall and very dark; and a distinguishing mark seems to be extreme redness of the eyes. One describes them as "always on the lookout, full of superstition, and long, exciting tales." Another calls them "singular and queer, seeming always in a deep study, looking at some distant object," and adds: "I have never seen one that could look a man straight in the eyes. They never sleep like any one else. It's more like the sleep of a cat. At the slightest noise or pain they are up telling their fortunes to see if any one is trying to injure them."

One conjure doctor is pictured as having the remarkable gift of "turning as green as grass most, and when he was just as black as a man could very well be: and his hair covered his neck, and around his neck he had a string, and he had lizards tied on it. He carried a crooked cane. He'd throw it down and he would pick it up and say something, and throw it down, and it would wriggle like a snake, and he would pick it up and it would be as stiff as any other cane."

In one account, the conjure doctors are represented as "going along looking very sanctified, with leathern bags on their arms.["] They are not called conjure doctors in their presence but are addressed as doctor. They seem to have exacted respectful treatment, for we have testimony that a conjure doctor meeting a person who refused to bow to him, would threaten to conjure the person.

Powers of all kinds are attributed to these doctors. The healing art in various degrees is their gift, and the so-called "diseases" which they possess exclusive power to cure are, as one of our informers puts it, these: tricks, spells and poisons.

The power of snake-charming seems to be quite generally attributed to them. One is told of who claimed that he could turn a horse to a cow, and kill a man or woman and bring them to life again by shaking up his little boxes. He could also whistle in the keyhole after the doors were locked, and make them fly open. Others are told of who "can trick, put snakes, lizards, terrapins, scorpions and different other things in you, fix you so yon can't walk, can't sleep, or sleep all the time, and so you can't have any use of your limbs. They could put you in such a state that you would linger and pine away or so that you would go blind or crazy."

Source: Leonora Herron, "Conjuring and Conjure Doctors,"
Southern Workman 24 (1891): 117–118.

Commentary

This is one of the earliest treatments of conjure as a valid form of folklore. It was no coincidence that it appeared in the school newspaper of the Hampton Institute, a college founded to educate newly freed slaves and their children after the Civil War. Its author clearly continues to harbor a negative view of the practice. Nevertheless, she went on to summarize and analyze the practice from an at least moderately sympathetic standpoint, determining that its survival was a consequence of the racism that doomed African Americans to life as second-class citizens.

VOODOO/HOODOO AS MEDICALLY POTENT

From "Voodoo Poisoning in Buffalo New York"

It is well recognized that folk remedies may carry inherent risks. The diagnosis and subsequent treatment of many dangerous conditions are delayed, if not completely neglected, which results in needless morbidity and mortality. A less common, though no less dangerous, risk is the direct harmful effects caused by the application of the remedy itself. Such an occurrence is illustrated in the following case.

Report of a Case

A 24-year-old Alabama-born Negro construction worker entered the E. J. Meyer Memorial Hospital with complaints of severe epigastric pain, nausea, and vomiting of four days' duration. Although the patient claimed to have been in "perfect health" all his life, two hospital admissions in the preceding two months had shown him to have rheumatic heart disease. On these admissions the patient's complaints had been similar but less severe, and had been preceded by heavy labor on a double shift.

Physical examination on this admission revealed an apparently healthy young man complaining of epigastric discomfort. Oral temperature was 100 F (37.8 C), blood pressure was 102/70 mm Hg, and pulse rate was 140 beats per minute and irregular. There were 18 respirations per minute. Neck veins were not distended. The chest was clear to percussion and auscultation. There was cardiac enlargement to the sixth interspace in the anterior axillary line. Murmurs indicative of both mitral and aortic stenosis and regurgitation were audible. Diffuse abdominal tenderness and muscle guarding were present. The liver extended 4 cm below the costal margin and was tender. There was no costovertebral angle tenderness, edema, or clubbing.

An electrocardiogram on admission revealed atrial fibrillation, ventricular hypertrophy on the left, and digitalis effect. An x-ray film of the chest on admission showed increased pulmonary vascular markings and enlargement of both the atrium and ventricle on the left. Laboratory-values included a normal hematocrit (44%) but a leukocytosis with a white blood cell count (WBC) of 19,000/cu mm, with a slight shift to the left. Urinalysis revealed three to four red blood cells (RBC) and one to two WBC per high-power field. Serum electrolyte concentrations were as follows: sodium, 138 mEq/liter; potassium, 6.9 mEq/liter; chloride, 95 mEq/liter; and carbon dioxide, 15 mEq/liter. The blood urea nitrogen (BUN) level was 43 mg/100 ml. At this time a diagnosis of subacute bacterial endocarditis and renal failure was entertained. Blood cultures were taken, and digoxin was administered. Polystyrene sodium sulfonate (Kayexalate) was given rectally.

By the second day, however, the patient had voided only 300 ml despite infusions of 1,500 ml. The patient had gained 1½ pounds, and the BUN level was now 50 mg/100 ml. A diuresis then ensued. By the third day the patient complained less of abdominal pain, had stopped vomiting, and was afebrile. Urinalyses revealed a few WBC and moderate numbers of bacteria: proteinuria and microscopic hematuria did not recur. . . . Serum enzymes were not drawn until the ninth day of illness, and were grossly abnormal. The serum glutamic pyruvic transaminase (SGPT) level was still abnormal on the 14th day of disease. No satisfactory explanation was recorded at the time to account for these enzyme elevations. The patient remained asymptomatic, and bed rest was prescribed for the rheumatic carditis.

However, several months later during a change of service, a new observer noted the original high SGPT values and postulated that the acute hepatic and renal episodes were related and more likely ascribable to a hepatorenal toxin than to congestive heart failure. This contention was strengthened by the patient's status during the two previous admissions when no evidence of impaired hepatic or renal function was found (BUN level, 7 mg/100 ml; normal serum glutamic oxalacetic transaminase [SGOT], 7 units, with a nonpalpable liver). The patient was accordingly questioned regarding the use of alcohol, ingestants, inhalants, and industrial exposures. All of this he denied. However, the patient did relate reluctantly that four days before admission his anxiety over possible cardiac surgery had led him to consult a Voodoo priestess who heard his story and advised him that surgery would kill him. She prepared for him a "large bottle" of special white liquid which had a peculiarly sweet taste. The patient paid $50 for these services and immediately drank all of the liquid. Within six hours he felt nauseated. Over the following three days, increasing abdominal pain and vomiting led the patient to the hospital for aid. The patient identified the priestess who was found to be an American Negro who was a former hospital attendant. Attempts to obtain a similar potion from her were unavailing, although she did prescribe other drugs and procedures for a Negro investigator.

Comment

The history of Voodooism can be traced to the religious practices that African slaves brought to the Americas between the late 17th and early 19th centuries. Central to the belief is the worship of a deity through a medium who serves not only as a priest and general counselor but, as in the case reported, as a healer. "Healing" is accomplished by means of curses, charms, and potions. Difficulties in correct diagnosis of Voodoo drug effects most likely stem from two factors. Folk medicines rarely occupy much time in history taking, especially where the possibility of poisoning is unsuspected. In addition, the Voodoo devotee may hesitate to reveal such information.

The number of agents that are associated with simultaneous hepatic and renal damage are few. In addition to the most commonly encountered substance, carbon tetrachloride, diethylene glycol and tetrachlorethylene have also been reported to induce simultaneous hepatic and renal injury. The earliest manifestations of carbon tetrachloride poisoning are nausea and vomiting, beginning from several hours to as long as six days after exposure. The patient often becomes dehydrated, passing small quantities of urine with high specific gravity. Abdominal pain is a frequent accompaniment. Characteristic toxic effects on liver and kidney usually appear by the third or fourth day. These may include hepatomegaly and jaundice, chemical findings of hepatocellular damage, and less often, fever. Glomerular and tubular damage are manifested by anuria or oliguria, isosthenuria, proteinuria, and microscopic hematuria. Uremia occurs in proportion to the severity of the renal injury. If the patient recovers, a spontaneous diuresis generally occurs within one to two weeks. Although the kidney may not regain normal concentrating power for up to two months, recovery of renal (and hepatic) function is the rule.

A comparison of the present patient's clinical manifestations with reported severe instances of organic hepatorenal toxins indicates that the postulated exposure was rather minor in quantity. Undoubtedly, other ingredients besides a hepatorenal toxin comprised the major portion of the ingested potion. The identity of the toxin as carbon tetrachloride is considered possible but not proved.

Source: J. Robin Saphir, Arnold Gold, James Giambrone, and James F. Holland. "Voodoo Poisoning in Buffalo, NY." *The Journal of the American Medical Association* 202 (1967): 437–438. Endnotes were removed. Copyright © 1967, American Medical Association. All rights reserved.

Commentary

Starting in the 1940s, anthropologists began to investigate curses as medical phenomena. By the 1960s and 1970s, case studies about the effects of magical curses and cures were common in medical literature. Numerous examples dealt with the role of Voodoo and hoodoo in African American life. Most such studies resembled the one here, which depicts conjure as a potential health problem that needs to be recognized to effectively treat patients. The generally negative view of hoodoo reflects physicians' preoccupation with curing illness through scientific means and their longstanding competition with folk practitioners more than it does the broader population's racially charged view that the practice of magic is a sign of backwardness or an expression of evil intent. In recent years, works such as Wonda Fontenot's *Secret Doctors: Ethnomedicine of African Americans* (1994) have been more open to positive interpretations of African American and Afro-Caribbean supernaturalism.

It must be pointed out, however, that the authors of the preceding text had a valid concern for the welfare of a seriously ill patient. Many hoodoo practitioners recognize both "natural" diseases, which are medically treatable ailments, and "unnatural" diseases that are the result of evil spells and can be cured only by magic. It appears that the Voodoo priestess in question either did not accept the distinction or did not care. Alternatively, her client may have ignored instructions to gradually ingest the liquid rather than drinking it all at once.

HOODOO AS FOLK PSYCHIATRY

From "Indigenous Therapists in a Southern Black Urban Community"

Traditionally, cross-cultural psychiatry has been a field restricted to psychiatrists with an unusual knowledge of anthropology or a special personal interest in other cultures. With the development of community mental health centers often serving widely divergent cultural groups, it has become mandatory for all psychiatrists to become at least acquainted with the manner in which mental illness is perceived and treated in cultures other than their own. In the crossing of cultural interfaces the scientifically oriented Western trained physician will inevitably find himself confronted by the indigenous therapists of the new culture whose practice and concepts of health and disease are often at variance with his own beliefs and training. Understanding and appreciating the indigenous practitioner within our own country has only recently been recognized as an essential prerequisite for the effective delivery of health care among our own poor and minority groups.

An indigenous therapist may be defined as a member of a community using sociological circumstances peculiar to the predominant ethnic and cultural groups of that community in an attempt to correct mental or physical disorders. This is similar to the definition for mental health counselors used in the 1965 report of the Joint Commission on Mental Health. That report listed "clergymen, family physicians, teachers, probation officers, public health nurses, sheriffs, judges, public welfare workers, scoutmasters, county farm agents, and others." But as Lubchansky et al have noted this does not include the "informal community caretaker: persons whose relevance is derived from other than formal organizations." Most of the indigenous therapists of the ghetto fall into this latter group.

Studies describing the practices of indigenous therapists in rural North American subcultures have appeared in the anthropological and sociological literature for many years. More recently the psychiatric literature has contained studies of indigenous therapists in Nigeria, the Ivory Coast, Trinidad, and the Puerto Rican community of New York City. . . .

To date little has been reported on the function of indigenous therapists in the black subcultures of the American South. This paper reports on a preliminary study of such a group in a large urban setting where community mental health services were being introduced for the first time.

Methods

The study conducted among the indigenous therapists of the Price Neighborhood, a black ghetto community on the southside of Atlanta with a population of approximately 28,000. Most of the residents living in the area are extremely poor. Of the families in the community, 56% have an annual income under $2,400 per year, with the average family consisting of two adults and three children. Since 1965 the community has had only one private general practitioner.

From 1955 to 1965 there was no private practitioner of medicine in the area as it underwent a period of rapid population growth and socioeconomic decline from an established middle-class black community to its present status as an urban slum. The only medical service available to most of the Price residents for several generations was the county funded, university staffed, municipal hospital more than a mile away. In 1967 the Office of Economic Opportunity (OEO) established a neighborhood health center which is intended to serve as the primary health care facility for the families of the area. Mental health services were not available at this center until 1969, when a community mental health center funded by the National Institute of Mental Health in conjunction with the OEO Health Center was established. Prior to this time health services were nonexistent except for commitment to the State Hospital or occasional crisis intervention at the county hospital.

While many indigenous therapists were known to practice in the area, they were often hard to locate, fearing criticism from the authorities and from the medical establishment. Through informal discussions with receptive community members contact was gradually established with many of these practitioners. During a six-month period, interviews and semiparticipant observations were made with representative individuals from each of the major categories of indigenous therapists in the area.

In the formal interviews an attempt was made to focus attention on the treatment approach used by these therapists and the significance of their methods as a reflection of the belief systems and other patterns of cultural thought found in the Price community. At the same time, much of the interviewing served merely to establish rapport with these individuals so they would more willingly permit the investigators to directly observe their work. . . .

[Authors proceed to divide indigenous therapists into four broad categories: (1) root-workers, (2) faith healers, (3) magic vendors, and (4) neighborhood prophets]

Comment

The most important findings of this study to date have been (a) the documentation of the existence of functional indigenous therapists in a southern black ghetto community, (b) the categorization of these therapists according to their predominant belief systems, and (c) the identification of the functions and roles of these indigenous therapists in their community.

Of extreme importance in the functioning of all indigenous therapists in this community was the lack of a clear distinction between mind and body that existed in the culture. Psychiatric problems were frequently couched in somatic terms and, even when a problem was clearly identified as psychological, herbs or potions were frequently sought as the most appropriate treatment. Similarly, spiritual cures for physical ailments were frequently the treatment of choice. Hence, therapeutic modalities which orthodox physicians would classify as either primarily psychiatric or medical are without such distinction in this culture.

Historically, the use of a mind-body dualism in Western medical thought was the outgrowth of the necessity of communication in a scientific medical language. This difficulty with communication persists in cultures such as the one in this study with unitarian belief systems. It is characteristic of the people of this culture to turn to those therapists whom they feel offer the most understandable explanation of the illness or problem in question.

The physicians now available to the community residents who have learned to explain the causes and treatment of illness in a manner that fits with the cultural belief systems of the community are increasingly the therapists of choice for most medical and surgical problems. An increase in the number of physicians available to residents of this community in the last few years has also helped. In a recent study, well over 98% of the population polled gave some form of orthodox medical care facility as their primary source of treatment for such disorders.

The manner in which the scientific medical model interacts with the traditional belief systems in the culture is demonstrated by the following example:

Mr. B. was a 64-year-old retired clerk who quite suddenly developed an erythematous, desquamating rash on his trunk and extremities. He presented to the neighborhood OEO Health Center after his wife accused him of having syphilis as a result of his infidelity many years prior to the onset of his illness. This explanation was rejected by the physician at the health center, but unfortunately he could not immediately offer an alternative explanation for the skin disorder. A story began to circulate among the health assistants employed at the center, most of whom came from the community, that the wife believed the rash to have been caused by a "fix" the patient's illicit lover had placed on him. As the physician apparently fumbled for a more adequate diagnosis and explanation, the assistants, despite their own training in scientific medical techniques, were adamant that "medicine didn't know everything yet," and that perhaps black magic was operating against the patient.

The diagnosis of an autoimmune reaction to malignancy was established, however, and the stories of "hexing" began to disappear. Witchcraft in this case provided an explanation that science did not immediately provide. The health assistants, though having absorbed medical training, easily slipped into more traditional cultural beliefs of the cause of disease when no scientific explanation was immediately available or easily understandable.

While explanations of physical illness are increasingly accepted in scientific terms, mental illness as a concept in this culture remains poorly perceived. This is partly because of the inability of most psychiatrists to offer an explanation for the conditions they treat in culturally acceptable terminology. Culturally, the religicomagical explanation of the indigenous therapist is generally more acceptable in this area. In addition, the complete lack of orthodox mental health care facilities explains why most of the psychopathology in this culture has been and continues to be treated by indigenous, and therefore more culturally and ethnically attuned, therapists.

The indigenous therapists are most easily classified and identified by the belief system they use to communicate with their clients. With the herbalist, the primary source of healing power is not the therapist, but the roots and herbs to which he is largely the intermediary. For the prophets of both types [faith healers and neighborhood prophets], God is the only source of healing power and is obtainable by faith and supplication of prayer. This was the case with both the lay and denominational ministers. Also seen was the belief that healing was available only through one who has been "chosen" and who must make the supplication for the ill, as with the prophet and faith healer, or through the use of herbs and roots, as was the case with another herbalist interviewed.

In each case the belief system identifies a particular source of healing power and dictates how it should be delivered to the believer. A more culturally determined point was exactly who qualified as a believer. [An] older prophetess, for example, recognized the gross psychosis of some of her patients and referred them to a physician as well as offering them prayer. Severely physically or mentally ill persons were usually referred to physicians, but those who were psychoneurotic fell into a gray zone in which their illness was more easily identified as the result of magic or a breach of religious faith. It was these patients who made up the majority of the clients of the indigenous therapists.

It is interesting to note that in its interaction with the community the OEO Health Center and the Mental Health Center have created a new class of indigenous therapists. By training community people, mainly women, as health assistants and "community mental health workers" a new class of helping agents has been created. These people in general enjoy the trust of the community and have authority brought about by their training and the backing of physicians and nurses. However, as the primary contact point for patients seeking assistance in these facilities, they make physicians as physically inaccessible as they were previously when the patients went to the original indigenous therapists. Despite this, the community is now receiving a substantially better level of health care.

Several attempts have been made to incorporate the community's indigenous therapists into the practice of the Health Center. These efforts have been almost universally unsuccessful. This is largely due to the fact that the people are not only threatened by the awesome magnitude of the medical operation, but they also see little advantage to themselves in an alliance with such facilities. While successful collaborative relationships have been achieved elsewhere, this has not been the case in Atlanta where the efforts to date have always been one sided.

The problem of identifying the source and the channelling of healing power has frequently been noted in the literature; Graubard described it as the "Frankenstein Syndrome." He puts forth the idea that the very thin line between today's scientific fact and yesterday's myth and magic is brought into focus by the concept of the magician-scientist who may employ his knowledge in black or white magic. The assumption that knowledge is power and therefore both valuable and dangerous persists in most societies. Advances in knowledge are characteristically associated by men with a withdrawal of taboos ascribing certain areas to the gods.

Because adequate medical care has never been available in this community, there has been a reluctance to accept scientific explanations of illness. As long as the indigenous therapists remained the only source of healing power available to most of the residents of the area, the belief systems on which the therapists based their cures were perpetuated. There is little advantage to subscribing to the concepts of a system to which one has no access and rejecting the beliefs of those to whom one is obliged to go to seek help.

Most of the younger people in the community dismiss the indigenous therapists as quacks and their support mostly comes from the older age groups. Medical care through the OEO and other sources is becoming increasingly available to all residents of the area. In addition, an increasing effort is now being initiated to incorporate these therapists into the orthodox medical system as has been done so effectively in other cultures; whether this will help to maintain their identity and credibility or serve to make them vanish completely remains to be seen.

Source: Arthur L. Hall and Peter G. Bourne, "Indigenous Therapists in a Southern Black Urban Community." *Archives of General Psychiatry* 28 (1973): 137–142. Endnotes were removed. Copyright © 1973, American Medical Association. All rights reserved.

Commentary

Psychologists and psychiatrists have been much more willing to find a positive side of conjure than other scientists. In this article, hoodoo doctors appear as practitioners of an ethnicity-specific brand of psychiatry. As such, they help their clients make sense of their world, adjust to difficult situations, and otherwise achieve mental health. This positive interpretation has helped undermine older notions of conjurers as charlatans who cheat their clients or as threatening criminals whose goal is to harm. In addition, as demonstrated in the preceding article, mental health specialists sometimes seek the aid of such "indigenous therapists" to improve the health of the communities they serve.

HOODOO AS CENTRAL TO IDENTITY

From "Hoodoo in America"

Veaudeau is the European term for African magic practices and beliefs, but it is unknown to the American Negro. His own name for his practices is hoodoo, both terms being related to the West African term juju. "Conjure" is also freely used by the American Negro for these practices. In the Bahamas as on the West Coast of Africa the term is obeah. "Roots" is the Southern Negro's term for folk-doctoring by herbs and prescriptions, and by extension, and because all hoodoo doctors cure by roots, it may be used as a synonym for hoodoo.

Shreds of hoodoo beliefs and practices are found wherever any number of Negroes are found in America, but conjure has had its highest development along the Gulf coast, particularly in the city of New Orleans and in the surrounding country. It was these regions that were settled by the Haytian emigrees at the time of the overthrow of French rule in Hayti by L'Overture. Thousands of mulattoes and blacks, along with their white ex-masters were driven out, and the nearest French refuge was the province of Louisiana. They brought with them their hoodoo rituals, modified of course by contact with white civilization and the Catholic church, but predominantly African.

These island Negroes had retained far more of their West African background than the continental blacks. Many things had united to bring this about. When an island plantation was stocked with slaves, they remained together, as a rule, for the rest of their lives. Whole African families and even larger units remained intact. They continued to carry on their tribal customs in their new home without even the difficulty of struggling with a new language. The system of absentee landlords afforded scant white contact and the retention of African custom was relatively uninterrupted and easy. Moreover, the French masters were tolerant of the customs of others, even slaves, and the Negroes were encouraged to make themselves as much at home as possible in their bondage. So the African customs remained strong in their new home.

On the North American continent the situation was different. Slaves were traded like live stock or any other commodity. They were bought for speculation and shipped here and there. No thought was given even to family ties, to say nothing of tribal affiliations. Virginia sold slaves to Georgia; Alabama swapped black men with Texas. The owners with their families lived on their plantations and were in constant contact with their slaves. In consequence the tribal customs, and the African tongue, were soon lost. The strong African admixture of words and construction in any West Indian dialect does not occur among southern Negroes except on the Sea Islands on the Coast of South Carolina, the swamps of the adjacent mainland, and the sparsely populated lands in the vicinity of the O'Geechy rivers in Georgia.

For these reasons the Negroes fleeing Hayti and Santo Domingo brought to New Orleans and Louisiana, African rituals long since lost to their continental brothers.

This transplanted hoodoo worship was not uninfluenced by its surroundings. It took on characteristics of the prevailing religious practices of its immediate vicinity. In New Orleans in addition to herbs, reptiles, insects, it makes use of the altar, the candles, the incense, the holy water, and blessed oil of the Catholic church—that being the dominant religion of the city and state. But in Florida, no use is made of such paraphernalia. Herbs, reptiles, insects, and fragments of the human body are their stock in trade.

Source: Zora Neale Hurston, "Hoodoo in America." *Journal of American Folklore* 44 (1931): 317–318. Reprinted with permission.

Commentary

Although few expected it during Zora Neale Hurston's lifetime, her writing became the most important force for positive redefinitions of Voodoo and hoodoo. As can be seen in this selection from "Hoodoo in America," her first literary foray into the world of conjure, Hurston clearly saw hoodoo as a vital aspect of just who African Americans are. To her, it was a link to an African past that whites had tried hard to break. The survival of hoodoo proved blacks' strength in the face of adversity. She elaborated on this theme much more explicitly in her *Mules and Men.* Hurston's work inspired the modern scholarly, literary, and artistic celebration of hoodoo.

HOODOO AS AN ART FORM

From Conjure in African American Society

The art most strongly affected by hoodoo has been music. Songs referring to conjure were already in circulation by the nineteenth century. . . . A worker from the Federal Writers' Project recorded one such song during the 1930s:

> Keep 'way from me, hoodoo and witch, Lead my path from de porehouse gate;
> I pines for golden harps and sich, Lawd, I'll jes' set down and wait. Old Satan
> am a liar and a conjurer, too—If you don't watch out, he'll conjure you.

Others told stories of conjure. Henry F. Pyles remembered an example. The words recount the process by which a nineteenth-century hoodooist named Old Bab made his charms:

> Little pinch o' pepper,
> Little bunch o' wool.

Mumbledy-mumbledy.

Two, three Pammy Christy beans,
Little piece o' rusty iron.

Mumbledy-mumbledy.

Wrop it in a rag and tie it with hair,
Two from a boss and one from a mare.

Mumbledy, mumbledy, mumbledy.

Wet it in whiskey
Boughten with silver;

That make you wash so hard your sweat pop out,
And he come to pass, sure!

Such songs foreshadowed blues music about hoodoo. . . .

Conjurers have been common in African American literature as well. In the 1899 book *The Conjure Woman* Charles W. Chesnutt told of Uncle Julius, a prolific teller of conjure tales, and his relationships with whites. Chesnutt's stories, which often depict the hardships of slavery, were also an implicit critique of America's racist society. Today nationalist authors such as poet Ishmael Reed depict hoodooists as tricksters who undermine white power with magic. One need not be a nationalist, however, to use conjurers in one's writing. For many female African American authors conjure women are examples of powerful, independent black women. Alice Walker's *Third Life of Grange Copeland* provides an example. One character, Sister Madelaine, is a two-headed doctor who uses her income from conjure and fortunetelling to send her son to college. Though the son initially disdains his mother's "superstition," he comes to admire her profession and its attendant power after joining the civil rights movement. A similar character appears in Toni Morrison's *Sula*. Like Sister Madelaine, Morrison's conjurer is a strong black woman. Even the book's narrator, who ostensibly condemns her as evil, nevertheless expresses her admiration for the hoodooist's knowledge, child-rearing skills, magical acumen, and even her physical appearance.

> *Source:* Jeffrey E. Anderson, *Conjure in African American Society* (Baton Rouge: Louisiana State University Press, 2005), 154–155. Endnotes were removed.

Commentary

One outgrowth of the acceptance of hoodoo as a worthy part of black identity is that it has become a fixture of both popular and high culture. Conjure and Voodoo have long figured prominently in blues music and its predecessors. More recently, they have gained a place in the visual arts. Hoodoo has been most at home in literature, however. In particular, African American female writers have been inspired by the works of Zora Neale Hurston, most notably *Mules and Men,* to depict conjure as an essential element of blackness. The preceding passage describes this development.

VOODOO AS RELIGION

From Voodoo in Haiti

Certain exotic words are charged with evocative power. Voodoo is one. It usually conjures up visions of mysterious deaths, secret rites—or dark saturnalia celebrated by "blood-maddened, sex-maddened, god-maddened" negroes. The picture of Voodoo which this book will give may seem pale beside such images.

In fact—what is Voodoo? . . . Its devotees ask of it what men have always asked of religion: remedy for ills, satisfaction for needs and the hope of survival.

> *Source:* Alfred Métraux, *Voodoo in Haiti,* translated by Hugo Charteris and with an Introduction by Sidney W. Mintz (New York: Schocken, 1972), 15.

From Secrets of Voodoo

Voodoo encompasses an exceedingly complex religion and magic with complicated rituals and symbols that have developed for thousands of years—perhaps longer than any other of today's established faiths. The believer in Voodoo . . . centers his hopes and fears as strongly on it as does a follower of Christianity, Judaism, Buddhism, or Islam. Indeed, the Haitian atmosphere seems ever impregnated with it—as if with a rich, mystical aroma of Africa—to the extent that individuals as well as families are conscious of Voodoo's effect upon their lives with a curious mixture of glory and dread.

> *Source:* Milo Rigaud, *Secrets of Voodoo,* translated by Robert B. Cross (New York: Arco, 1969; reprint, San Francisco: City Lights, 1985), 7.

From The Complete Idiot's Guide to Voodoo

If you think all there is to voodoo are black magic, pins stuck in dolls, and the living dead, you're about to discover a powerful spiritual system that can bring immediate benefits. . . . Voodoo encompasses so much more than mere magic. It developed out of the slaves' struggle for freedom and to preserve their African heritage, and it touches every part of its practitioners' lives. It encompasses a broad pantheon of immortal spirits; rituals characterized by drumming, dancing, and the miracle of spirit possession; a personal relationship with the divine; and the healing power of herbal medicine.

> *Source:* Shannon R. Turlington, *The Complete Idiot's Guide to Voodoo* (Indianapolis: Alpha, 2002), xvii.

Commentary

Since the early years of the twentieth century, viewpoints of hoodoo and Voodoo have shifted from highly negative to highly positive among some groups. In addition to folklorists who now view African American supernaturalism as a legitimate practice and artists and activists who see the practice of hoodoo as an expression of blackness, many scholars and popular authors have begun to attack outdated representations of Voodoo and Vodou. In particular, studies that depict Haitian Vodou as a genuine religion rather than a threatening sorcery cult have proliferated since the mid-twentieth century. These excepts represent a series of short selections from works that seek to tear down stereotypes and redefine Vodou for modern audiences.

INSIDERS' VIEWS

From Narrative of the Life and Adventures of Henry Bibb,
An American Slave

There is much superstition among the slaves. Many of them believe in what they call "conjuration," tricking, and witchcraft; and some of them pretend to understand the art, and say that by it they can prevent their masters from exercising their will over their slaves. Such are often applied to by others, to give them power to prevent their masters from flogging them. The remedy is most generally some kind of bitter root; they are directed to chew it and spit towards their masters when they are angry with their slaves. At other times they prepare certain kinds of powders, to sprinkle about their masters dwellings. This is all done for the purpose of defending themselves in some peaceable manner, although I am satisfied that there is no virtue at all in it. I have tried it to perfection when I was a slave at the South. I was then a young man, full of life and vigor, and was very fond of visiting our neighbor slaves, but had no time to visit only Sundays, when I could get a permit to go, or after night, when I could slip off without being seen. If it was found out, the next morning I was called up to give an account of myself for going off without permission; and would very often get a flogging for it.

I got myself into a scrape at a certain time, by going off in this way, and I expected to be severely punished for it. I had a strong notion of running off, to escape being flogged, but was advised by a friend to go to one of those conjurers, who could prevent me from being flogged. I went and informed him of the difficulty. He said if I would pay him a small sum, he would prevent my being flogged. After I had paid him, he mixed up some alum, salt and other stuff into a powder, and said I must sprinkle it about my master, if he should offer to strike me; this would prevent him. He also gave me some kind of bitter root to chew, and spit towards him, which would certainly prevent my being flogged. According to order I used his remedy, and for some cause I was let pass without being flogged that time.

I had then great faith in conjuration and witchcraft. I was led to believe that I could do almost as I pleased, without being flogged. So on the next Sabbath my conjuration was fully tested by my going off, and staying away until Monday morning, without permission. When I returned home, my master declared that he would punish me for going off; but I did not believe that he could do it while I had this root and dust; and as he approached me, I commenced talking saucy to him. But he soon convinced me that there was no virtue in them. He became so enraged at me for saucing him, that he grasped a handful of switches and punished me severely, in spite of all my roots and powders.

But there was another old slave in that neighborhood, who professed to understand all about conjuration, and I thought I would try his skill. He told me that the first one was only a quack, and if I would only pay him a certain amount in cash, that he would tell me how to prevent any person from striking me. After I had paid him his charge, he told me to go to the cow-pen after night, and get some fresh cow manure, and mix it with red pepper and white people's hair, all to be put into a pot over the fire, and scorched until it could be ground into snuff. I was then to sprinkle it about my master's bedroom, in his hat and boots, and it would prevent him from ever abusing me in any way. After I got it all ready prepared, the smallest pinch of it scattered over a room, was enough to make a horse sneeze from the strength of it; but it did no good. I tried it to my satisfaction. It was my business to make fires in my master's chamber, night and morning. Whenever I could get a chance, I sprinkled a little of this dust about the linen of the bed where they would breathe it on retiring. This was to act upon them as what is called a kind of love powder, to change their sentiments of anger, to those of love, towards me, but this all proved to be vain imagination. The old man had my money, and I was treated no better for it.

One night when I went in to make a fire, I availed myself of the opportunity of sprinkling a very heavy charge of this powder about my master's bed. Soon after their going to bed, they began to cough and sneeze. Being close around the house, watching and listening, to know what the effect would be, I heard them ask each other what in the world it could be, that made them cough and sneeze so. All the while, I was trembling with fear, expecting every moment I should be called and asked if I knew any thing about it. After this, for fear they might find me out in my dangerous experiments upon them, I had to give them up, for the time being. I was then convinced that running away was the most effectual way by which a slave could escape cruel punishment.

Source: Henry Bibb, *Narrative of the Life and Adventures of Henry Bibb, an American Slave*, 3rd ed., with an Introduction by Lucius C. Matlack. (New York: Privately printed, 1850), 25–28.

A Description of Conjure by William Adams, an Ex-Slave Practitioner

Thar am lots of folks, an' edumacated ones too, dat says weuns believes in superstition. Well, 'tis 'cause dey don' undahstan'. 'Membah dat de Lawd, in some of His ways, am mysterious. De Bible says so. Thar am some things de Lawd wants all folks to know, some things jus' de chosen few to know, an' some things no one should know. Now, jus' 'cause yous don' know 'bout some of de Lawd's laws, 'taint superstition if some udder person undahstan's an' believes in sich.

Thar are some bo'n to sing, some bo'n to preach, an' also some bo'n to know de signs. Thar are some bo'n undah de powah of de devil an' have de powah to put injury an' misery on people, an' some bo'n undah de powah of de Lawd fo' to do good an' overcome de evil powah. Now, dat p'oduces two fo'ces, lak fiah an' wautah. De evil fo'ces stahts de fiah, an' I's have de wautah fo'ce to put de fiah out.

How I's larnt sich? Well, I's don' larn it. It come to me. W'en de Lawd gives sich powah to a person, it jus' comes to 'em. It am 40 yeahs ago now w'en I's fust, fully 'ealized dat I's have de powah. However, I's was always interested in de wo'kin's of de signs. W'en I's a little piccaninny, my mammy an' udder folks use to talk about de signs. I's heah dem talk about w'at happens to folks 'cause a spell was put on 'em. De ol' folks in dem days knows mo' 'bout de signs dat de Lawd uses to reveal His laws dan de folks of today. It am also true of de cullud folks in Africa, deys native lan'. Some of de folks laugh at thar beliefs an' says it am superstition but it am knowin' how de Lawd reveals His laws.

Source: William Adams, interview by Sheldon F. Gautier (TX), in George P. Rawick, ed., *The American Slave: A Composite Autobiography* (Westport: Greenwood, 1972–78), supp. 2, 2, pt. 1:16–17.

An 1878 Letter to the Editor of the Southern Workman

Dear Teacher:

Being requested by you to tell you what I know about conjure Doctors, I will endeavor to do so, according to the best of my ability. I remember once being at a woman's house, and there were six men and five girls there, and a conjure Doctor passed, his name was ———, but the people called him Dr. ———. He passed the house, and there were three men with him, and after he had passed the woman's house, about a half a mile, those that were at the woman's house, began to talk about him and make fun of him, with the young girls, and the woman told those at the house, that they had better stop talking about that conjurer; she said, "If you don't he will conjure you all." The men said to her, "He doesn't know that we are talking about him." She replied, "You need not fool with those conjurers, for they will conjure you by looking at you," but they would not stop. The conjure Dr. said to the men with him, that he had to go back to that woman's house—which he had passed about a mile back. He said, "They are talking about me and making fun of me;" and he turned round, and went back, and when be got in sight of the house they all got so afraid that some got under the bed and some went up the stairs, and the head woman of the house got almost frightened to death, but he went in and told them to come from down the stairs, and get from under the bed, for he said, "I have something to tell you all," and they all looked as if they were condemned to die, but he said to them, "Don't be uneasy," and he told them every word they said about him and not one could deny it. He said "honeys, I won't do anything about it this time, by you not knowing who I am, but when you are talking about me, you had as well be talking about Jesus Christ, for I can do you as much good, and I can do you as much harm." They all begged him to excuse them, and told him that they would never say anything about him again, and thanked him for not hurting them in any way; and you could not hear one of those men say any harm about him after that. All they would say would be that they would never say any thing about another conjurer as long as they lived, and after he had gone, he said to those men that were with him that those people were talking as well about him now as they were talking bad about him at first.

In 1873 I was going down the street and came across a conjure Dr. and he asked me where did a certain lady live, and I told him, and he went there; and when he got there the woman told him she had some kind of pain in her head and side, and told him something kept coming up in her throat and she did not know what to do, and she said, "I want you to look over for me," and he went and got his cards and shuffled them, and told her to take them in her hands, and she did so, and he told her to hand them back to him, and she did so, and he began to tell her what was the matter with her and he told her she was conjured and told her what it was about. And he told her she had better do something for it very soon, for if she didn't she would be under the ground very soon; and she told him she did not know what to do, and she asked him if he could do her any good, and he told her yes, he could cure her in two days. She said "All right," and he told her she was conjured by drinking a cup of tea at a wedding, and he looked in his sack, and got out his roots and made her a cup of tea and told her she would see what that was in her, and he told her to drink the tea, and she did so, and in five minutes a scorpion came out of her mouth. That frightened several of them, and after this thing was seen, they all got on the right side of that conjure Dr. and the next day she was all right, and she paid this conjurer twenty-five dollars and gave him as much as he could carry home with him, that is, such as meal and meat, and flour and lard.

At home there was a conjure Dr. that did a crime. He said he was going to kill a man, and this man whom he said he was going to kill had him put in jail, and as fast as the jailor would lock one door and turn his back, this conjurer would come out behind him, and they put him in there three times, and he did the same thing every time, and they started to put him in for the fourth time, and he said he was not going in there any more. So the sheriff took hold of one side of him, and the constable hold of the other, and just as soon as they fastened him, scorpions would run out of his coat sleeves and run on them, and they would turn him loose. Every time they would take hold of him the same thing would occur, so they turned him loose. I remember once of being at a woman's house, and a conjurer came there, and by the time he got in the house he told her that she was conjured and she asked him to look and see how her time would run. And he threw his cards to the top of the room and called them out one by one until he called them all down. And he looked over them, and told her that she was badly off and told her if she would put it into his hands he would fix things. And she told him all right, and he said, "Before I will do anything, you shall see who conjured you, and the one that conjured you shall come and make a great to do over you;" and he told her not to say any thing to him. That evening the man came and tried to make them believe that he believed he knew who did it, but they did not say anything much to him. But this conjure Doctor was off in the woods fixing for the man who conjured that woman, and when he went away, this conjure Dr. went back and asked the woman if she wanted him killed, and she told him to do as he chose. And he said, "What he conjured you with will kill you in five days;" and he said, "I shall turn it back on him;" and he did so, and he died in three days, and this woman got better. This conjure Dr. is known by both white and colored, and he has made his fortune, almost, by conjuring. I heard him say out of his own mouth that he made over five hundred dollars a week sometimes. The people believe a great deal in conjure Drs. some of them can throw down there walking stick and it will turn to a snake. In 1876, I was in ——— County working, and there was a lady there by the name of Clarinda ———, and they say round there that she is as dangerous as a rattlesnake.

If any one would go to her, you might hear her scream for a quarter of a mile, and she would begin to tell them whatever they wanted to know. There was a man went to her while I was over there, and she told him who conjured him, and this man went and got after him about it, and he said no one would tell him he did it, and the man asked him who told him that he conjured him, and he said Dr. ———; and this man went to this con-conjurer's house, to shoot her, and when he got there he pulled the trigger and tried to shoot her, but she had tricked his gun and he took it down, and just as soon as he took it down both barrels went off and liked to have killed him, and she told him he would have to crawl home, or some one would carry him, and he started home and before he had gotten two hundred yards from the house he could not do anything but crawl, and a cart came along and carried him home, and when he got home he was so badly off that he did not live but half a day. This conjurer had conjured him so badly that he could not live.

At my home once a conjurer was caught in a man's orchard, up a tree, and the man got his gun and shot after him, and this conjurer told the man to shoot again, and he shot him again, and this conjurer told him to come and get his shot, and the man went and the conjurer looked under his arm and gave him his shot. The people at my home believe in these conjure Drs. more than they do in the Physician Dr. These conjurers can get their money time the work is done because the people are afraid of them, and I believe they make more money than the white Dr.

I now will close by saying that I believe in the conjure Drs., and all this that I have written I can vouch for myself.

Yours truly

R.

Source: R., L., G., and A., "Conjure Doctors in the South,"
Southern Workman 7 (1878): 30.

The Text of a 1920s Chicago Defender Spiritual Supply Shop Ad

THE 6th AND 7th BOOKS OF MOSES OR MOSES' MAGICAL SPIRIT ART
Contains over 125 Seals used by Moses, Aaron, the Israelites and Egyptians in their magical arts. Price $1.00; no C.O.D. Money back guarantee. Seal of Love (printed on parchment) FREE. Other rare Black and White Magic books, Lodestone, Magnetic Sand, Seals, Incense, Parchment, Fairy Stones, Herbs, etc. Catalog Free. S. DEAN CO., Newark, MO.

Source: The Chicago Defender, July 2, 1927, 1:11.

Three Accounts by Modern Practitioners

"Vodou" by Mary Traversi, White Female

No problem with explaining my religion, because it is a religion. Vodou (Voodoo) actually means a drum beat in my religion. In Haiti it is called "serving the Spirits." This is quite

An advertisement for a divination service that appeared in a prominent African American newspaper. Note the use of a stereotypical Indian imagery to promote the effectiveness of the product. *The Chicago Defender*, July 5, 1924, 2:7.

interesting, because it is called that in all of the Afro-Caribbean religions. The Southern Hoodooists also make references to this.

Serving the Spirits is pretty much a way of life. I compare the LWA (Les Lois) to friends, because they all have personalities and have their preferences. They choose you. One does not choose the Spirits. This does not always make sense to people, because not everyone becomes initiated even though they serve the Spirits.

I was about 23 almost 24 when I found my way to Vodou. I was referred to my first Houngan when I was teaching a Tarot class. One of my pupils was a Santeria priestess. I live in California and Santeria is the primary Afro-Caribbean Diaspora religion. My first Houngan was an oddity in these parts. My first marriage was crumbling and I was willing to take any help I could get.

My first Houngan told me, "The Spirits like you. They want the best for you." I knew some information on Vodou and thought it was a ploy, because being Haitian is almost a prerequisite for being in the religion. Even today there are A LOT of houses in Haiti who will not give a true initiation to a non-black Haitian. They will take their money and give them a fake one though. Of course, the LWA are color blind and like who they like.

My first Houngan was an Afro-American male who traveled to Haiti in 1949 to become initiated. He had quite a few problems finding the right house for initiation. The Spirits led him to the right house and he went through it. As they did me.

Here is the caveat about initiation that people do not understand about Vodou. It is NOT for the practitioner, but for the LWA. If a person was dense going into the devjo, they will be dense getting out. Initiation does not bequeath power, it is a way to say "thank you" to the LWA. I have an obligation as a Mambo Asson to tell about the LWA and to uphold my religion. I do this with gratitude and awe.

It has been an amazing road with the LWA. They have guided me, protected me, and just been the best friends one can have. The LWA have taught me to trust my instincts and my own power, because YOU know you better then anyone else. They have also said, "we will be with you when everything blows up." The beauty of the religion is the ability to choose.

There is no "black or white" concept. The religion understands that humans are all really shades of grey. This is one of my favorite sayings from my first Houngan, "can't get mad at the Devil, 'cause he's just doin' his job."

I have studied Wiccan, Pagan, Hinduism, and Faery Faith, but Vodou was the path that touched my heart. It just made the most sense to me and it helped me to heal. It helps me to understand how to take life on its on terms.

As far as Vodou being connected to Hoodoo, they actually work very well together. I find a lot of spells in Vodou correspond with spells in Hoodoo. I call the LWA to help me with my Hoodoo work. They actually do come from different tracts though.

Marie Laveau was NOT a Vodousant. She was a Hoodooist and root worker. I see no record of her ever going to Haiti for initiation. Only in the last maybe ten to twenty years has New Orleans had an upsurge in people going to Haiti for initiations. This is where the two get confused. Voodoo in the U.S. is generally another name for Hoodoo.

I am white of French, German, and Portuguese descent. I am 36 years old, married, and live in Oakland, CA. I have a college degree and currently getting my MFA in creative writing at University of San Francisco. I am a free-lance travel writer. I was born and raised in San Francisco, CA. I do teach Tarot and have a long suffering psychic practice on the side. I practice Hoodoo for my family. I will teach a person Hoodoo or Vodou spell if I see it can help the situation.

"I Become a Conjure Lady" by Susan Santer, White Female

It started when a supervisor came on the scene, in our research lab. This individual was arrogant, impatient, but had few skills. As time went on, the ineptitude of the supervisor became ever more apparent; every day was a trial and because he was the spouse of our well-liked boss, we felt powerless to do anything about him.

Except put a spell on him.

As a way of lightening the burden of his presence we began searching the internet for fun ways of cursing this guy. Because I am a researcher, naturally I began to categorize what I read—"No, not Vodou, that's a religion" "no not Wicca that's just ridiculous" and found my way to the Lucky Mojo website. I was very impressed with the large amount of information and the style of presentation. And, as a history enthusiast, it was all very interesting. So, reading more and more, and combing the university library for information became the occupation of my free time.

I joined an online study group, and started frequenting the Detroit-area candle shops. Every time I took our dog for a walk I came home with handfuls of plants picked along the way. I started remembering all the herbal lore I had read as a teenager. I asked people about old-time cures they heard from their grandparents. And then, one day after our supervisor had a tantrum after a failed experiment, I crossed the line and said two words to myself, "Hotfoot powder."

Allowing myself the freedom to think magically has been an amazing thing. It's as if I found a well-loved book I had misplaced for many years. I realize now that I spent all my adult life turning away from a range of empathic skills, because I thought they did not fit with my science background. I now have so much more knowledge about non-European cultures, beyond the Buddhism I had studied previously. I credit conjure with broadening my interests and allowing me greater insight into other people.

Conjure is quite serious work and must be done with responsibility, but it has a fun side too, especially for a middle-aged woman. I absolutely love doing things that require me to slip off into the dark! Again, this is like finding that long-lost book from childhood.

And yes, our supervisor left us forever, after suffering from a case of foot numbness for which his physician could find no cause.

"A Dallas Clientele" by Valentina Burton, White Female

I am a card reader in Dallas, Texas. I read at a luxury boutique hotel near downtown and have a small private office and conjure supply shop. I am a graduate of the Lucky Mojo hoodoo correspondence course, and so I do much hoodoo consultation with clients. I find hoodoo to be extremely practical and successful in solving real-world problems, even for folks who haven't ever even imagined trying a magical solution.

I have had many amusing incidents related to me by my clients.

Due to my situation at the hotel I now tend to have a very upscale clientele, including a hilarious group of sophisticated, vibrant young women who actually refer to themselves as "The 'Sex in the City' Girls." One of "the Girls," an adorable and perky blonde, was moaning about how she was worried about a job interview the next day. I explained an old trick to get a job, using just salt. You tell the salt your intention, then carry some in your pocket into the interview, and try to get some of the salt actually on the person conducting the interview. I elaborated on ways to do this with some subtlety, and she seemed to understand. Not much more than a month after, they all swirled back in, nearly bursting to tell me what had happened. She told of how she had talked to the salt, loaded her pocket, and gone to the office. In the interview room she was successful in getting a few grains on the floor. They sat to begin, and the interviewer asked if she'd like a soda or coffee first and got up to get it for her. Seeing her opportunity, our girl carefully sprinkled a light dusting of salt in the chair. The interviewer returned, sat in the chair, was enchanted by the young lady, and immediately offered her the job!

One night at the hotel, I read for a charming girl. Her cards told me that things were really good in her life, just maybe not progressing quickly enough for her.

She said that all she really wanted was to find her "true love."

I explained how to do a traditional hoodoo salt bath, followed by a honey-jar to bring in exactly what she wanted in love.

A few weeks later she appeared back at my little table, and pulled me aside to tell me what had happened as a result of the work. I couldn't help giggling as she related that she hadn't had the nerve to do the honey-jar yet, because forty-eight hours after the salt bath she had received numerous phone calls . . . each call from a male friend declaring that he was so in love with her, that he was her true love. She was overwhelmed by the result, and was really worried about what to expect from the honey-jar! . . .

I think the results folks get with hoodoo are wonderful just because they frequently are "too much." There is no mistaking that something has actually happened, and this seems to create all sorts of conflicting emotions in the client. They swing from shock, to fear, to elation, and then finally to a true sense of wonder. It's really fun to watch!

Source: Contributions solicited by the author from members of the Lucky Mojo Curio Company's Hoodoo Rootwork Correspondence Course discussion group.

Commentary

Doctors, psychiatrists, folklorists, and the like have much to tell the world about hoodoo and Voodoo, but as outsiders they cannot capture quite what those who practice it experience. These selections are all by those who believe or at one time believed in conjure or Voodoo. Unlike most scholarly investigators, they tend to evaluate hoodoo not on the basis of things like social function, artistic value, or sometimes even religious content. Instead, what matters is whether or not it works.

These texts represent a variety of viewpoints, ranging from the skeptical to the faithful practitioner. The first two selections are from those who had their first experiences with hoodoo while slaves. Bibb tried it and found it lacking. Adams, on the other hand, not only believed it but found in his own practice the workings of God. The third document—a letter to the editor of the *Southern Workman,* school newspaper of the Hampton Institute—is a rare example of an educated and presumably socially advancing African American admitting to his faith in magic during a time when most blacks of his station were striving to purge their society of such "superstitions." As one might guess, the editor was rather disapproving. The next selection is an example of the text from a typical twentieth-century hoodoo newspaper advertisement. As it clearly demonstrates, conjure adapted to the times, even to the point of using mass media marketing.

The final three accounts were submitted to the author in 2007 by members of a hoodoo correspondence course taught by Catherine Yronwode, proprietor of the Lucky Mojo Curio Company. Lucky Mojo is one of the most prominent modern conjure businesses and does most of its business online. As the stories indicate, members of the course are no less modern than the company. Most notably, their beliefs and practices not only show their faith in Vodou and hoodoo but demonstrate an outlook shaped by the spiritual eclecticism that has so influenced the United States since the 1960s.

WORKS CITED

Anderson, Jeffrey E. *Conjure in African American Society.* Baton Rouge: Louisiana State University Press, 2005.

Bibb, Henry. *Narrative of the Life and Adventures of Henry Bibb, an American Slave.* 3rd ed. With an Introduction by Lucius C. Matlack. New York: Privately printed, 1850.

Cable, George Washington. "Creole Slave Songs." With illustrations by E. W. Kemble. *The Century Magazine* 31 (1886): 807–828.

Chicago Defender, The. July 2, 1927, 1:11

Hall, Arthur L. and Bourne, Peter G. "Indigenous Therapists in a Southern Black Urban Community." *Archives of General Psychiatry* 28 (1973): 137–142.

Herron, Leonora. "Conjuring and Conjure Doctors." *Southern Workman* 24 (1891): 117–118.

Hurston, Zora Neale. "Hoodoo in America." *Journal of American Folklore* 44 (1931): 317–318.

Métraux, Alfred. *Voodoo in Haiti.* Translated by Hugo Charteris and with an Introduction by Sidney W. Mintz. New York: Schocken, 1972.

Page, Thomas Nelson. *Red Rock: A Chronicle of Reconstruction.* Charles Scribner's Sons, 1898.

R., L., G., and A. "Conjure Doctors in the South." *The Southern Workman* 7 (1878): 30–31.

Rawick, George P., ed. *The American Slave: A Composite Autobiography.* Westport: Greenwood, 1972–78.

Rigaud, Milo. *Secrets of Voodoo.* Trans. by Robert B. Cross. New York: Arco, 1969; reprint, San Francisco: City Lights, 1985.

Saphir, J. Robin, Arnold Gold, James Giambrone, and James F. Holland. "Voodoo Poisoning in Buffalo, NY." *The Journal of the American Medical Association* 202 (1967): 437–438.

Turlington, Shannon R. *The Complete Idiot's Guide to Voodoo.* Indianapolis: Alpha, 2002.

Four

Scholarship and Approaches

The subjects of hoodoo, conjure, and Voodoo are unusual in that there is not a great body of scholarship surrounding them. Most of what has been written appeared before the 1940s. As one might guess, these older works were none too complimentary. In fact, their usual purpose was to illustrate the supposed backwardness of American blacks. Sometimes the depictions were prime examples of racial denigration, designed to convince whites of the need to control the alleged barbarians in their midst. This openly hostile approach was most common during the nineteenth century, when white fear of the revolutionary potential of African American slaves and freedmen was at its height.

Other works adopted a condescending rather than condemnatory approach, which became the preferred viewpoint after whites had confined blacks to second-class status by implementing discriminatory laws and practicing widespread lynching during the late nineteenth and early twentieth centuries. These works used the study of hoodoo and Voodoo as pretexts to depict magical and religious ceremonies in ways that were variously exotic, titillating, or laughable to white readers. Condescension was certainly less overtly hostile to African Americans. At the same time it helped prevent whites from even considering equality for blacks by insidiously defining the latter as superstitious beings who were therefore inferior to whites in intellectual attainment.

Most of those writing about African American supernaturalism were whites. Such authors composed their books and articles primarily to entertain readers rather than from the conviction that hoodoo had any real power. Of course, any assumption that whites could not be believers would be patently false. For instance, many accounts of New Orleans Voodoo ceremonies describe them as including Caucasian participants. On the other hand, most whites were nonbe-lievers. They consequently had an inherent bias against black supernaturalism, especially during the nineteenth and early twentieth centuries, when race rela-tions were especially tense.

Average African Americans, who typically believed in and often practiced con-jure, were far less hostile than whites. Occasionally their more moderate views made it into print. Such was the case with many slave narratives, including the well-known autobiographies of Frederick Douglass, Henry Bibb, and William Wells Brown. Charles W. Chesnutt, an African American writer of fiction, felt comfortable enough with hoodoo to make it the subject of his 1899 collection of short stories, *The Conjure Woman.*

In contrast, many late nineteenth- and early twentieth-century African American leaders overwhelmingly accepted whites' viewpoints on conjure. In keeping with the prevailing stereotypes of their day, they considered the survival of African-derived magic and religion in black society as a blot on their race. There was a difference in how the races viewed hoodoo and conjure, however. Whites saw its presence as defining the black race as inferior. African Americans saw it as a negative feature of their society that cast them in a bad light—in other words, a tool whites used to define them as second-rate humans. This viewpoint is excellently illustrated in several letters to the editor and articles that appeared in the *Southern Workman,* the school newspaper of the Hampton Institute. They both record information on conjure for future generations while lamenting the continued practice of what one author called "a curious conglomerate of fetich-ism, divination, quackery, incantation and demonology" (Herron, 117).

Fortunately, since the mid-twentieth century, a new breed of scholarship has developed that sees conjure as not simply worthwhile as a relic of the past but as a practice worthy of celebration. Poems by Ishmael Reed laud the power of conjurers, depicting them as a force for liberation from white dominance. Many doctors and mental health specialists recognize beneficial effects of hoodoo and Voodoo. Even scholars like Martha Ward have come to see black supernaturalism as a vital part of what it has meant to be African American. At present, such positive understand-ings of conjure are largely confined to believers, practitioners, and their intellectual supporters, but the new viewpoint is growing in prominence among the general public as well. The following discussion examines just how today's approach to conjure developed from the outright hostility of the nineteenth century.

HOODOO AS THREAT

White authors have always considered African American spirituality frighten-ing. During slavery's long tenure in the United States, this feeling was much more intense than in later days. Conjure and Voodoo seemed to threaten the existing

A hoodoo practitioner burning a "Voodoo doll," the embodi-
ment of threatening hoodoo. Virginia Frazier Boyle, *Devil
Tales,* with illustrations by A. B. Frost (1900; reprint, Freeport:
Books for Libraries Press, 1972), facing p. 98.

order. At times, it was the prevailing Christian religion that felt itself assailed
by black beliefs. That New Englanders accused African Americans of witchcraft
during the seventeenth century testifies to whites' fears for their faith. Seen from
a European American viewpoint, conjurers' magic worked to undermine religious belief. By definition, practitioners were servants of Satan (McMillan, 104;
Breslaw, 535–556).

Just as common as the fear that conjure could undermine religion was the belief that hoodoo was a threat to the South's racist labor and social systems. Under
slavery, blacks' rebellious activities included the casting of spells to help them
escape from bondage and the manufacture of charms to prevent mistreatment
by their masters. Sometimes, they focused on more than self-protection and
struck back, using magical poisons to sicken or kill their owners. Whites feared
the potential of African American supernaturalism, especially when it came to
their own health. Numerous antebellum laws prohibiting slaves from practicing medicine were almost certainly designed to prevent rootworkers from using
their knowledge to harm their masters (Bibb, 26–27; Douglass, 41–42; Wilkie,
136–146; Fett, 142, 162–164).

Whites were even more afraid of conjurers' potential as revolutionary figures.
They had good reason to be. The Haitian Revolution, the only successful slave
uprising in modern history, was supposedly inspired by Vodou. In the United
States, there were examples of smaller insurrections that featured conjurers among

their leaders. Perhaps the most prominent was the Denmark Vesey Revolt. One of Vesey's chief lieutenants was Gullah Jack Pritchard, a native East African. Gullah Jack reportedly promised supernatural protection to Vesey and his men. Similar conjurer-leaders were reported across the South (Wilkie, 136–146; Fett, 142, 162–165, 244 n87; Anderson, *Conjure,* 87).

The fear that conjurers were a threat to society persisted much longer than did slavery itself. White slaveowners clung to the belief that they had been benevolent masters, who had conferred the blessings of civilization on their bondspeople. Without the continued oversight of the supposedly superior race, the planters feared that blacks would revert to what whites believed was their natural state: barbarism. Of course, such savagery was marked by faith in supernaturalism. In 1889, Philip A. Bruce wrote, "There is no peculiarity of the negro that is more marked in its influence on his conduct than his superstitiousness, and in the individual of no other race is the same trait more fully developed." He attributed this supposed fact to the "obtuseness and narrowness of his intellect" (Bruce, 111). Any loss of power to such a people was an overriding concern for racist whites. Bruce ominously stated that blacks did occasionally escape from the control of whites. Large landholders, he recorded, sometimes had to force conjurers off their plantations to retain command of their African American workforce. Other sources report a more serious loss of white control. Lieutenant Governor C. C. Antoine of Reconstruction-era Louisiana, was accused of practicing Voodoo by those whites who hated him because of both his race and the conquering North that he represented. Marie Laveau was herself credited with considerable political influence in the immediate post–Civil War period. In the eyes of whites, Antoine, Laveau, and others like them threatened southern civilization (Bruce, 120; Dillon, "Marie the Great," 28–29).

One particularly unusual fear attached to conjurers was that they threatened the much-vaunted purity of white women. Antebellum legal documents record instances of unmarried white women claiming that conjurers had magically forced them to engage in intercourse (Wyatt-Brown, 313, 315–316, 424–425). Although whites' fear of black sexuality was strong throughout the slave era and beyond, outright rape was not the only way conjure sullied the honor of white females. In 1904, Helen Pitkin published a novel entitled *An Angel by Brevet,* which described Voodoo and white Creoles' contact with it. Although it includes much useful information on the faith, its plot centers on Angèlique a young white woman who is drawn to Voodoo as a way to win the man she loves. The result is the near death of her romantic rival, which afflicts Angèlique with guilt and eventually drives her to repentance.

Just what could happen to a white female who became too deeply involved in Voodoo was explained in a tale of an unnamed but beautiful white girl first recorded in an 1869 article that appeared in New Orleans' *Daily Picayune.*

According to the story, the girl was French but had fled political turmoil with her parents during the mid-nineteenth century. After arriving in Louisiana, tragedy struck. Her parents died, leaving the girl in the hands of strangers. Her guardians proved unfit for the task, allowing her to become involved with black Voodoo practitioners. Participating in Voodoo rituals, the article states, had robbed her of both sight and reason. Her only option was to serve as a priestess of the religion, rejected by whites but adored by her black followers—an appalling fate in the eyes of nineteenth-century whites (Dillon, "Famous Wangateurs," 18).

Whites' dread of hoodoo was strongest before the twentieth century, although unease continues to linger even today. For instance, the recent book *Whisper to the Black Candle: Voodoo, Murder, and the Case of Anjette Lyles* explicitly ties African American beliefs to crime. The murder in question, however, had no direct link to either Voodoo or hoodoo. Similarly, the current publisher of Newbell Niles Puckett's *Folk Beliefs of the Southern Negro,* a classic work on conjure, Voodoo, and other aspects of black supernaturalism, includes it in the Patterson Smith Reprint Series in Criminology, Law Enforcement, and Social Problems. Other titles in the series address prison discipline, delinquency, and the parole system. In these cases and many others, the authors do not intend to denigrate blacks' beliefs. Instead, they simply reflect the disquietude with African American magic that has plagued whites since colonial times.

HOODOO AS CHARLATANRY

The idea that hoodoo is a form of charlatanry has been present since colonial times as well. Not until after emancipation, however, did this view take precedence over the idea that conjure and Voodoo were dangerous. The new focus reflected the Jim Crow racial system in place by the late nineteenth and early twentieth centuries. With African Americans safely defined as segregated inferiors, conjurers and Voodoo priestesses were no longer as threatening figures as in the past. Increasing numbers of whites defined them as little more than mere con artists who cheated their supposedly simple-minded black clients.

In the eyes of whites—and many blacks as well—conjure and Voodoo might not be threats to society, but they were certainly vices. As such, they were to be suppressed. Few if any African Americans were prosecuted for practicing magic or being members of Voodoo congregations. Constitutional freedom of religion made laws against expressions of spirituality difficult to pass and enforce, especially after ratification of the Fourteenth and Fifteenth Amendments gave African Americans at least an illusion of equal standing as American citizens. Practitioners instead faced charges stemming from assumedly false representations of their abilities. Jean Montanée, the famed New Orleans hoodoo practitioner, occasionally ran into legal trouble for fraud, usually because of dealings with whites who did not achieve the results they sought. One famous effort to prosecute a well-known conjurer was the work of High Sheriff James McTeer, who attempted to arrest Dr. Buzzard of St. Helena Island, South Carolina, on charges that he practiced medicine without a license. McTeer, himself an amateur conjurer, recorded his failures in *Fifty Years as a Low Country Witch Doctor.* Many other practitioners faced charges of mail fraud, violating local laws against selling charms or fortune-telling, or simple vagrancy (Long, *Voudou Priestess,* 137–139; Long, *Spiritual Merchants,* 131).

An 1894 fictional account of a hoodoo-related prosecution clearly illustrates white viewpoints. Entitled "A Case of Hoodoo," it tells of Washington Webb, a

THE KING OF THE VOODOOS.

A prominent Missouri hoodoo doctor, appearing as little more than a drunk charlatan in this illustration. Mary Alicia Owen, *Old Rabbit, the Voodoo and Other Sorcerers,* with an Introduction by Charles Godfrey Leland, with Illustrations by Juliette A. Owen and Louis Wain (London: T. Fisher Unwin, 1893; reprint, Whitefish, MT: Kessinger Publishing, 2003), p. 172.

fortuneteller and dabbler in conjure, who is on trial for fraud. Webb is a distinctly unsympathetic figure. The author of the tale, William Cecil Elam, describes him in a manner calculated to elicit repulsion. Webb was "colored, a simple-looking fellow, of a dull, dead-black complexion, with staring pop-eyes, projecting and flapping ears that seemed to grow out of the corners of his wide mouth, and a profusion of reddish, sunburnt hair growing into tight little standing twists all over his head" (Elam, 138). Jefferson Hunks, a former client of Webb who is pressing charges against the conjurer, is none too admirable himself. His grounds for accusation are that he purchased charms and had his fortune told by Webb, only to convert to Christianity a few days later. In keeping with his new beliefs, he has eschewed supernaturalism as a work of Satan. Now, he wants the $1.39 he paid Webb returned. The judge refuses to return Hunks's money, but he does determine that the conjurer is a swindler of the "ignorant and credulous" and a vagrant. Webb receives a jail term, designated to last until he can pay a $200 fine (Elam, 140–141). The author's point was clear—conjurers are fakes, and those who patronize them are fools.

This take on hoodoo remained strong well into the twentieth century. An example of its power was an article by George J. McCall entitled, "Symbiosis: The Case of Hoodoo and the Numbers Racket." The essay is an interesting look at how conjure and illegal lotteries interact. McCall's conclusion is that they support each other. Lottery players buy charms, candles, and dreambooks from hoodoo doctors and shops to gain spiritual assistance with their gambling. Those running the numbers games likewise benefit. Many players become convinced that they can win against the odds, increasing the amount they bet (and usually lose). In addition, the widespread use of books that purport to predict one's winning numbers based on the dream he or she had the night before placing a bet means that the wagers tend to cluster around certain numbers linked to common dreams. Those who run the lotteries commonly remove these numbers from the pool or lessen the payouts for those who chose them, helping the "bank" maximize its profits by ensuring that a disproportionate number will lose.

McCall was likely correct when he wrote that hoodoo and illegal gaming are linked, or at least that they were at the time of his writing; however, he uncritically assumed that those conjurers and shops that catered to gamblers were charlatans. This assumption is abundantly clear in McCall's comment that, "if a separation of clientele [of hoodoo practitioners and the operators of lotteries] could be effected, both operations might be substantially weakened, possibly resulting in considerable saving of ill-spent cash for many Negro families" (McCall, 370).

Works defining conjure as charlatanry have been on the decline since at least the 1970s. One reason is a shift in outlook. Popular promotion of multiculturalism has helped lessen both white and black condemnation of hoodoo. Multiculturalist thinking makes it difficult to condemn Voodoo priestesses and conjurers because the philosophy defines them as expressions of black culture, on par with spiritual specialists from any other society. Scholars' adoption of postmodernism, which includes the denial of objectivity as one of its central tenets, has also weakened Americans' belief in authoritative spirituality and their ability to deny the validity of supernaturalism. For many Americans, condemning conjure or Voodoo as vice would mean violating deeply held beliefs in relativism (Anderson, *Conjure,* 18–24).

The belief that conjure and Voodoo are mere charlatanry will never entirely disappear, however. After all, examples of spells failing to achieve desired results abound. Refunds are rare in such cases, guaranteeing dissatisfied customers. As with any professional or amateur pursuit, one can safely assume that many practice conjure because of a love for tradition. Some do so as an expression of their spirituality. Others do so for profit alone and do not particularly care whether or not they help their clients. Simply assuming that the belief system is itself a fraud and that believers are dupes is wholly unwarranted.

VOODOO/HOODOO AS SUPERSTITION

By far the greatest number of authors have approached conjure and Voodoo as superstition. The chief difference between this view and other negative conceptions of hoodoo is that it does not necessarily assume that anyone will be harmed by its practice. On the contrary, this softer approach sees conjure and Voodoo simply as signs of backwardness. As such they are things to poke fun at or even sources of entertainment. Because these practices are so strongly linked to African Americans, it is easy for racism to become a part of this approach, especially when authors describe Voodoo and conjure as uniquely black superstitions without parallel in white society. Of course, many have described practitioners as parasites who prey on the otherwise harmless superstition of their clients, transforming what might otherwise be deemed amusing, outdated beliefs into sheer foolishness that was best avoided.

Thaddeus Norris provided an excellent illustration of the problems with the hoodoo-as-superstition approach in his 1870 article, "Negro Superstitions." Condescending racism is present throughout the brief essay, making it quite offensive to modern readers. The introductory paragraphs of the work draw a clear line between the refined "myths" of whites and the "repulsive" superstitions of blacks, thereby rendering conjure and other aspects of black folk belief uniquely backward. Later in the essay, Norris described Voodoo—called "Hoodoo" in the text—as one of these superstitions. Although the article does acknowledge that Voodoo involved worship and "heathenish rites," the only feature of the religion Norris detailed was a firsthand account of a hoodoo poisoning by which a slave Norris had known years before supposedly developed a condition in which tadpoles infested his blood. In this case, a white man became a charlatan—although Norris never describes him as one—curing the supposed infestation by bleeding the victim and then secretly pouring live tadpoles into the basin that held the blood. After seeing the blood and tadpoles, the slave rapidly recovered. In addition to the fraud, Norris's description of Voodoo is especially troubling because he refused to treat it as a religion. To him, it was merely one of many entertainingly primitive black superstitions.

The most prominent author to treat African American conjure and Voodoo as superstition was Robert Tallant, whose popular *Voodoo in New Orleans* remains in print more than 60 years since its initial publication. According to Tallant, Voodoo and hoodoo were exotic, sensual, and mysterious practices. They could also be threatening, and their practitioners were charlatans in his view. Tallant's work was never intended to be a scholarly examination of Voodoo/hoodoo. His purpose in writing was clearly to turn a profit by entertaining his audience. To this end, much of his information is basically accurate, although he had no problems exaggerating or even inventing grotesque details of Voodoo. Despite its flaws, *Voodoo in New Orleans* remains the most accessible source for information on the Crescent City's version of African American religion and supernaturalism. As such, it continues to influence the outlook of both scholars and everyday readers.

A popular tourist-oriented Voodoo shop on New Orleans's Bourbon Street. Outdated understandings of the religion continue to draw visitors to the Crescent City, many hoping to catch a glimpse of grotesque superstition or threatening magic. Author's personal collection.

HOODOO AS FOLKLORE

In most people's minds, little differentiates superstition from folklore. Modern scholars disagree. They see folklore as an ever-evolving set of beliefs that is never outdated because it adapts to new conditions; however, folklorists' ideas had to undergo their own evolution to reach this point. Some of the earliest folkloric approaches to conjure and Voodoo were exceedingly similar to the popular understanding of black supernaturalism as superstition in that they treat conjure and Voodoo as relics of the past. Folklorists merely recorded details of the practices for future generations who would not have the supposed misfortune of experiencing them firsthand. Such was the case with numerous articles that appeared in the *Southern Workman* during the last three decades of the nineteenth century. Several essays in the *Journal of American Folklore* from the same period likewise give the impression that they were preserving a record of outdated practices. One article, "Some Bits of Plant Lore," displays the blurred lines between folklore and superstition in the minds of nineteenth-century whites when it introduced the topic of herbalism by stating, "The newness of the country, the practicality of a wealth-seeking nation furnishes poor soil for the dreamy, poetic traditions and scraps of traditions about trees and plants that have been brought to us from older countries" (Bergen, "Bits of Plant-Lore," 19).

Despite many early folklorists' assumption that conjure was a relic of earlier days, they nevertheless produced some highly influential works on hoodoo. The first to discuss conjure in depth was Newbell Niles Puckett, about a quarter of whose 1926 *Folk Beliefs of the Southern Negro* specifically addressed conjure and Voodoo. Puckett unabashedly saw himself as a collector of superstitions. In his judgment, the superstitions held by "backward" African Americans in his own day were the survivals of beliefs they had picked up from more "advanced" whites during previous centuries. Whites had cast off these superstitions, Puckett

Rabbit, a conjurer according to Missouri folklore. Mary Alicia Owen, *Old Rabbit, the Voodoo and Other Sorcerers*, with an Introduction by Charles Godfrey Leland, with Illustrations by Juliette A. Owen and Louis Wain (London: T. Fisher Unwin, 1893; reprint, Whitefish, MT: Kessinger Publishing, 2003), p. 140.

believed, but blacks had proven unable to do so (Puckett, 1–3, 520–521). Despite his problematic approach to African American supernaturalism, Puckett included a wealth of information from personal observation, interviews, and print sources in his work. It remains a valuable source today.

Over the years, folklore has largely evolved beyond its early racist assumptions and developed an analytical approach to the study of hoodoo. The drive to preserve fading beliefs has persisted, sometimes producing vitally important works, most notably Harry Middleton Hyatt's five-volume *Hoodoo-Conjuration-Witchcraft-Rootwork*. Though an invaluable book, it consists almost entirely of transcribed oral histories with hundreds of conjurers. Folklore's increasingly analytical focus has proven more innovative. During the second half of the twentieth century, serious attempts to study hoodoo rather than to simply collect stories and spell formulae have appeared. One example was Norman E. Whitten's 1962 article "Contemporary Patterns of Malign Occultism among Negroes in North Carolina," which analyzed the configuration of evil conjure in a single state. In 1980, Michael E. Bell completed his as-yet-unpublished dissertation, "Pattern, Structure, and Logic in Afro-American Hoodoo Performance," an ambitious attempt to dispel longstanding assumptions that conjure was without logic in its prescriptions for both good and evil intent.

Arguably the most important outgrowth of the folkloric viewpoint has been a widespread reassessment of African American supernaturalism and religion as positive features of black society. More than anyone else, Zora Neale Hurston assaulted Americans' assumptions about hoodoo. Hurston, a student of anthropology great Franz Boas, undertook the study of hoodoo during the late 1920s. Hurston, a black woman, was reacting to the artistic and literary movement known as the Harlem Renaissance. Like other African Americans of her day, she saw black folk culture as something to celebrate. Hoodoo—by which term she designates what others would separate into conjure and Voodoo—became one of her chief subjects of study. To Hurston, hoodoo was to be neither forgotten nor simply preserved in print form. On the contrary, she celebrated its refusal to be suppressed in the face of widespread condemnation and frequent criminal prosecution. Many features of conjure that had been universally villified by earlier writers acquired positive features in her skilled hands. Even casting spells to cause death did not make hoodooists murderers in Hurston's eyes. Instead, doing so showed the strength of African American magic and its practitioners (Hurston, *Mules and Men,* 176; Anderson, "Voodoo in Black and White").

Hurston's contribution to the study of conjure was enormous, largely because she believed and took part in what she wrote about. She described her foray into the world of African American magic in a lengthy 1931 article entitled "Hoodoo in America" that was partially reproduced in her later book *Mules and Men.* Hurston not only wrote about working magic but claimed to have undergone multiple initiations into Voodoo and to have encountered hoodoo spirits. Hurston's work contains details of conjure and Voodoo recorded nowhere else. Still, like white folklorists of her day, she feared that hoodoo might disappear and saw herself as rescuing the "shreds" that remained. To this end, she appended lists of hoodoo spells and magical materials to the end of her article (Hurston, 318, 411–417).

Hurston's writings on hoodoo, however, are deeply problematic. For one thing, she plagiarized extensively from an early twentieth-century conjure manual and passed off the information as oral folklore. Also, some of the conjure stories she included in her article were fabricated. Her accounts of elaborate initiations may have been as well. Similarly, Hurston's writing tends toward sensationalism. In fact, its style is not so different from that of whites who used African American "superstition" as entertainment. Despite her many flaws, Hurston succeeded in persuasively reinterpreting hoodoo as something to be celebrated, a fact that all modern researchers must remember (Long, *Spiritual Merchants,* 123; Anderson, "Voodoo in Black and White").

VOODOO/HOODOO AS MEDICALLY POTENT

Much of the conjure- and Voodoo-related scholarship of the second half of the twentieth century and beyond has approached African American supernaturalism as medically effective. This understanding has not been wholly confined to recent decades. Believers, of course, did not question the power of the supernatural to either harm or heal. Even nonbelievers had little doubt that hoodoo could affect one's health. For instance, James C. Neal's 1891 condemnation of midwifery entitled "Legalized Crime in Florida" addressed a variety of conjure-related practices that its author believed negatively affected black midwives' ability to deliver infants. The author assumed that conjure designed to ease childbirth had no beneficial qualities and was both a hindrance to safe deliveries and a damning indicator of "superstitious" black midwives' medical incompetence.

A profound shift in how medical specialists viewed conjure began with the publication of Walter B. Cannon's 1942 essay "'Voodoo' Death." Despite its title, Cannon's article had little to do with African American religion and supernaturalism. On the contrary, it was a wide-ranging investigation that lumped all instances of death-by-magic under the misleading heading of "Voodoo." Nevertheless, Cannon's conclusion, that curses could kill by causing extreme excitement leading to fatal falls in blood pressure, has proven highly influential. Several authors followed in his footsteps, offering modified or alternative explanations for the effectiveness of curses. Some even addressed African American supernaturalism. Although such authors had no intention of improving the negative image of conjure and Voodoo, they did begin the process by arguing that at least negative hoodoo was not charlatanry. It could, in fact, be quite effective.

By no means did Cannon and his successors deal a death blow to the traditional view of the medical establishment. The assessment of hoodoo as a form of quackery persisted well beyond the early twentieth century. It was so strong during the second half of the century that an author of one 1972 article assumed his readers would hold this view, entitling his investigation of the powers of conjurers "Can a 'Root Doctor' Actually Put a Hex On?" Although the author felt it necessary to devote most of his work to arguing that evil hoodoo could work, he nevertheless took conjure seriously, referencing multiple experts and recording verified stories of magical ailments (Michaelson).

Despite persistent doubts surrounding hoodoo's effectiveness, many physicians have accepted that it must be understood to properly treat believers. Those who have adopted this view are principally concerned with ways health care professionals can cure patients who believe themselves to be cursed or otherwise under supernatural influence. For example, Chase Patterson Kimball's 1970 article "A Case of Pseudocyesis Caused by 'Roots'" recorded the story of a woman who believed a conjurer was working to break up her marriage. The hoodooist, she thought, had caused her to experience a case of false pregnancy to help bring about this result. Kimball was unable to offer specific advice for treating those who believed themselves afflicted with a similar ailment, although he did suggest that physicians employ rootworkers in like situations. Other researches have recommended the same approach or suggested that doctors familiarize themselves with conjure. They reasoned that patients who believe themselves cursed should be treated not just with scientific medicine but with supernatural cures as well. Those who consider themselves under the influence of malign spiritual forces respond best to those who honor their beliefs during treatment.

Doctors have typically depicted hoodoo—whether effective or not—as a barrier to good health. This viewpoint should not be surprising. After all, physicians' primary occupation is healing ailments. Moreover, many of their rootwork-related cases involve curses, showing them the most threatening side of hoodoo. In recent years, however, some scholars have come to see benefits in African American supernaturalism. One prominent scholarly work dealing with conjure as an beneficial healing practice is Wonda L. Fontenot's *Secret Doctors,* which defines African American supernatural healing practices as *ethnomedicine*—in other words, a legitimate, culturally specific form of treatment. A popular work that endorses a similar viewpoint is Faith Mitchell's *Hoodoo Medicine: Gullah Herbal Remedies,* a collection of traditional herbal remedies collected in the South Carolina Sea Islands. Mitchell not only lists dozens of herbs and their traditional usage but also frequently includes their traditional function in Euro-American and/or Native American practice and their officially recognized pharmacological properties.

Recent works addressing African American magic as effective medicine are valuable contributions to the study of hoodoo. Their major drawback is that they present only the positive side of conjure. To some extent, this focus provides a counterbalance to decades of scholarship that depicted rootwork as a collection of curses. At the same time, they risk reducing hoodoo to a mere conglomeration of healing remedies by obscuring both its supernatural import and its malevolent features.

HOODOO AS FOLK PSYCHIATRY

Closely linked to the understanding of hoodoo as medically potent is the view that it is a form of folk psychiatry. Like health care professionals, psychiatrists and psychologists turned their attention to conjure in the wake of scholarship addressing Voodoo death, which Cannon had argued was at its heart a phenomenon resting on victims' belief in curses—thus an essentially psychological ailment (Cannon, 189–190). Unlike doctors, mental health care providers were quick to see conjure and Voodoo as healthful practices, forms of folk psychiatry that helped believers cope with difficult situations. Writing in 1973, Arthur L. Hall and Peter G. Bourne referred to the conjurer as an "indigenous therapist," which they defined "as a member of a community using sociological circumstances peculiar to the predominant ethnic and cultural groups of that community in an attempt to correct mental or physical disorders" (Hall and Bourne, 137) Such ethnopsychiatrists, they argued, can cure a variety of mental ailments because they understand and empathize with their clients. Of course, in some cases, mental disorders express themselves physically. When hoodoo practitioners help cure the underlying problem, they likewise alleviate the physical symptoms. For instance, Hall and Bourne recorded the case of a schizophrenic woman who responded better to orthodox therapy after consulting with a rootworker who provided her with a tea to remove the curse believed by the woman to have caused her mental turmoil (Hall and Bourne, 137–139).

In addition to their role in reinterpreting hoodoo in a positive light, some mental health researchers have divided African American supernatural healers into analytical categories. Hall and Bourne, for example, divided African American indigenous therapists into four types. First were rootworkers, who sold herbal remedies for a variety of mental and physical disorders. A second category was faith healers, who claimed the ability to cure ailments because of their offices as ministers of spiritual powers. Magical vendors who sold not only herbal remedies but magical items for a variety of nonmedical uses made up a third group. Last were neighborhood prophets, who claimed their power to heal from God and who treated clients with emotional and other personal problems (Hall and Bourne, 138–141). Other researchers have suggested different categories. Hans Baer, for instance, divided healers into broad categories of cultic and independent healers. He argued that these categories could be further divided into eight types of specialists and six types of general practitioners ("Black Folk Healers," 331).

HOODOO AS CENTRAL TO IDENTITY

From colonial days through at least the early twentieth century, whites judged conjure and Voodoo as indelibly tied to blackness. Rarely did that connection imply anything remotely positive. Whites' definition of black identity used conjure and Voodoo as symbols of black inferiority. This fact should come as no surprise. After all, whites long viewed hoodoo as threatening (Anderson, *Conjure,* 1–24).

Unsurprisingly, the height of the symbolic use of conjure as an indicator of white superiority came during the days when whites strove to bind blacks into the Jim Crow system of discrimination and segregation. Whites seized on the hoodoo practitioner as a powerful image of the depths to which African Americans could sink without the supposedly benevolent rule of whites. Tales of threatening conjurers were common. One prominent example came from the popular author Thomas Nelson Page, whose novel, *Red Rock: A Chronicle of Reconstruction,* includes a hoodoo practitioner who both leads the newly freed blacks and attempts to rape the central female character (see Chapter 3). Helen Pitkin's cautionary tale of a white Creole sinking into the practice of Voodoo expressed the same links among African Americans, supernaturalism, and the need for white supremacy. Even works not particularly hostile to blacks stressed the role of conjure and Voodoo in their lives. Numerous authors of popular books on black folklore, including Joel Chandler Harris, author of the Uncle Remus stories, prominently included conjurers in their tales of African American animal heroes.

Taking their cues from white society, educated black leaders judged conjure and Voodoo as things of which to be ashamed. Many sought to hide its practice or even suppress it. Even those African Americans who recorded the folklore surrounding it rarely lamented its anticipated rapid demise. Charles Waddell Chesnutt, the first African American author to write a book built around the belief and practice of hoodoo, certainly did not celebrate it. Chesnutt's the *Conjure Woman* is a collection of short stories chronicling the interaction between a northern couple, John and Annie, who had recently purchased a southern plantation, and their black servant Julius. In "Po' Sandy," for example, Julius tells the story of Sandy, a slave whose conjure woman lover transformed him into a tree. Unfortunately for Sandy, his unsuspecting master cut him down, sawed him up, and built his remains into an outbuilding on the very plantation now occupied by his employers. According to Julius, the building was haunted by Sandy's ghost ever after. Julius' purpose in telling the story was to persuade the emotive Annie to grant him the use of the building. He achieved his goal, despite John's doubts.

Chesnutt used hoodoo as a vehicle for relating a tale of African American re-sourcefulness. Readers are likely to marvel that anyone could fall for the seeming absurdity of Julius' fantastic story. Chesnutt's evaluation of conjure was not as harsh as that of many whites, but he certainly did little to rehabilitate the image of hoodoo as backwardness (Chesnutt, 36–63).

Hoodoo remains a prominent part of black identity today, although its valuation has changed dramatically. The average white American knows little of conjure and considers Voodoo to be evil magic, but scholars and many black writers now argue that hoodoo is a vital and positive feature of black history and culture. Why the shift in viewpoint? In part, the influence of the 1920s literary and artistic movement know as the Harlem Renaissance and the 1960s and 1970s black power movement have taught both blacks and whites that African American history and culture have value. In this light, the celebration of hoodoo is no longer off limits. Moreover, the modern tendency to understand all of African American history as a drive toward civil rights has inspired writers of all stripes to see conjure and Voodoo as liberating. Those scientific studies pointing out possible healthful benefits from conjure have further undermined the bias against it. Whites, in particular, have also been influenced heavily by postmodern philosophy and its religious expression, the New Age/neopagan movement. Both reject any hierarchy of spirituality, emphasizing cultural relativism and frequently extreme individualism. In the postmodern/New Age mindset, Voodoo is the equal of Christianity, and making a mojo is the metaphysical equivalent of saying a prayer (Anderson, *Conjure,* 18–24, 136–149).

Many now see conjure and Voodoo as symbols of African American strength, and especially black feminine power. African American writers have taken the lead in this reassessment. Alice Walker's *Third Life of Grange Copeland,* Toni Morrison's *Sula,* and Gloria Naylor's *Mama Day* each feature female conjurers as emblems of strong black womanhood. Ishmael Reed's poetry has likewise celebrated conjure. To Reed, hoodoo is subversive—a means by which African Americans undermine white domination (Lindroth).

Scholars have adopted much the same course as novelists. One groundbreaking work in this vein was Theophus Smith's *Conjuring Culture.* Smith argues that African American understandings of the Bible are rooted in supernaturalism. In 2001, Carolyn Morrow Long produced *Spiritual Merchants: Religion, Magic, and Commerce,* which discusses the rise of the modern spiritual supplies industry and includes numerous personal accounts of visits to hoodoo shops and manufacturing companies. Two years later, religious studies scholar Yvonne Chireau published a scholarly account of conjure that focused on the nineteenth century. Most recent has been Jeffrey E. Anderson's *Conjure in African American Society,* a general history of hoodoo from colonial times to the present. In each case, the authors depict conjure as an example of how African Americans have used supernaturalism to resist or cope with the abysmal conditions of slavery and the

The final resting place of Marie Laveau, which remains an object of devotion to modern believers, as well as tourists. Faintly visible cross marks on the grave are evidence of those seeking her aid. Author's personal collection.

Jim Crow South. At times magical redress for wrongs was all black Americans could hope for. In other cases, resorting to practices like rootwork were not the remedies blacks desired. They were simply all they could afford.

The historical Voodoo queen Marie Laveau has particularly seized the attention of scholars and popular writers alike. In addition to recent biographies by Martha Ward, Ina Fandrich, and Carolyn Morrow Long, Jewell Parker Rhodes has written two novels about her, *Voodoo Dreams* and *Voodoo Season*. In most of these books, Laveau has appeared as a model of black strength. Often she is an overt champion of civil rights as well. Long's *New Orleans Voudou Priestess: The Legend and Reality of Marie Laveau* is an exception to general adulation, taking a more sober view of her contributions. Although clearly fascinated by Laveau and her role in African American Voodoo practice, she repeatedly points out that it is easy to exaggerate the Voodoo Queen's influence and her supposed, but undocumented, civil rights activities. The tendency to exaggerate the positives of hoodoo is an ever-present feature of modern scholarship, however, much as was the tendency to demonize it only a few decades ago.

HOODOO AS AN ART FORM

Hoodoo has long featured prominently in African American art and literature. Charles Waddell Chesnutt, for instance, wrote his tales of conjure during the late nineteenth century. Supernaturalism has been even more prominent in music. A Virginia spiritual collected by Carl Sandburg, called "Satan's a Liah," described the devil as a conjurer (Chesnutt, 250–251). Many blues songs likewise referenced hoodoo. The most famous of them is probably Muddy Waters's "Hoochie Coochie Man," in which bluesman referenced many conjure charms and prophetic signs while describing his power over women (Clar, 177–189). To such artists, conjure was a persistent feature of everyday African American life.

In contrast, many now see hoodoo as a driving force in their work. Some musicians, such as modern blues artist Malcolm John Rebennack Jr., adopt stage names linking them to conjure. Rebennack calls himself Dr. John, after the well-known nineteenth-century Voodoo practitioner, Jean Montanée. Visual arts are no less open to hoodoo. In the early twenty-first century, graphic artist Kenjji introduced a uniquely black comic book superhero named the WitchDoctor who relied on the power of Voodoo to fight evil. Sculptors Betye and Alison Saar have likewise used hoodoo and Vodou as images of African American spiritual power in their artworks ("Dr. John"; Blair 4.16; Judith Wilson, 113–116).

By far the most prominent conjure-driven artistry of today is the literary hoodoo movement. Prominent participants include but are not limited to Ishmael Reed, Arthur Flowers, and Gayl Jones. Literary hoodooists consider their works not merely entertainment but vital links to the African past and its traditions. According to scholar Patricia R. Schroeder, literary hoodoo is about preserving an authorial line of descent from Africa to the present, looking to slave narratives, Chesnutt, Hurston, and others as the necessary links. Schroeder further argues that although literary hoodooists use a European-American form of written communication, they function as the modern African American embodiments of the *griot*, the West African preserver of peoples' oral traditions. Such authors tell their stories to create the "visions necessary for the survival of the race." As a matter of course, hoodoo and other folk traditions figure prominently in them (Schroeder, 264).

VOODOO AS RELIGION

Haitian Vodou and Mississippi Valley Voodoo have been some of the most misunderstood religions in modern history. Since Médéric Louis-Élie Moreau de Saint-Méry wrote the earliest surviving account of a Vodou ceremony, whites have tended to see it as threatening, even satanic (Moreau de Saint-Méry, 45–51). Writers have often depicted it as nothing more than superstitious magic, mis-understanding or deliberately ignoring its developed cosmology and complex rituals. Americans quickly adopted this prejudicial approach to Vodou after the publication of works like Spencer St. John's *Hayti or the Black Republic,* which includes sensationalistic and derogatory depictions of Vodou.

The U.S. occupation of Haiti heightened American interest in the religion but did little to improve its citizens' understanding of the faith. The most popular book that addressed Vodou to emerge from the era was William B. Seabrook's *Magic Island.* In one lurid account of a Vodou ceremony, Seabrook described the interaction between a sacrificial goat and a female participant. At one point in the ceremony he wrote, "The goat's lingam became erect and rigid, the points of the girl's breasts visibly hardened and were outlined sharply pressing against the coarse, thin, tight-drawn shift that was her only garment. Thus they faced each other motionless as two marble figures on the frieze of some ancient phallic temple" (Seabrook, 65). Clearly, Seabrook's intent was to entertain and titillate, although considering the bestialistic content, one must question just who he expected to make up his audience.

The appearance of English-language works on Vodou also spurred interest in Mississippi Valley Voodoo. Most notably, Zora Neale Hurston wrote *Mules and Men* as the American occupation of Haiti was winding down. Beginning dur-ing the late 1930s, Robert Tallant researched Voodoo, eventually leading to the publication of *Voodoo in New Orleans* and later *Voodoo Queen,* a fictionalized bi-ography of Marie Laveau. With the exception of *Voodoo Queen,* these books and various shorter works from the era are just as sensationalistic as Seabrook's *Magic Island,* albeit far less condemnatory.

The general public continues to demonize Voodoo and related faiths, such as Santería, but modern scholars rightly understand it as a true religion. To a large extent, this shift is a result of the positive interpretation of black supernaturalism and religion offered by Zora Neale Hurston and her imitators. Just as important were the writings of anthropologist Melville Herskovits, who argued forcefully for the importance and value of African-derived features of New World societies in his groundbreaking 1941 book, *Myth of the Negro Past.* In addition, he had earlier written a scholarly interpretation of Haitian life, entitled *Life in a Haitian Valley,* which devoted substantial space to Vodou. Herskovits's works, which promoted the concept of cultural relativism, proved to be models for future research.

Inspired by Hurston and Herskovits, numerous scholars and laypersons have produced insightful examinations of the religion. One of the most accessible and comprehensive such works is Alfred Métraux's *Voodoo in Haiti,* which cov-ers a wide array of Vodou-related topics, ranging from its history to its rituals to its interaction with Christianity. Whereas Métraux originally wrote in French, several English-language works have also explored Vodou in considerable depth. Probably the best known of these is Maya Deren's *Divine Horsemen: The Living Gods of Haiti.* These "divine horsemen" are humans possessed by Vodou deities during ceremonies. In this relationship, Vodou practitioners refer to the possessed by the Kreyol term for *horses* and the process of possession as *mounting.* Both the English translation of Métraux and Deren's book saw print in the 1950s. A more recent title on the subject is Leslie G. Desmangles' *Faces of the Gods: Vodou and Roman Catholicism in Haiti.* For those interested in the personal side of Vodou, Karen McCarthy Brown has provided an engaging biography of a Haitian-American manbo in *Mama Lola: A Vodou Priestess in Brooklyn.* Those who shy away from scholarly works entirely have a wealth of Internet sources at their fingertips as well as a recent title by Shannon R. Turlington, the *Complete Idiot's Guide to Voodoo.*

Although substantial scholarship on Haitian Vodou has corrected many of the old interpretive errors, there has been no comparable work on North American hoodoo. True, Mississippi Valley Voodoo has begun to garner some respect, but scholarship on the topic remains sparse. The fullest recent accounts of Voodoo are two chapters in Carolyn Morrow Long's biography of Marie Laveau and an article by Jeffrey Anderson scheduled to appear in the forthcoming *Encyclopedia of African American Religious Culture* (Long, *Voudou Priestess,* 93–148). Surprisingly, some authors have depicted conjure as something of a religion. Zora Neale Hurston was the first to do so, comparing it to a suppressed religion in *Mules and Men* (Hurston, 176). In *Conjuring Culture,* Theophus Smith supported a similar interpretation by describing the conjuring mindset as the basis for African American theology. Hurston and Smith's views on conjure are not widespread among scholars, practitioners, or the general public.

Much work remains to be completed on the subject of hoodoo. Scholars of conjure have made a good start, but much more could be said, especially on the subject of Voodoo. Likewise, scholarly examinations tend to oversimplify hoodoo, depicting it as merely a hidden civil rights movement, glorifying prominent practitioners, and otherwise reducing it to a one-dimensional system of beliefs. In short, conjure and Voodoo have yet to occupy their rightful place among either scholars or laypeople. Rather than being judged as vital parts of African American culture and history, they remain a mere curiosity to most.

WORKS CITED

Anderson, Jeffrey E. *Conjure in African American Society.* Baton Rouge: Louisiana State University Press, 2005.

———. "Voodoo." In *Encyclopedia of African American Religious Culture.* Anthony Pinn, ed. Santa Barbara, CA: ABC– CLIO, 2009.

Baer, Hans. "Toward a Systematic Typology of Black Folk Healers." *Phylon* 43 (1982): 327–343.

Bell, Michael E. "Pattern, Structure, and Logic in Afro-American Hoodoo Performance." Ph.D. diss., Indiana University, 1980.

Bergen, Fanny D. "Some Bits of Plant-Lore." *Journal of American Folklore* 5 (1892): 19–22.

Bibb, Henry. *Narrative of the Life and Adventures of Henry Bibb, an American Slave.* 3rd ed. With an Introduction by Lucius C. Matlack. New York: Privately printed, 1850.

Blair, Jayson. "X-ray Vision Is Needed to Find Black Superheroes." *The New York Times,* May 5, 2002, 4.16.

Breslaw, Elaine G. "Tituba's Confession: The Multicultural Dimensions of the 1692 Salem Witch-Hunt." *Ethnohistory* 44 (1997): 535–556.

Brown, Karen McCarthy. *Mama Lola: A Vodou Priestess in Brooklyn.* Updated and expanded. Berkeley: University of California Press, 2001.

Brown, William Wells. *Narrative of the Life of William Wells Brown, an American Slave.* London: Charles Gilpin, 1850.

Bruce, Philip A. *The Plantation Negro as a Freedman: Observations on His Character, Condition, and Prospects in Virginia.* New York and London: G. P. Putnam's Sons, 1889.

Cannon, Walter B. "Voodoo Death." *American Anthropologist* 44 (1942); reprinted in *Psychosomatic Medicine* 19 (1957): 182–190.

Chesnutt, Charles W. *The Conjure Woman.* With an Introduction by Robert M. Farnsworth. Ann Arbor: University of Michigan Press, 1969.

Chireau, Yvonne. *Black Magic: Religion and the African American Conjuring Tradition.* Berkeley: University of California Press, 2003.

Clar, Mimi. "Folk Belief and Custom in the Blues." *Western Folklore* 19 (1960): 173–189.

Deren, Maya. *Divine Horsemen: The Living Gods of Haiti.* London and New York: Thames and Hudson, 1953.

Desmangles, Leslie G. *Faces of the Gods: Vodou and Roman Catholicism in Haiti.* Chapel Hill: University of North Carolina Press, 1992.

Dillon, Catherine. "Voodoo, 1937–1941." Louisiana Writers' Project, folders 118, 317, and 319. Federal Writers' Project, Cammie G. Henry Research Center, Watson Memorial Library, Northwestern State University, Natchitoches, LA.

"Dr. John, Always in the Right Place." *National Public Radio* Website. 2007. http://www.npr.org/templates/story/story.php?storyId=4833036 (19 July 2007)

Douglass, Frederick. *Narrative of the Life of Frederick Douglass.* With an introduction by William Lloyd Garrison, a letter from Wendell Phillips, and a new introductory note. New York: Dover, 1995.

Elam, William Cecil. "A Case of Hoodoo." *Lippincott's Monthly Magazine* 54 (1894): 138–141.

Fett, Sharla. *Working Cures: Healing, Health, and Power on Southern Slave Plantations.* Chapel Hill: University of North Carolina Press, 2002.

Fontenot, Wonda L. *Secret Doctors: Ethnomedicine of African Americans.* Westport and London: Bergin & Garvey, 1994.

Hall, Arthur L. and Bourne, Peter G. "Indigenous Therapists in a Southern Black Urban Community." *Archives of General Psychiatry* 28 (1973): 137–142.

Harris, Joel Chandler. *Uncle Remus: His Songs and His Sayings.* New and revised ed. With illustrations by Arthur Burdette Frost. New York: Grosset and Dunlap, 1921.

Herron, Leonora. "Conjuring and Conjure Doctors." *Southern Workman* 24 (1891): 117–118.

Herskovits, Melville J. *Life in a Haitian Valley.* New York: Alfred A. Knopf, 1937.

———. *The Myth of the Negro Past.* With a new introduction by Sidney W. Mintz. Boston: Beacon P, 1990.

Hurston, Zora Neale. "Hoodoo in America." *Journal of American Folklore* 44 (1931): 317–417.

———. *Mules and Men.* In *Folklore, Memoirs, and other Writings,* selected and annotated Cheryl A. Wall. The Library of America. New York: Literary Classics of the United States, Inc., 1995.

Hyatt, Harry Middleton. *Hoodoo-Conjuration-Witchcraft-Rootwork.* 5 vols. Memoirs of the Alma Egan Hyatt Foundation. Hannibal: Western, 1970–1978.

Kimball, Chase Patterson. "A Case of Pseudocyesis Caused by 'Roots'." *American Journal of Obstetric Gynecology* 107 (1979): 801–803.

Lindroth, James. "Images of Subversion: Ishmael Reed and the Hoodoo Trickster." *African American Review* 30 (1996): 185–196.

Long, Carolyn Morrow. *A New Orleans Voudou Priestess: The Legend and Reality of Marie Laveau.* Gainesville: University Press of Florida, 2006.

———. *Spiritual Merchants: Religion, Magic, and Commerce.* Knoxville: University of Tennessee Press, 2001.

McCall, George J. "Symbiosis: The Case of Hoodoo and the Numbers Racket." *Social Problems* 10 (1963): 361–371.

McMillan, Timothy J. "Black Magic: Witchcraft, Race, and Resistance in Colonial New England." *Journal of Black Studies* 25 (1994): 99–117.

McTeer, James Edwin. *Fifty Years as a Low Country Witch Doctor.* Beaufort: Beaufort Book Company, 1976.

Métraux, Alfred. *Voodoo in Haiti.* Translated by Hugo Charteris and with an Introduction by Sidney W. Mintz. New York: Schocken, 1972.

Michaelson, Mike. "Can a 'Root Doctor' Actually Put a Hex On?" *Today's Health* March 1972: 38–41, 58, 60.

Mitchell, Faith. *Hoodoo Medicine: Gullah Herbal Remedies.* Columbia: Summerhouse Press, 1999.

Moreau de Saint-Méry, Médéric Louis-Élie. *Description topographique, physique, civile, politique et historique de la partie française de l'île de Saint-Domingue.* 2 vols. Philadelphia, 1797.

Morrison, Toni. *Sula.* New York: Knopf, 1974.

Naylor, Gloria. *Mama Day.* New York: Ticknor and Fields, 1988.

Neal, James C. "Legalized Crime in Florida." In *Proceedings of the Florida Medical Association: Session of 1891,* 42–50. Jacksonville: Times-Union, 1891.

Norris, Thaddeus. "Negro Superstitions." *Lippincott's Monthly Magazine* 6 (1870): 90–95.

Page, Thomas Nelson. *Red Rock: A Chronicle of Reconstruction.* Charles Scribner's Sons, 1898.

Puckett, Newbell Niles. *Folk Beliefs of the Southern Negro.* Patterson Smith Reprint Series in Criminology, Law Enforcement, and Social Problems, no. 22. Chapel Hill: University of North Carolina Press, 1926; reprint, Montclair: Patterson Smith, 1968.

Reed, Ishmael. *Conjure: Selected Poems, 1963–1970.* Amherst: University of Massachusetts Press, 1972.

———. *Mumbo Jumbo.* Garden City: Doubleday, 1972.

Rhodes, Jewell Parker. *Voodoo Dreams: A Novel of Marie Laveau.* New York: Picador USA, 1993.

———. *Voodoo Season: A Marie Laveau Mystery.* New York: Atria, 2005.

St. John, Spencer. *Hayti or the Black Republic.* London: Smith, Elder, and Company, 1884.

Schroeder, Patricia R. "Rootwork: Arthur Flowers, Zora Neale Hurston, and the 'Literary Hoodoo' Tradition." *African American Review* 36 (2002): 263–272.

Seabrook, William B. *The Magic Island.* New York: Harcourt, Brace, 1929.

Smith, Theophus H. *Conjuring Culture: Biblical Formations of Black America.* New York and Oxford: Oxford University Press, 1994.

Tallant, Robert. *Voodoo in New Orleans.* New York: Macmillan, 1946; reprint, Gretna: Pelican, 1998.

———. *The Voodoo Queen.* New York: Putnam, 1956; reprint, Gretna: Pelican, 2000.

Turlington, Shannon R. *The Complete Idiot's Guide to Voodoo.* Indianapolis: Alpha, 2002.

Walker, Alice. *The Third Life of Grange Copeland.* New York: Harcourt, Brace, Jovanovich, 1970.

Ward, Martha. *Voodoo Queen: The Spirited Lives of Marie Laveau.* Jackson: University Press of Mississippi, 2004.

White, Jaclyn Weldon. *Whisper to the Black Candle: Voodoo, Murder, and the Case of Anjette Lyles.* Macon, GA: Mercer University Press, 1999.

Whitten, Norman E. "Contemporary Patterns of Malign Occultism among Negroes in North Carolina." *Journal of American Folklore* 75 (1962): 310–325.

Wilkie, Laurie A. "Magic and Empowerment on the Plantation: An Archaeological Consideration of African-American World View." *Southeastern Archaeology* 14 (1995): 136–148.

Wilson, Judith. "Down to the Crossroads: The Art of Alison Saar." *Callaloo* 14 (1991): 107–123.

Wyatt-Brown, Bertram. *Southern Honor: Ethics and Behavior in the Old South.* New York and Oxford: Oxford University Press, 1982.

Five
Contexts

Since the first slaves suffered the rigors of the Middle Passage across the Atlantic Ocean, African-derived religion and supernaturalism have been important aspects of American culture. Nevertheless, most modern whites and many blacks view conjure, hoodoo, and Voodoo as superstitious relics of a bygone era—and certainly not a lamented one at that. Such stereotypical understandings of the place of creole supernaturalism and religion have obscured their rightful place in American society. Instead of being curious, marginal beliefs, they are pervasive, although little recognized, aspects of African American life.

To be sure, the place of hoodoo, conjure, and Voodoo is not a consequence of the recent spate of scholarly and popular works on the subjects. The writings of slaves like Frederick Douglass testify that hoodoo was important long before it was consciously identified as such. The resonance of works by Charles Waddell Chesnutt and Zora Neale Hurston demonstrate the continued vitality of the practices during the late nineteenth and early twentieth centuries. Blues music does the same. Considering that supernaturalism could function as a magical means of addressing problems, its popularity should come as no surprise. After all, African Americans have had more than their fair share, ranging from racial injustice to grinding poverty.

VOODOO AND HOODOO IN UNEXPECTED PLACES

Some aspects of hoodoo are easy to analyze. Others are not. Identifying the lineage of African creole beliefs, for instance, is simple. Things like hoodoo shops and magical roots are easy to trace to their American regional and transatlantic origins. In contrast, the influence of hoodoo on other aspects of society has been subtler, making it much more difficult to recognize. Still, the marks of Voodoo, hoodoo, and conjure are visible in a number of places where they might be unexpected.

Some versions of Christianity, especially among black congregations, have been clearly influenced by African magical and religious concepts. Of course, many African Americans explicitly rejected old faiths and magic after becoming Christians. That others did not is shown by many conjurers' decisions to adopt the title of *reverend.* In both cases, blacks found it unnecessary to abandon African understandings of religion (R., L., G., and A., 30–31; Joyner, 149–150). Theophus H. Smith, author of *Conjuring Culture,* maintains that black interpretations of Christianity are saturated with African magical concepts. The chief expression of such readings is a widespread African American view of the Bible as a book that can be used to transform culture, chiefly when believers emulate the lives of its important characters.

Specific instances of African beliefs transformed into Christian practices have also been uncovered. The ring shout, a sacred dance widely practiced during the era of slavery and beyond, had African precedents and resembles spiritual dances present in several Afro-Latin religions. Baptism also had a distinctly African side to it. The nineteenth-century Georgia practice of praying to Kongo-derived *simbi* spirits before immersion demonstrates this aspect of an otherwise Christian rite. One could argue, however, that this specific facet of African American Christianity was transitory. After all, the prayers appear to have died out by the early twentieth century. Nevertheless, baptism remained a feature of African American faith. It likewise continued to be influenced by the presence of spirits (Raboteau, 68–74; Georgia Writers' Project, 113, 125, 131; Brown, "'Walk in the Feenda'," 312–313).

Carl Carmer, a white observer from New York, described a 1930s Alabama Baptist river immersion that strongly resembled the possessions seen in some Spiritual Churches and at one time in Voodoo ceremonies (Carmer, 23–27). One African American participant in the ceremony, he wrote emitted a "a high shrick" and began "babbling wild indescribable sounds." Carmer continued, "I saw men converging on a tall writhing figure. . . . Her long body jerked spasmodically and with terrific force—breaking the hold of the men again and again. Her eyes rolled wildly, and from her mouth came sounds so incoherent and strange that I felt cold shudders" (Carmer, 27). This had not been one of the emotional but tame events common in white Baptist churches. Carmer failed to describe just what spirit or spirits were responsible for what he evidently judged to be a shocking display. Considering the context, it is likely that the participants perceived the Holy Spirit at work. The African spirits may have departed, but their legacy remained.

Some modern types of Christianity show stronger African religious influence than others. With the exception of Spiritual Churches, the denominations most closely akin to Voodoo and other African American faiths are some varieties of

Pentecostalism. Miraculous cures, prophecy, and other signs of sanctification have clear precedents in biblical Christianity. At the same time, an African heritage of reverence for such overt displays of spiritual power has made Pentecostalism especially appealing to African Americans. In fact, many of the movement's early leaders were African Americans. That some of them used such apparently magical items as roots and glass eyes to divine God's will and to otherwise give signs of sanctification backs up the assertion that African magic and traditional faiths influenced such groups (MacRobert, 295–309; Synan, 70–71, 167–186; Wacker, 65, 91–92, 104–105, 153, 206–207, 226–235; Chireau, "Conjure," 248–257; Anderson, *Conjure,* 157–158).

Another area over which African American supernaturalism has been influential is race relations. Since well before the Civil War, typical whites have frowned on supernaturalism, including magic of any sort, seeing it as superstition and a marker of backwardness or even inferiority. Referring to someone as superstitious was certainly not a compliment. As discussed in the previous chapter, whites used such stereotypical views to define conjure and Voodoo—and by inference African Americans—as inferior. It is vitally important to understand that these attitudes were no mere abstractions. They affected everyday life. For example, Joel Chandler Harris, a famous collector of black folklore and author best known for his Uncle Remus stories, occasionally addressed supernaturalism in his tales. On a few occasions, a rabbit conjure woman named Mammy-Bammy Big-Money has dealings with her fellow animals. As her name suggests, she is not meant to be taken seriously, at least by anyone other than the child audience for whom the book was intended. For Harris, writing in an era that popularized a mythology of loyal slaves who loved their masters, their belief in such superstitions was quaint and amusing. At the same time, acceptance of this view shielded whites from doubts that their self-defined benevolent rationalism was necessary for the survival of what they assumed were inherently irrational blacks. Perhaps without realizing it, Harris was furthering racism (Harris, 244–246).

The writings of some of Harris's many imitators make the negative connotations of hoodoo and Voodoo much clearer. For late nineteenth-century author Charles Colcock Jones, Jr., conjure was anything but endearing. Writing of conjure among coastal blacks he stated, "Comparatively few there were who could lift themselves entirely above the superstitious fears born in Africa and perpetuated by tradition in their new home" (169). He went on to record that antebellum planters felt it necessary to suppress the practice to keep conjure women from creating "strife and disquietude" (171). Obviously, Jones believed the survival of such "superstition" justified white oppression. Writing a few years later, Mary Alicia Owen recorded an incident of an African American woman from Missouri who lost a luck ball. Owen summed up the woman's disquietude: "Her superstitious terrors when she discovered the loss were really pitiable" (*Old Rabbit,* 169).

When belief remained so strong, conjurers retained their power as well. On at least one occasion, a group of South Carolina planters relied on "military interference" to suppress a revival of African religion and supernaturalism following emancipation. Whites' views of supernaturalism had tangible consequences for African Americans (Joyner, 144). Viewpoints on hoodoo did not create slavery, Jim Crow laws, segregation, or lynching, but they helped ensure that African Americans remained the focus of racism by marking them as inferior members of the human race.

Only recently have large numbers of African Americans rejected the negative definitions of hoodoo. During the late nineteenth century, most black leaders fully understood the effect that Voodoo and conjure had on African Americans' place in the American South. The Folk-Lore and Ethnology column of the *Southern Workman,* school newspaper of the historically black Hampton Institute, often stressed the disreputable nature of conjure. One 1893 issue made it clear that folk beliefs were to be something abandoned as blacks overcame their "ignorance" ("Ethnology and Folk-Lore," 180). Such embarrassment about hoodoo is understandable when one recognizes the degree to which whites used it to oppose black aspirations.

Fortunately, this view is now in a slow retreat. Many of the writings of Zora Neale Hurston, Ishmael Reed, Alice Walker, Toni Morrison, and others have been attempts to redeem this much-maligned aspect of African American life from its thralldom to white stereotyping. Instead of something of which to be embarrassed, conjure, hoodoo, and Voodoo have become things to celebrate—living bonds to an African heritage. Modern recognition of African American equality, although incomplete, has rescued hoodoo. Proponents of the new interpretation hope that their version of African American supernaturalism and religion will have positive effects capable of overcoming the harm done by past misappropriations of black beliefs.

THE FUTURE

The future of hoodoo, Voodoo, and conjure is difficult to predict. In some ways, each appears to be suffering from a longstanding decline in followers. Voodoo as an organized faith was largely gone by the close of the nineteenth century, although some ceremonies appear to have continued into the 1940s. Likewise, several well-known hoodoo shops have closed in recent years. Even the terminology of African American supernaturalism has declined. Although *Voodoo* remains a household term, the number who could accurately define it are almost certainly a small minority. The words *conjure* and *hoodoo* have fallen out of general usage to the extent that researchers frequently have to explain the terms to potential informants, as well as their intended audiences (Dillon, sec. "Voodoo Openings," 19–28; Long, *Spiritual Merchants,* 52, 147–150).

A modern spiritual supply shop in an urban area. It supplies both traditional herbs and manufactured items. Author's personal collection.

Nevertheless, several shops and practitioners continue to ply their supernatural trade. In *Spiritual Merchants,* Carolyn Long listed 67 spiritual supply stores that she had either visited or purchased products from while conducting research in the 1990s (253–261). This list is certainly a small fraction of the total currently in operation, which can be found across the nation in large cities, small towns, and on the Internet. Moreover, some practitioners continue to ply a trade along the lines of their nineteenth-century forebears. Such was the case with a Bessemer, Alabama, hoodoo doctor, who by the twenty-first century was one of the last to claim the ability to remove reptiles from the bodies of conjure victims (Deborah [pseudonym], interview by author).

The Latin kin of hoodoo and Voodoo are not merely surviving. They are flourishing. Vodou, the best known of them, remains the popular faith of average Haitians. Cuban Santería similarly shows little sign of decline, despite periodic repression at the hands of dictator Fidel Castro's communist regime (Brown, *Mama Lola,* 5; Brandon, 99–103). Others flourish as well.

In addition, as in the late eighteenth and early nineteenth centuries, the contacts between such faiths and North American incarnations of African American supernaturalism are on the rise, largely a result of increased immigration during the last 50 years. Cubans, in fact, have proven to be more devoted to Santería in the United States than they had been in Cuba (Brandon, 104). The growing prominence of African creole religions in the United States has given African American practices an increasingly Latin hue. Most of New Orleans's modern Voodoo practitioners are actually adherents of Haitian Vodou rather than an indigenous Mississippi Valley variety. Throughout the country, shops catering to the supernatural needs of those faithful to Vodou, Santería, and similar faiths often double as hoodoo shops. The level of African American interest is demonstrated by the number of handbooks found in most spiritual supply shops that describe how to properly worship Santerían orishas. Similar works grace the shelves of major book chains and include in their number the *Complete Idiot's Guide to Voodoo* (Chamani, interview by author; Glassman, interview by author; Williams, interview by author; Anderson, *Conjure,* 145–146).

American journalists and scholars' fascination with all things African likewise made a vast store of information on Afro-Latin and African American religion and supernaturalism available to the public. At one end of the spectrum of such works is Christine Wicker's *Not in Kansas Anymore: A Curious Tale of How Magic is Transforming America.* It is a highly readable personal account of her investigation of supernatural beliefs in the United States. At the other extreme are a variety of erudite works on various aspects of African creole beliefs, including but not limited to Claude F. Jacobs and Andrew J. Kaslow's *Spiritual Churches of New Orleans,* Robert Farris Thompson's *Flash of the Spirit,* and Jeffrey E. Anderson's *Conjure in African American Society.* Unlike earlier days, when finding accurate information on such beliefs was always difficult and sometimes impossible for most Americans, a trip to a local bookstore can provide any information one is likely to desire about Santería, Vodou, Voodoo, or conjure.

This current American fascination with the supernatural has the potential for reviving hoodoo. The growing acceptance of conjure and Voodoo among African American artists and intellectuals has already been noted. In addition to simply admitting the role of supernaturalism in their culture, some of them have begun to practice hoodoo themselves. One example is Phoenix Savage, who studied hoodoo as part of graduate work in medical anthropology and went on to become a practitioner for family and friends. To Savage and others like her, supernaturalism is a source of "strong African ancestral energy" and link to their heritage. A more extreme case is Oba Oseigeman Adefumni I, founder of Oyotunji village, a Yoruba-style village in South Carolina. Adefumni founded the self-proclaimed independent country on the basis of West African traditional religion, which he first encountered as a practitioner of Santería (Savage, interview by author; Davis, *American Voudou,* 182–186).

What is more surprising in light of its history is the degree to which whites are embracing the once shunned and feared beliefs of their onetime bondspersons. Following the postmodern/New Age legitimation of magic, the degree to which whites have adopted African American religion and supernaturalism has slowly but steadily increased. Sometimes these practitioners have gained prominence, which has been the case with Sallie Ann Glassman, a New Orleans-based manbo of Haitian Vodou who has emerged as one of the country's best-known practitioners. Catherine Yronwode of Forestville, California, has gained comparable renown through her online hoodoo business, the Lucky Mojo Curio Company. Many others have followed similar paths without achieving the recognition of Glassman or Yronwode. The degree to which the larger society has embraced hoodoo is illustrated by the fact that over 1,100 students have taken Yronwode's Hoodoo Rootwork Correspondence Course since its 2003 inception (Yronwode, *Lucky Mojo*, http://www.luckymojo.com/mojocourse.html). Considering the wide availability of books and Web sites addressing seemingly endless aspects of African American magic, this number is all the more striking.

In addition to the revival of magic, Voodoo has also returned to some of its former range. The last reliable reports of historical Voodoo initiations appeared in the late 1930s, although they had ceased to be common decades earlier (Dillon, sec. "Voodoo Openings"). During the late twentieth century, however, Voodoo began to reappear. As had happened around the turn of the nineteenth century, it came in the form of believers in Haitian Vodou or modified versions thereof. This time, however, many have been converts rather than immigrants. Among their number, the most prominent have been African Americans Ava Kay Jones and Miriam Chamani and white practitioner Sallie Ann Glassman. There are many others, although the depth of their belief and commitment to the religion varies considerably (Bodin, 74–82; Chamani, interview by author [2001]; Glassman, interview by author [2001]).

Despite the apparent upturn in supernatural practices, the long-term prospects for conjure and Voodoo remain uncertain. Americans involved in the supernatural regularly change their interests. Despite the current attractiveness of conjure and Voodoo, their allure might fade. This has happened to numerous religions before. One striking example was the Spiritualism of the nineteenth century, which was once a prominent faith but had almost died out by the late nineteenth century. Hoodoo, it should also be remembered, was a favorite topic for scholarly and popular writers from the 1920s to the 1940s. They lost interest rapidly thereafter. Without widespread interest in hoodoo and Voodoo, the economic base for the hoodoo industry would shrink, rendering shops and traditional practices commercially unviable and thereby threatened with extinction.

Hoodoo and Voodoo are also vulnerable to the same events and developments that affect other aspects of American culture. Hurricane Katrina's impact on New Orleans is a striking example of just how devastating a blow events outside the spiritual realm can deal to belief systems. New Orleans, long touted as *the* American Voodoo capital, remains a shadow of its former self. With a population only 60 percent of its prestorm level and a depressed tourist trade, the city's hoodoo shops and Voodoo practitioners are struggling. Many Spiritual Churches have also disappeared, perhaps never to return. It is unlikely that New Orleans will ever fully lose its reputation for the supernatural. The practices that gave the city its character,

A modern New Orleans shop that not only caters to Voodoo but also a wide range of other alternative religions. Author's personal collection.

however, could very well disappear (Warner, http://www.nola.com/news/t-p/front page/index.ssf?/base/news-8/1186642536113410.xml&coll=1 and http://www. nola.com/news/t-p/frontpage/index.ssf?/base/news-/1186642536113410. xml&coll=1&thispage=2; Williams, interview by author [2007]; Chamani, interview by author [2007]; Glassman, interview by author [2007]).

At the very least, hoodoo of the future will doubtless differ from historical forms. Modern conjurers are as likely to be white as black. Voodoo adherents might also practice Wicca or a variety of New Age religions on the side. Alternatively, it might be that they prefer a side of Voodoo with their Wicca. Then, again, change is not foreign to African American religion and supernaturalism. From the earliest days of the American colonies, change has been the rule. African Traditional Religions became creole faiths in the New World, adopting elements of Christianity and Native American beliefs to adapt to the new situation in which enslaved Africans found themselves. Over the centuries, African Americans have welcomed innovations from Spiritualism, Afro-Latin religions, and a host of lesser sources. In light of the past, the future of hoodoo, Voodoo, and conjure looks far from bleak. Survival in the face of change has always characterized them.

WORKS CITED

Anderson, Jeffrey E. *Conjure in African American Society.* Baton Rouge: Louisiana State University Press, 2005.

Bodin, Ron. *Voodoo: Past and Present.* Lafayette: University of Southwestern Louisiana, 1990.

Brandon, George. *Santeria from Africa to the New World: The Dead Sell Memories.* Bloomington and Indianapolis: Indiana University Press, 1993.

Brown, Karen McCarthy. *Mama Lola: A Vodou Priestess in Brooklyn.* Updated and expanded. Berkeley: University of California Press, 2001.

Brown, Ras Michael. "'Walk in the Feenda': West-Central Africans and the Forest in the South Carolina—Georgia Lowcountry." In *Central Africans and Cultural Transformations in the American Diaspora,* ed. Linda M. Heywood, 289–317. Cambridge and New York: Cambridge University Press, 2002.

Carmer, Carl. *Stars Fell on Alabama.* With an Introduction by J. Wayne Flynt. Tuscaloosa, AL and London: University of Alabama, 1985.

Chamani, Miriam. Interview by author. November 15, 2001, New Orleans, LA. Notes and audio recording. Author's personal collection, Monroe, LA.

———. Interview by author. October 26, 2007. New Orleans, LA. Notes. Author's personal collection, Monroe, LA.

Chireau, Yvonne. "Conjure and Christianity in the Nineteenth Century: Religious Elements in African American Magic." *Religion and American Culture: A Journal of Interpretation* 7 (1997): 225–246.

Davis, Rod. *American Voudou: Journey into a Hidden World.* Denton: University of North Texas Press, 1999.

Deborah [pseudonym]. Interview by author. July 15, 2002, Bessemer, AL. Notes. Personal collection, Monroe, LA.

Dillon, Catherine. "Voodoo, 1937–1941." Louisiana Writers' Project, folders 118, 317, and 319. Federal Writers' Project. Cammie G. Henry Research Center, Watson Memorial Library, Northwestern State University, Natchitoches, LA.

Folk-Lore and Ethnology. *Southern Workman* 22 (1893): 180–181.

Georgia Writers' Project, Savannah Unit. *Drums and Shadows: Survival Studies among the Coastal Negroes.* With an Introduction by Charles Joyner and photographs by Muriel and Malcolm Bell, Jr. Athens: University of Georgia Press, 1986.

Glassman, Sallie Ann. Interview by author. November 14, 2001, New Orleans, LA. Notes and audio recording. Personal collection, Monroe, LA.

———. Interview by author. October 19, 2007. New Orleans, LA. Notes. Author's personal collection, Monroe, LA.

Harris, Joel Chandler. *The Complete Tales of Uncle Remus.* Compiled by Richard Chase. With illustrations by Arthur Burdette Frost, Frederick Stuart Church, J. M. Condé, Edward Windsor Kemble, and William Holbrook Beard. Boston: Houghton Mifflin, 1955.

Jacobs, Claude F. and Andrew J. Kaslow. *The Spiritual Churches of New Orleans: Origins, Beliefs, and Rituals of an African-American Religion.* Knoxville: University of Tennessee Press, 1991.

Jones, Charles Colcock Jr. *Gullah Folktales from the Georgia Coast.* With a Foreword by Susan Miller Williams. Athens and London: University of Georgia Press, 2000.

Joyner, Charles. *Down by the Riverside: A South Carolina Slave Community.* Urbana and Chicago: University of Chicago Press, 1984.

Long, Carolyn Morrow. *Spiritual Merchants: Religion, Magic, and Commerce.* Knoxville: University of Tennessee Press, 2001.

MacRobert, Iain. "The Black Roots of Pentecostalism." In *African-American Religion: Interpretive Essays in History and Culture,* ed. Timothy E. Fulop and Albert J. Raboteau, 295–309. New York and London: Routledge, 1997.

Owen, Mary Alicia. *Old Rabbit, the Voodoo and Other Sorcerers.* With an Introduction by Charles Godfrey Leland. With Illustrations by Juliette A. Owen and Louis Wain. London: T. Fisher Unwin, 1893; reprint, Whitefish, MT: Kessinger Publishing, 2003.

R., L., G., and A. "Conjure Doctors in the South." *The Southern Workman* 7 (1878): 30–31.

Raboteau, Albert J. *Slave Religion: The "Invisible Institution" in the Antebellum South.* Oxford and New York: Oxford University Press, 1978.

Savage, Phoenix. Interview by author. July 28, 2002, phone call between Birmingham, AL and Nashville, TN. Notes. Personal collection, Monroe, LA.

Smith, Theophus H. *Conjuring Culture: Biblical Formations of Black America.* New York and Oxford: Oxford University Press, 1994.

Synan, Vinson. *The Holiness-Pentecostal Tradition: Charismatic Movements in the Twentieth Century.* 2nd ed. Grand Rapids and Cambridge: William B. Eerdmans, 1997.

Thompson, Robert Farris. *Flash of the Spirit: African and Afro-American Art and Philosophy.* New York: Random House, 1983.

Turlington, Shannon R. *The Complete Idiot's Guide to Voodoo.* Indianapolis: Alpha, 2002.

Wacker, Grant. *Heaven Below: Early Pentecostals and American Culture.* Cambridge and London: Harvard University Press, 2001.

Warner, Coleman. "N.O. Headcount Gains Steam." *Times-Picayune.* 9 August 2007. http://www.nola.com/news/t-p/frontpage/index.ssf?/base/news-8/1186642536113410.xml&coll=1 and http://www.nola.com/news/t-p/frontpage/index.ssf?/base/news-/1186642536113410.xml&coll=1&thispage=2 (November 6, 2007).

Wicker, Christine. *Not in Kansas Anymore: A Curious Tale of How Magic is Transforming America.* New York: HarperCollins, 2005.

Williams, Claudia. Interview by author. November 16, 2001, New Orleans, LA. Notes. Author's personal collection, Monroe, LA.

———. Interview by author. October 23, 2007. New Orleans, LA. Notes. Author's personal collection, Monroe, LA.

Yronwode, Catherine. *Lucky Mojo Curio Company* Website. 1995–2006. http://www.luckymojo.com.

Glossary

Cross references are set in SMALL CAPITALS.

Adam and Eve Root. name for the conjoined double roots of various orchid species, usually indicating *Aplectum hyemale*. These roots are most commonly used in love spells.

African Diaspora. name for the dispersion of Africans across the world as a result of the international slave trade.

African Traditional Religions. common term for the many indigenous religions of Africa, including VODU. The term is useful in differentiating these faiths from the Christianity and Islam practiced by many Africans, but it is somewhat misleading because it can convey an impression that the many peoples of Africa share almost identical beliefs. There are, indeed, features common to many African Traditional Religions. A few of these are belief in a remote supreme deity, faith in an array of lesser GODS, ANCESTOR VENERATION, and belief in animistic SPIRITS.

Akan. a group of peoples from the African GOLD COAST who contributed a small but ever-present contingent of slaves to the various regions of North America. The importance of women in matrilineal Akan societies may have contributed to the openness of CONJURE to women. The Akan also placed considerable importance on ANCESTOR VENERATION.

Alexander, "King." a Missouri conjurer featured prominently in the works of MARY ALICIA OWEN.

"Alleged." *see* DISCLAIMERS.

Altars. sometimes used in HOODOO, especially in the LATIN CULTURAL ZONE. Although altars are common in Africa, American manifestations more commonly resemble the raised platform of Catholic practice than African versions, which often depicted specific deities. HOODOO altars serve primarily as a ritual space for the performance of spells, especially those requiring an extended period of time. For example, spells involving CANDLES and LODESTONES are frequently performed on altars.

Ancestor Veneration. the widespread African practice of ranking dead family among the important inhabitants of the spirit world. Offerings, prayers, and ceremonies for the ancestors are common throughout the continent, although they are particularly associated with the GOLD COAST and WEST CENTRAL AFRICA. They are also prominent in the VODU practiced in the BIGHT OF BENIN. Many of these practices also survive in Haitian VODOU and were at one time known in the U.S. South, especially in places where VOODOO was present. Today, CONJURE relies on the powers of the dead primarily in the form of GOOPHER DUST and to a lesser extent BONES.

Anderson, Jeffrey Elton. author of *Conjure in African American Society* (2005) and of this volume and a leading modern scholar of African American folk magic and religion.

Anderson, Leafy. reputed founder of New Orleans's SPIRITUAL CHURCHES. Anderson had reportedly been involved in SPIRITUALISM in Chicago before arriving in New Orleans sometime around 1920. Although Anderson undoubtedly had a major impact on the rise of the SPIRITUAL CHURCHES, many of their beliefs predate her.

Anglo Cultural Zone. the portion of the United States initially settled by the English and characterized by the presence of CONJURE. This area began as a strip of land along the Atlantic coast and gradually spread westward until it approached the LATIN CULTURAL ZONE along the Mississippi River. In the Anglo Zone, the AFRICAN TRADITIONAL RELIGIONS once associated with magic faded quickly, partly because of the Protestantism of most British settlers, which left little room for SYNCRETISM. As a result, conjure proper has rarely been associated with African GODS, INITIATIONS, or elaborate CEREMONIES.

Àshe. in YORUBA belief, a commanding power that originated with the supreme being and is incarnate in various humans, animals, plants, and objects.

Assonquer. a god of good fortune in Mississippi Valley VOODOO.

Bakulu. in KONGO belief, the SPIRITS of the ancestors.

Bass, Ruth. author of "Mojo: The Strange Magic That Works in the South Today" (1930) and "The Little Man" (1935), both of which appeared in *Scribner's Magazine.* Both of these deal with CONJURE and address such topics as SPIRITS and multiple SOULS. *see* OLD DIVINITY.

Bible. widely used a magical text in African American magic. Practitioners write down or quote verses while performing spells or making HANDS. The Bible itself is sometimes used as a JACK for DIVINATION. *see* SMITH, THEOPHUS.

Bight of Benin. African region centered on the coast of modern-day Benin, formerly the Kingdom of Dahomey. Slaves from this area were few compared with those of SENGAMBIA, the BIGHT OF BIAFRA, or WEST CENTRAL AFRICA. Nevertheless, groups like the FON, YORUBA, and EWE were important to the development of both Haitian VODOU and Mississippi Valley VOODOO and HOODOO.

Bight of Biafra. African region centered on modern-day Nigeria. Many African slaves were imported from this region, particularly by the colony/state of Virginia. The single most important ethnic group from this region were the IGBO, who composed the dominant African people group in Virginia and were prominent elsewhere as well.

Black Cat Bone. bone of a black cat usually obtained by boiling the feline alive. The bone that floats to the topic of the pot or cauldron is said to confer magical powers on its owner, most notably the ability to become invisible.

Black Hawk. a SAINT revered by the SPIRITUAL CHURCHES of New Orleans. Black Hawk is likely identical to the well-known Native American leader of the same name. Most often, he appears as a benevolent protector, although a few claim he is an evil SAINT.

The reverence for Black Hawk and Indians in general was likely introduced to this denomination by followers of mainstream SPIRITUALISM during the nineteenth century. Some, however, argue that Black Hawk was chosen by African Americans as a spirit worthy of reverence because of his legacy of resistance to white aggression.

Black Power Movement. along with the NEW AGE MOVEMENT, it indirectly transformed perceptions of CONJURE. Black Power advocates promoted the destruction of the white-based society and culture of the United States. In its place, they hoped to build a new society based on African American ideals. Although HOODOO was rarely mentioned in this context, the Black Power vision indirectly changed African Americans' view of CONJURE by means of its positive valuation of African features of black life. In short, the movement made it possible for African Americans to abandon the stereotype that conjure was a practice of the ignorant that should be abandoned. Today, many consider HOODOO a valuable link to U.S. blacks' African roots.

Blanc Dani. one of the names for an important snake deity in Mississippi Valley VOODOO.

Blue Gums. an indication of a conjurer. Some claimed that African Americans with blue gums had a poisonous bite.

Blues. an African American musical style strongly linked to HOODOO. References to MOJOS, GOOPHER OR GOOFER DUST, and the like have been common in blues recordings since their origin in the early twentieth century. The works of musician Muddy Waters provide several excellent examples.

Bokor. Haitian term for an evil sorcerer.

Bones. prominent in African and African American magic as an embodiment of the SPIRITS of the dead. Human bones are particularly powerful and have historically been highly sought-after items. Many have placed special value on the bones of Native Americans. *See* BLACK CAT BONE.

Books. see DO-IT-YOURSELF BOOKS *and* DREAMBOOKS.

Boyle, Virginia Frazer. author of *Devil Tales* (1900). Her book is a work of fictionalized folktales addressing CONJURE, usually in the context of practitioners' battles with the DEVIL. *Devil Tales* is part of the "moonlight and magnolias" school of southern literature in that it hearkens back to idealized plantation days. Compared with the writings of more popular authors like THOMAS NELSON PAGE, Boyle's tales are darker in theme, and African Americans, rather than whites, are central to the storyline.

Brick Dust. obtained by pulverizing bricks, preferably red ones. Red brick dust has long been used to protect oneself from evil, particularly by African Americans living in the LATIN CULTURAL ZONE. Believers usually place the POWDER on or near the thresholds of their homes to keep evil from entering their dwellings.

Buried Treasure. one of the many pursuits to which HOODOO is allegedly useful. Treasure hunting has long been a popular pastime. The lure of hidden gold was particularly strong for poverty-stricken African Americans after the Civil War. Legend had it that Confederate gold was buried across the South. Magical rods, crystal balls, and many other items have proven popular tools of treasure seekers and remain so today, although the invention of metal detectors seems to have lessened their appeal considerably.

Cable, George Washington. author of multiple works containing references to VOODOO, most notably the *Grandissimes* (1891), a novel of antebellum New Orleans.

Candle Shop. a business that sells SPIRITUAL SUPPLIES. The name refers to the prevalence of CANDLES in modern HOODOO practice.

Candles. historically used in New Orleans VOODOO, they are now common in HOODOO throughout the United States, largely because of the influence of Latin American folk religions like SANTERÍA. Modern candles are often encased in glass, on which the figure of a Catholic saint or other illustration is printed. Manufacturers often print instructions for their use on the opposite side. The SAINT pictured on the candle and/or the color of the candle generally indicates its use. For instance, red candles are often used in love spells, whereas black ones are intended to cause harm or death to victims.

Ceremonies. rituals prominent in African and African American supernaturalism. CONJURE and HOODOO frequently involve small ceremonies performed for clients, including but not limited to ritual baths, candle burning, and formal divination. VODU, VODOU, and VOODOO have their own unique rituals. These include complex INITIATIONS and, in the United States, the famous but now defunct SAINT JOHN'S EVE gathering on the shores of Lake Pontchartrain.

Chireau, Yvonne. author of *Black Magic: Religion and the African American Conjuring Tradition* (2003). Along with CAROLYN MORROW LONG and JEFFREY ELTON ANDERSON, she is one of the leading modern scholars of African American CONJURE.

Claremont, Lewis de. popular HOODOO manuals of the early twentieth century appeared under this author's name, which was almost certainly a pseudonym. The most popular of his works today is *Legends of Incense, Oil, and Herb Magic.* He may have been the same person as HENRI GAMACHE.

Cologne. often used in HOODOO love spells. Popular brands include Hoyt's and Jockey Club. Although manufacturers did not make colognes with magical uses in mind, they had become staples of modern CONJURE by the 1920s. *see* SPIRITUAL SUPPLIES.

Conjure. the most common designation for African American folk magic outside of the Mississippi Valley and coastal regions until the early twentieth century. Today, many use the term as a synonym for HOODOO. The word originated in English, where it was widely used to describe a sorcerer who called up and controlled SPIRITS.

Conquer-John. *see* JOHN THE CONQUEROR.

Contagion. magical principle that objects once in contact continue to influence each other even if separated. Along with the principle of SIMILARITY and belief in SPIRITS, contagion is a common part of most magical systems. In HOODOO, it is exceptionally prominent. Practitioners' use of dirt from enemies' FOOT TRACKS in spells designed to drive them away is one example of contagion at work.

Court Case Spells. common element of HOODOO since the late nineteenth century. Spells and charms designed to silence witnesses, sway judges and juries, or otherwise hinder successful prosecution are common. Some authors have referred to CONJURE men as "poor men's lawyers," although their services can be quite pricey. Typically, court case magic relies on POWDERS, rituals involving the names of judges or jurors, and the like. DOCTOR BUZZARD, however, could supposedly cause buzzards to enter the courtroom in order to break up trials. Some researchers credit hoodoo doctors' success to their temporal influence.

Creole. cultures arising in the New World that have Old World bases. The term originally referred to Africans, and later Europeans, born in the Americas. When capitalized, it refers to mixed race persons of color from southern Louisiana, as well as Louisianans of French or Spanish ancestry.

Crime. persistently associated with CONJURE and VOODOO. Nineteenth- and early twentieth-century critics frequently accused practitioners of murder and human SAC-RIFICE. Successful use of magical POISONS has taken place, but incidents have been rare. At the same time, evildoers have resorted to spells designed to cause illness or death much more frequently, although their effectiveness is difficult to prove. In more recent days, charges against conjurers of fraud and practicing medicine without a license have been common. *see* DISCLAIMERS.

Cross Marks (×). powerful symbols in African American CONJURE and HOODOO, usually for protection. For instance, conjurers and believers will draw cross marks along the paths they are traveling and spit on them. The marks are to prevent enemies from fol-lowing them. Visitors to the grave of MARIE LAVEAU also make three such marks on her tomb as a way of imploring her favor. Recent scholarship connects cross marks to the KONGO cosmogram, a religious symbol consisting of an upright cross within an oval or circle, with each arm of the cross terminating in a disk outside the bounds of the central oval. Although Kongo influences are likely, the folkloric protective powers of the Christian cross almost certainly influenced their use as well.

Crossroads. feature prominently in HOODOO ritual. Most notably, folklore records that they are the appropriate place to sell one's soul to the DEVIL.

Cures. process whereby victims of CONJURE are cured, usually in two steps. First, the source of the malady must be discovered. Typically, practitioners seek out a buried or otherwise hidden packet that caused the initial illness and destroy it. Then the HEALER must remove the symptoms of the spell. In the case of LIVE THINGS IN YOU, this would mean removal of animals from the body. Sometimes the cure also involves TURNING BACK. HOODOO doctors frequently succeed in removing evil spells, but vic-tims who wait too long sometimes find that their ailments become incurable. *see* DIAGNOSIS.

Danbala. an important VODOU deity, envisioned as a serpent.

Dédé, Sanité. an early nineteenth-century VOODOO QUEEN and MARIE LAVEAU'S best-known predecessor.

Devil. features prominently in CONJURE folklore. Most often the devil figures as a source of power. Formulas for gaining power by ritually selling one's soul to Satan—usually by night at a CROSSROADS—are legion. In reality, few practitioners admit to having done so, although ZORA NEALE HURSTON claimed to have met a man who called on the devil for aid. Occasionally, the devil appears as the foe of HOODOO doctors, as in the stories of VIRGINIA FRAZER BOYLE.

Devil's Shoe String. one of a variety of long, stringlike roots widely used in CONJURE, usu-ally for protection or good luck. *see* NATIVE AMERICAN CONTRIBUTIONS TO CONJURE.

Diagnosis. determining whether someone has been conjured or is merely physically ill. One common method is to wear a silver dime on a string around one's ankle. If the dime turns black, then the wearer is a victim of magic. HOODOO DOCTORS may also use DIVINATION to determine whether clients have been cursed. Determining who laid the curse is a common second step of diagnosis. Attempted CURES usually follow im-mediately after diagnosis.

Dibia. an IGBO system of supernatural wisdom, which developed into North American UBIA.

Dirt Dauber Nest. mud nests made by a type of wasp. HOODOO practitioners collect and use these nests, usually but not exclusively to control or harm victims. Use of dirt dauber nests is much rarer today than in earlier centuries.

Disclaimers. phrases attached to manufactured CONJURE items designed to avoid making supernatural claims for products. By refusing to state that items have specific benefits, manufacturers and retailers minimize their likelihood of facing fraud charges. HOODOO entrepreneurs, of course, rightly assume that believers will disregard such disclaimers.

Divination. a common feature of African and African American supernaturalism. Common methods of divination include observing eggs broken in water, card reading, and using objects suspended from strings to determine courses of action. Divination is commonly linked to finding winning numbers for games of chance, including modern lotteries. *see* JACKS *and* DREAMBOOKS.

Do-It-Yourself Books. during the late nineteenth century, rising African American literacy created a market for HOODOO manuals. The most prominent of these have been DREAMBOOKS that are used for DIVINATION. Other manuals popular with CONJURE believers have been books describing how to burn CANDLES for magical results, works explaining how to make magical oils and POWDERS, and eclectic collections of spells from various times and places. These books have influenced conjure by introducing magical elements from Jewish, Amish, Afro-Caribbean, and many other cultures to modern African American practice. In addition, manuals along with other SPIRITUAL SUPPLIES have increased the uniformity of hoodoo across the country, reducing the regional distinctions once prominent in African American supernaturalism. It is because of them that *hoodoo, Voodoo,* and *conjure* have become synonyms in the minds of most Americans.

Doctor Buzzard. best-known CONJURE man of the ANGLO CULTURAL ZONE. There have been many Dr. Buzzards, however, apparently beginning with a white practitioner from the area of Beaufort, South Carolina, who died late in the nineteenth century. Today, most remember STEPHANEY ROBINSON, the white rootworker's successor, as *the* Dr. Buzzard. Robinson had become enormously influential by the early twentieth century, to the extent that his name was known across the South. In addition, his fame was such that many imitators adopted his title. According to legend he also became very wealthy operating a mail-order SPIRITUAL SUPPLIES business. Although he died in 1947, folktales continue to be told about him. *see* MCTEER, JAMES *and* DOCTOR EAGLE.

Doctor Eagle. DOCTOR BUZZARD's best-known competitor. He also resided near Beaufort, South Carolina. Unlike Doctor Buzzard, Dr. Eagle befriended JAMES MCTEER. Dr. Eagle's given name was P. H. Washington.

Double Head. common term for a HOODOO practitioner. The origins of the word are unknown, although it may derive from the belief that being born with a caul gave people magical powers.

Dragon's Blood. a resin from the Asian palm species *Daemonorops draco* or *Dracaena draco*. Dragon's blood, although an imported product, had entered HOODOO by the early twentieth century. Believers use it to draw luck, love, and money and for protection. *see* SPIRITUAL SUPPLIES.

Drawing. name for a class of spells and charms designed to bring something to believers. Common versions include love drawing HANDS and money-drawing MOJOS.

Dreambooks. encyclopedic books of dream interpretations, usually designed to help users pick winning lottery numbers. These are legion and have been common since at least the late nineteenth century. Today, they are the most popular published books on HOODOO. In southern states with lotteries, these can often be found in places where lottery tickets are sold, including gas stations. *see* DO-IT-YOURSELF BOOKS.

Dye, Caroline. HOODOO practitioner of Newport, Arkansas. Although born a slave, she had built a powerful reputation by the time of her death in 1918. She was also rumored to have died wealthy. A few blues songs about and postcards of the CONJURE woman testify to her fame. Dye was unusual in that she was rarely if ever accused of doing any "bad work," which cannot be said of MARIE LAVEAU or DOCTOR BUZZARD. Instead, she was best known for her DIVINATION and other positive magic.

European Contributions to Conjure. evident throughout U.S. HOODOO practice. European elements in CONJURE include spiritual concepts, such as belief in the Christian God and the power of SAINTS. In addition, many items of European origin have become common conjure paraphernalia. Some notable examples include CANDLES, the BIBLE, and a variety of herbal curios, including at least one version of JOHN THE CONQUEROR.

Ewe. a people of the GOLD COAST and BIGHT OF BENIN who traditionally practice VODU. The Ewe are widely (and rightly) considered one of the major sources for the beliefs of Haitian VODOU and Mississippi Valley VOODOO and HOODOO. Their influence on the conjure of the ANGLO CULTURAL ZONE was much less profound.

Ezili. one of various female VODOU GODS. Ezili Freda, a particularly beloved manifestation, is the goddess of love and beauty.

Fandrich, Ina. author of *The Mysterious Voodoo Queen, Marie Laveaux: A Study of Powerful Female Leadership in Nineteenth-Century New Orleans* (2005), a feminist study of the life of Marie Laveau. Unlike fellow authors MARTHA WARD and CAROLYN LONG, Fandrich writes from a strongly theoretical viewpoint.

Federal Writers' Project (FWP). federally funded support program overseen by the Works Progress Administration as part of Franklin D. Roosevelt's New Deal. FWP workers collected vast amounts of folkloric data from both whites and blacks. In the South, much of the material addresses either CONJURE or VOODOO. ZORA NEALE HURSTON once worked as part of the Florida division of the FWP.

Feeding the Hand. traditional CONJURE charms require feeding. If not fed with blood, whiskey, OILS, or some other liquid specified by the maker, HANDS will lose their power. This idea rests on the assumption that the charms possess indwelling SPIRITS.

Five Finger Grass. a EUROPEAN CONTRIBUTION TO CONJURE, commonly used for obtaining good fortune, love, money, and the like. Called cinquefoil by whites (*Potentilla reptans, canadensis,* and related species), Europeans used it as a witch and demon repellent during the early modern period.

Fix. to place a curse on someone. The phrase "I'll fix you" likely originated with this meaning of the term.

Fon. an African people related to the EWE who live in the BIGHT OF BENIN region. Like the Ewe, they practice a form of VODU and contributed heavily to VODOU and Mississippi Valley VOODOO and HOODOO. Their impact on ANGLO CULTURAL ZONE CONJURE was much less significant. The Fon were once a very warlike people who organized them-selves into the Kingdom of Dahomey. The wars of the Fon kings produced many slaves sold to European slavers. Dahomey changed its name to Benin in 1975.

Foot Tracks. conjurers use dirt from them in CONJURE. Practitioners most commonly use foot track dirt in spells designed to drive off or keep away enemies, although numerous other uses are known.

Frizzly Chickens. Powerful protectors against evil CONJURE. Believers maintain that they will dig up buried HOODOO items that are designed to harm the chickens' owners. Similar beliefs in the protective powers of chickens are common throughout much of Africa.

Gamache, Henri. an author working under this name produced popular HOODOO manu-als during the early twentieth century. The most popular of his works today is *The Master Book of Candle Burning: How to Burn Candles for Any Purpose.* He may have been the same person as LEWIS DE CLAREMONT.

Geechee. an African American people group of coastal Georgia. Like the GULLAHS of South Carolina, they are much studied because of their distinctive language and strong folk culture, which preserves many Africanisms, including a strong belief in magic. The origin of the term *Geechee* has proven difficult to determine, although the most popular theories are that it derives from the name for a West African people group or from the name of Georgia's Ogeechee River.

Gods. figure prominently in VODU, VODOU, and VOODOO. In each religion, the deities are numerous. Vodu has a pantheon of minor deities, which are called on for aid by believers, as well as a supreme creator god, who made the earth then distanced himself from it. These African beliefs made their way into Haitian Vodou, although with significant additions from other portions of Africa, most notably the region cen-tered on the Kingdom of the KONGO. In addition, Afro-Haitians drew equivalencies between their gods and specific Catholic SAINTS. In the United States, most Voodoo gods were of the West African variety, hailing primarily from the BIGHT OF BENIN region, although Kongo deities were not unknown. Some of the more important Voodoo deities are the serpent god Blanc Dani (from the Fon and Ewe Dañh-gbi) and the trickster deity Papa Lébat (from the Fon and Ewe Legba). As in Haiti, many had SAINT equivalents. Outside of the Mississippi Valley and portions of Florida, the gods had largely died out by the antebellum era. In the ANGLO CULTURAL ZONE, many if not most African Americans had adopted the Christian God as the source of CONJURE.

Gold Coast. region of Africa approximately corresponding to today's Ghana. This region most notably contributed to the Atlantic South and likely supported WEST CENTRAL Africans in their focus on ancestral SPIRITS. Peoples of the AKAN linguistic family were the most important arrivals from this region.

Gombre. rare Virginia term for CONJURE. It may derive from *ngombo,* a KONGO term referring to DIVINATION. This seems unlikely, however, considering Virginia's small number of slaves originating in WEST CENTRAL AFRICA.

Goopher or Goofer. synonym for *CONJURE* and HOODOO, probably derived from the KiKongo term *kufwa,* meaning "to die." The modern term *goofy* may be a descendant of this word. *see* KONGO.

Goopher or Goofer Dust. common name for earth taken from a grave or for a POWDER that incorporates such dirt. It can be used for both good and evil purpose. The character of the person from whose grave the dirt is taken can be an important factor. For instance, charms designed to protect or give power to their bearers might use dirt from the plot of a soldier.

Grand Zombi. A powerful VOODOO spirit, perhaps identical to BLANC DANI.

Graveyard Dirt. *see* GOOPHER DUST.

Gregory Bag. *see* GRIS-GRIS.

Gris-gris. a term once common in Haiti and the Mississippi Valley referring to VODOU, VOODOO, and HOODOO charms. The word derives from *gree-gree, gerregerys,* or *gregory,* which West Africans from SENEGAMBIA to the BIGHT OF BENIN have long used to describe MOJO-like bag charms.

Guinea Pepper. commonly used for protection and driving away enemies. It is also sometimes mixed with GRAVEYARD DIRT to make GOOPHER DUST. Despite its name, Guinea pepper (*Capsicum annum*) is in part a NATIVE AMERICAN CONTRIBUTION TO CONJURE.

Gullah. an African American people that lives primarily in the South Carolina Lowcountry. Gullahs also inhabit coastal areas in parts of North Carolina, and if one includes the GEECHEES in their number, can be found as far south as northern Florida. The Gullahs have a strong belief in ROOTWORK, as exemplified by the career of DOCTOR BUZZARD. In addition to magical beliefs, the Gullah have also preserved many features of African culture, including a unique language and distinctive foods and crafts. Dispute about the origin of the term *Gullah* is ongoing. The oldest explanation is that the word derives from *Gola,* the name of a people who live in modern-day Liberia and Sierra Leone. A second popular theory is that the term is a corruption of *Ngola,* the name for a people of modern Angola.

Gullah Jack. a conjurer and Denmark Vesey's second in command during his 1822 plot to overthrow slavery. Jack was a native of Mozambique. After living first in Florida, GULLAH Jack later commanded a contingent of Vesey's forces in their planned attack on Charleston, South Carolina. According to popular belief, Jack could not be harmed by whites, although an executioner later proved this faith to be misplaced.

Hand. one of the names for a magic charm in HOODOO. Hands are designed for positive uses, ranging from bringing simply luck to drawing love to bringing success in gambling.

Harris, Joel Chandler. A nineteenth-century recorder of folklore and author of the famed Uncle Remus books. CONJURE performed by MAMMY-BAMMY BIG-MONEY frequently appears in these stories. *see* RABBIT.

Haskins, James. prolific author who wrote *Voodoo and Hoodoo: The Craft as Revealed by Traditional Practitioners* (1978), a popular work addressing African American magical practices. Haskins's book contains both a brief historical and folkloric overview of CONJURE practices and a large selection of HOODOO spells.·

Healer. CONJURE practitioner who performs beneficial magic. Some modern believers draw a distinction between "good" healers and "evil" HOODOO practitioners.

Hoodoo. modern synonym of *CONJURE* and historical synonym of *VOODOO*. During the nineteenth century, blacks from the Mississippi Valley portion of the LATIN CULTURAL ZONE referred to what is more commonly known as Voodoo as HOODOO. Today, however, the term has lost its religious connotations and has become a general word for African American magic. The origins of the word have been much disputed. Most likely, the word originated in the BIGHT OF BENIN, which contributed strongly to the black culture of the Mississippi Valley. According to Judy Rosenthal, author of *Possession, Ecstasy, and Law in Ewe Voodoo*, it is likely the same as the Mina word *hudu*, which literally means "blood eating" but symbolically refers to VODU rituals. A second possibility is that *hoodoo* might derive from a combination of the EWE word *hu*, one meaning of which is "spirit," with either *do*, which can be translated as "work," or *du*, which can mean "eating." For example, one meaning of the phrase *hu do* is "spirit work." Similarly, *hu du* can mean "spirit eating," which is the name of a specific Vodu ritual. Either source for the term is an excellent fit for the LATIN CULTURAL ZONE, where hoodoo would have specifically represented the ritual side of Voodoo. After later generations had abandoned the African GODS and INITIATIONS, only the magical rituals would have remained, effectively rendering *hoodoo* a synonym of *conjure*.

Hoodoo Doctor. a name for a practitioner of HOODOO. Occasionally, believers specify that hoodoo doctors only heal those harmed by other conjurers. *see* HEALER.

Horseshoe. used as lucky and protective charms when hung above doorways.

Hot Foot Powder. a preparation including but not limited to GUINEA PEPPER designed to drive rivals or enemies out of town. The name refers to the fact that walking away is necessary to cool one's feet after treading on or otherwise coming into contact with the POWDER.

Hurston, Zora Neale. with the possible exception of ROBERT TALLANT, the best-known author to address African American HOODOO and VOODOO. Her primary works on CONJURE are "Hoodoo in America" (1931) and *Mules and Men* (1935). Although her writings are rife with exaggeration and falsification, she has been highly influential. Most important, she imbued hoodoo with an air of legitimacy, convincing modern folklorists, historians, and literary scholars of its worth. After reading Hurston, most find it difficult to think of conjure as simply devil worship or fraud.

Hyatt, Harry Middleton. Christian minister and editor of the largest and most important collection of HOODOO folklore ever published, the five volume *Hoodoo-Conjuration-Witchcraft-Rootwork* (1970–1978). This work consists almost entirely of the phonetically transcribed interviews of well over 1,000 informants. These difficult-to-find volumes include a staggering amount of information of CONJURE that Hyatt collected throughout the South, primarily during the late 1930s, approximately the same time that the FEDERAL WRITERS' PROJECT was active. Hyatt's chief flaw is that he did not record information from those he saw as nontraditional conjurers, which included owners of SPIRITUAL SUPPLY shops.

Igbo. large African people group residing in the BIGHT OF BIAFRA region. As slaves they were particularly influential in Virginia, where they outnumbered all other ethnicities. Stories of flying Africans likely originated with this group as did the term UBIA.

Incense. common feature of modern HOODOO. These are burned for a variety of purposes. The name, odor, and/or color of the incense often indicates its intended use.

Initiations. one way to become an adept at African and African American folk religion and magic. In both African VODU and Haitian VODOU, initiations into various RELIGIOUS SOCIETIES are required to advance within the religions. In North American

CONJURE, HOODOO, and VOODOO, initiations have been rare since the nineteenth century, and very few have been recorded outside of the LATIN CULTURAL ZONE. In New Orleans, however, occasional initiations continued until at least the late 1930s, as evidenced by oral histories conducted by the FEDERAL WRITERS' PROJECT.

Insanity. a common result of a CONJURE curse. Victims of evil conjure often develop madness, either in connection with other symptoms or on its own. Of course, a successful HOODOO doctor can CURE magically induced insanity. If not identified and treated in time, however, it can lead to death. *see* LOCKED BOWELS *and* LIVE THINGS IN YOU.

Jack. a DIVINATION tool peculiar to HOODOO. A jack is usually a magical object suspended from a string. The direction the item points indicates answers to questions asked by the diviner. The suspended items are frequently magic roots or LUCK BALLS, although some prefer to use BIBLES. Some use *jack* as a synonym for *HAND*.

John the Conqueror. a variety of roots that convey power on their owners. Since at least the early twentieth century, many roots have gone by this name and have been recognized as falling into several categories, including High John, LOW JOHN, Chewing John, and Southern John. This entry refers only to High John. The original version of the plant appears to have been Solomon's seal (*Polygonatum biflorum*), a EUROPEAN CONTRIBUTION TO CONJURE. Since the advent of SPIRITUAL SUPPLIES, jalap (*Ipomea jalapa* and *Convolvulus panduratus*) has generally replaced the earlier version. It appears that during the antebellum era, slaves carried whole John the Conqueror roots in their pockets to prevent harsh treatment from their masters. Today, they are widely used in spells and charms designed for positive ends, including drawing love, money, or the like. *see* SLAVERY AND CONJURE.

Jomo. an uncommon near-synonym for *MOJO*. The chief difference between mojos and jomos, if one truly exists, is that the latter are as often evil by design as they are good. *see* HAND *and* TOBY.

Jordan, James Spurgeon. North Carolina's greatest CONJURE man, who in his day rivaled Dr. Buzzard in fame. Jordan, of Como, began practicing during the late nineteenth century and had built a national reputation by the time of the Great Depression. By the time of his death, he had amassed a fortune. His earnings from the practice of ROOTWORK allowed him to buy multiple farms, a logging company, and a baseball team. Jordan's fame was so great that a community grew up around his shop, which came to be known as Jordansville. The career of Jordan is particularly interesting in that his practice spanned the years during which traditional conjure developed into the SPIRITUAL SUPPLIES industry. Jordan himself participated in the shift, gradually incorporating HOODOO manuals and manufactured products into his own work.

Kongo. an important people group of WEST CENTRAL AFRICA. The Kongo, who call themselves BaKongo, once ruled a substantial kingdom centered in modern Congo and Angola. In 1491, the king converted to Christianity and invited missionaries to evangelize his country. Some recent scholars have argued that Christian elements made their way into Haitian VODOU and U.S. VOODOO from the Kongo rather than from white slave masters.

Lala. a New Orleans VOODOO QUEEN during the first half of the twentieth century. FEDERAL WRITERS' PROJECT workers met and interviewed her during the late 1930s. She features prominently in ROBERT TALLANT's *Voodoo in New Orleans* as the embodiment of modern VOODOO.

Latin Cultural Zone. portion of the modern United States originally settled by people of Latin origin, most notably the French and Spanish. The area extends across the Gulf Coast and up the Atlantic Coast to the northern border of Florida. The shores of the Mississippi River and its major tributaries extend this cultural area into the heart of the country. The Latin Cultural Zone was the original home of VOODOO, HOODOO, and NAÑIGO. These contrast with the CONJURE of the ANGLO CULTURAL ZONE in that they preserve many more features of magic and AFRICAN TRADITIONAL RELIGIONS from SENEGAMBIA, the BIGHT OF BENIN, and nearby areas of West Africa. The survival of complex INITIATIONS and African GODS stands out most prominently. On the other hand, WEST CENTRAL AFRICAN elements are comparably fewer in the LATIN CULTURAL ZONE. Slave importation patterns largely account for the differences. Although African religions throve in the region, they had virtually died out in the ANGLO CULTURAL ZONE by the antebellum area. The Spanish and French tendency to allow greater rights to their slaves accounts for this in some degree, as does the Catholic Church's willingness to accept only partial conversion of newly imported slaves.

Latour, Malvina. MARIE LAVEAU's most famous successor as VOODOO QUEEN.

Laveau, Marie. the most famous of New Orleans's VOODOO QUEENS. Born in 1801, she had become one of the nation's best known African American females by the time of her death in 1881. Her obituary is reported to have appeared in the *New York Times*. Laveau has become the stuff of legend; however, many of the claims made about her have proven false. For instance, although rumored to have become wealthy, she sometimes struggled to make ends meet. Likewise, although many recent authors claim that before the Civil War she secretly worked to undermine slavery, this does not appear to have been true. In fact, Laveau occasionally bought and sold slaves. One unsolved mystery surrounding Laveau involves just how many Marie Laveau's there were. Since the days of ZORA NEALE HURSTON, most authors have claimed that Laveau's daughter, generally known as Marie II, took over her mother's (Marie I) practice. Some, including Hurston, have argued that the mantle was later taken up by the granddaughter of Marie I. Most modern scholars support the idea that there were two VOODOO QUEENS named Marie Laveau. The problems are that all of Laveau's daughters had *Marie* as their first name and that the one usually identified as Marie II died nearly two decades before her mother. It is possible that folk memory mistakenly associated this daughter with MALVINA LATOUR, a younger VOODOO practitioner who rose to some prominence after Marie I's death.

Lébat. a deity who opens communication between humans and other GODS in Mississippi Valley VOODOO. He is related to the Haitian LEGBA.

Legba. the VODOU deity who opens communication between the GODS and humans.

Liberia. a small country of West Africa, founded as an American colony for former slaves. Of course, the area was already inhabited. This older population had supplied a small number of slaves to the New World. *see* SIERRA LEONE.

Live Things in You. a type of HOODOO poisoning when live animals inhabit the victim's body. These are typically reptiles, amphibians, or invertebrates, although SNAKES appear to have been the most common. The condition is often but not exclusively contracted by unknowingly swallowing the powdered body of the animal. The POWDER takes on the form of the living creature and can often be seen moving under the victim's skin or even peering from his or her mouth. One can only be cured of live things with the help of a CONJURE doctor. Cures usually involve induced vomiting to remove the live things. If the hoodoo practitioner does not arrive in time, the afflicted person will die. At the time of death or just before, the live things usually leave the body by way of the mouth. *see* LOCKED BOWLES *and* POISON.

Locked Bowels. a type of HOODOO curse in which victims die from constipation. Of the many types of evil CONJURE spells, this one is the most severe. Reports of cures are rare compared to those for other types of curses, such as LIVE THINGS IN YOU.

Lodestone. a stone used by HOODOO practitioners to attract money or love. Lodestones are naturally magnetic, hence their use to draw wealth and affection.

Long, Carolyn Morrow. along with JEFFREY ELTON ANDERSON and YVONNE CHIREAU, one of the leading modern researchers on African American HOODOO. Her book, *Spiritual Merchants: Religion, Magic, and Commerce* (2001), was the first to detail the rise of the SPIRITUAL SUPPLIES industry out of traditional CONJURE. In 2006, Long published a scholarly biography of Marie Laveau, entitled *A New Orleans Voudou Priestess: The Legend and Reality of Marie Laveau.*

Low John. a variety of JOHN THE CONQUEROR. Some call it Chewing John or Little John, although its common name is galangal (*Alpinia officinarum* or *Alpinia galangal*). Its most famous use was as a means of preventing abuse at the hands of slave masters. To ward off beatings, slaves would chew the root and spit its juice toward their owners or their overseers, believing that they would be thereby protected from harm. Believers continue to chew Low John as a means of protecting themselves or controlling others.

Luck Ball. a magical charm featured prominently in the writings of MARY ALICIA OWEN. Luck balls are a kind of hand carried in a bag. In effect, they are a type of MOJO, although the bag appears less an integral part of the charm than a simple carrying case.

Lwa. the Haitian term for major deities of VODOU. Older works typically spell the term *loa*.

Mammy-Bammy Big-Money. a CONJURE woman who appears in Joel Chandler Harris's Uncle Remus stories.

Mande. a language group of the SENEGAMBIA region of West Africa. The Mande appear to have contributed the term GRIS-GRIS to New Orleans VOODOO. The reason for preferring Senegambia over the BIGHT OF BENIN as the word's place of origin is that the majority of Africans brought to Louisiana during the early colonial period came from the former.

McTeer, James Edwin. a sheriff of the South Carolina Low Country who also became a CONJURE practitioner. McTeer was most active as both sheriff and rootworker during the second quarter of the twentieth century. His two books, *High Sheriff of the Low Country* (1970) and *Fifty Years as a Low Country Witch Doctor* (1976), provide considerable information on South Carolinian ROOTWORK.

Medical Effects of Conjure. heavily commented on by doctors and laypersons alike since the late nineteenth century. Before the 1960s, virtually all investigations focused on HOODOO's ability to harm or kill. Whether authors attributed the ill effects of CONJURE to the ignorance of well-meaning practitioners or to malevolent intent varied widely. After the 1960s, increasing numbers of physicians came to see HOODOO as a potential aid to healing. The most prominent scholarly treatment of the topic has been Wonda L. Fontenot's *Secret Doctors: Ethnomedicine of African Americans* (1994). General readers have preferred Faith Mitchell's *Hoodoo Medicine: Gullah Herbal Remedies* (1999), which lists specific herbal remedies and briefly analyzes their potential healthful qualities.

Minkisi. KONGO charms. *Minkisi* (singular *nkisi*) contained medicinal and/or magical ingredients, as well as a soul called a *mooyo*. *Minkisi* appear to have strongly influenced the American idea of the MOJO, which may have derived its name from *mooyo*. *see* UNCLE/UNKUS.

Mojo. Most commonly a name for a bag-style HAND. Mojo bags can be made of many different materials, but the most common traditional material is RED FLANNEL, probably because the color signified power. Roots, herbs, LUCK BALLS, and virtually any other HOODOO item found places in such charms. Conjurers' choice of materials depended primarily on the purpose of the hand. For instance, JOHN THE CONQUEROR carried in a mojo could bring its possessor luck, power, or protection. FIVE FINGER GRASS, in contrast, would draw money to its owner. Like other hands, these charms often lose their power unless they are regularly fed with whiskey, OILS, or other liquids. In some places, *mojo* is also used as a synonym for *CONJURE*. This usage is particularly common in the Mississippi Valley, especially in the area around Memphis, Tennessee. The word *mojo* may derive from the KONGO term *mooyo*, which originally signified the spirit that dwelt within an *nkisi* charm. *See* FEEDING THE HAND, JACK, *MINKISI, and* TOBY.

Morrison, Toni. a prominent African American author who sometimes uses CONJURE in her writings, most notably in her novel *Sula* (1974). *see* REED, ISHMAEL *and* WALKER, ALICE.

Nañigo. a SANTERÍA-like religion once practiced in parts of Florida, most notably the Tampa region and Key West. Both areas experienced significant Cuban migration during the late nineteenth century, when the religion was most active. In Cuba, *Ñáñigo* is a term for a RELIGIOUS SOCIETY. Nañigo's CEREMONIES and GODS derived primarily from the YORUBA people of West Africa and survived at least into the early twentieth century. The influx of Cuban followers of Santería during the second half of the twentieth century erased any remnants of the faith, causing them to be absorbed into the religion with which Nañigo shared a common origin. Some authors refer to it as *Ñañigo* or *Ñañigro*.

Native American Contributions to Conjure. Native American religious and magical beliefs both reinforced elements of AFRICAN TRADITIONAL RELIGIONS present in CONJURE and introduced unique features to HOODOO. As was true with many Africans, most Native Americans worshipped multiple GODS, manufactured charms, and esteemed traditional magic workers. For example, the importance of serpents in VOODOO doubtless originated in Africa, but the fact that their reverence persisted only in the LATIN CULTURAL ZONE was probably because the region's blacks had close and regular contact with Native Americans who shared similar beliefs. In contrast, the rest of the South was largely empty of Native American by the time of the Civil War. It is no coincidence that African Americans in the ANGLO CULTURAL ZONE had largely abandoned similar beliefs well before their traditional beliefs were recorded. On the other hand,

Native American elements are ever present in conjure throughout the United States. They are most evident in hoodoo's magical herbalism. Some prominent Native American botanical contributions are ADAM AND EVE ROOT, DEVIL'S SHOE STRING, puccoon root (*Sanguinaria canadensis* or *Lithospermum canescens*), and at least one version of JOHN THE CONQUEROR. The importance of Native Americans to the shaping of conjure is reinforced by the fact that many practitioners claim to have learned their art from Indians. *see* EUROPEAN CONTRIBUTIONS TO CONJURE.

New Age Movement. a widespread spiritual movement that began with imported Eastern mysticism adopted by members of the countercultural community during the 1960s. As it gained popularity during the 1970s and 1980s, the New Age Movement gathered a stunning variety of religious and magical practices under its wings, including various neopagan religions, Gnostic revivalism, and mystical Islam. Initially, many New Agers avoided HOODOO. To some degree this avoidance signified the widespread stereotype of CONJURE as evil "black magic" (or "magick," as they would say). At the same time, hoodoo was an American tradition, rendering it rather less than countercultural. Over time, however, the success of the movement undermined Americans' faith in science and helped legitimize magic in the eyes of many. Whites and blacks, who would have once scorned conjure as a backward practice of the foolish or uneducated, now see it as a form of folk wisdom. The result has been a resurgence of hoodoo practice, particularly among educated blacks looking for a link to their African past. *see* BLACK POWER MOVEMENT.

Nganga. the spirit-containing cauldron that is a central feature of PALO MONTE MAYOMBE.

Noodoo. a name for the practice of HOODOO found in Missouri.

Numbers. particular numbers are important to some HOODOO spells. Of particular significance is the number nine, which is considered lucky and powerful.

Nzambi Mpungu. the supreme being in KONGO belief. This being may have been the origin of VOODOO's GRAND ZOMBI.

Oils. a common feature of modern HOODOO. Oils gained prominence during the twentieth century, eventually supplanting POWDERS in prevalence. Today, they rival CANDLES as the most valued product of hoodoo shops. Oils can be used for virtually any purpose, with color and brand name indicating their use. Most commonly, oils are applied to other CONJURE items in order to activate them. Many MOJOS require periodic feedings with oils in order to maintain their power. *see* FEEDING THE HAND, SPIRITUAL SUPPLIES, *and* VAN VAN OIL.

Old Divinity. a Mississippi conjurer described by RUTH BASS. He reportedly had the ability to talk to trees, which taught him MOJO.

Openings. *see* INITIATIONS.

Owen, Mary Alicia. late nineteenth-century scholar who studied Missouri HOODOO. Most notably, she authored the book *Old Rabbit, the Voodoo and Other Sorcerers* (1893). *see* ALEXANDER, "KING" *and* NOODOO.

Page, Thomas Nelson. writer and chief architect of the "moonlight and magnolias" vision of the Old South, which depicted whites as heroic and paternal masters of childlike and submissive slaves. Despite the negative associations attached to this school of thought, Page was himself a supporter of the moderate version civil rights advocated by Booker T. Washington. CONJURE doctors are minor characters in some of his novels, most notably *Red Rock* (1898), where the evil Dr. Moses is a leader of the free blacks after the Civil War.

Palo Mayombe Monte. an Afro-Cuban religion, principally KONGO in origin. It is commonly associated with its most famous emblem, the *NGANGA* cauldron, in which a spirit lives and serves its possessor.

Peterkin, Julia. a white South Carolinian author whose fictional writings on the GULLAH frequently contain references to ROOTWORK. She was born in 1880 and died in 1961.

Poison. long associated with African and African American supernaturalism. In black belief, poison is not simply a toxic substance. Instead poisoning someone is the equivalent of cursing someone. To be sure, some magical substances administered to unsuspecting victims were poisonous. Others, however, might not even be ingested. Some popular types of poisonings are LOCKED BOWELS and LIVE THINGS IN YOU.

Powder. a common feature of African and African American magic. Some powders, such as those designed to cause LIVE THINGS IN YOU, are meant to be ingested. Much more commonly, however, the powders are scattered in places where the object of the spell will come into physical contact with them. For instance, common places for the deposit of powders are doorsteps and letters. The most famous traditional powder is GOOPHER DUST. A modern powder that has gained widespread fame is HOT FOOT POWDER. *see* SPIRITUAL SUPPLIES.

Psychological Effects of Conjure. significant topic of study beginning during the second half of the twentieth century. Ever since the 1942 publication of Walter B. Cannon's "Voodoo Death," which actually has nothing to do with VOODOO, many psychologists and psychiatrists have been interested in the mental effects of magic. By the 1960s, their attention had turned to CONJURE. These studies have focused on the theory that the effects of HOODOO curses are psychosomatic illnesses—ailments that originate in the mind though expressing physical symptoms. Most researchers suggest that patients exhibiting signs of such curses seek help from HOODOO DOCTORS as well as modern psychologists and psychiatrists. Some have gone further, arguing that the practice of positive conjure is itself a form of beneficial folk psychology that helps individuals maintain their mental health by helping them believe they are aided and protected by supernatural forces. *see* MEDICAL EFFECTS OF CONJURE.

Puckett, Newell Niles. author of *Folk Beliefs of the Southern Negro* (1926). Puckett's work was the most in-depth look at CONJURE available until the publication of HARRY MIDDLETON HYATT's massive *Hoodoo-Conjuration-Witchcraft-Rootwork* (1970–1978). Hyatt believed that most African American folklore had descended from European beliefs, but he made an exception in the cases of HOODOO and VOODOO, which he judged to be clearly African in origin. Puckett's work, although dated and racially condescending, has influenced virtually all scholarly works to address conjure and remains extremely valuable today.

Rabbit. the most popular character in traditional African American folklore. In some works, especially those by MARY ALICIA OWEN, he is a powerful conjurer.

Rabbit's Foot. a traditional lucky charm in African American society. To be most effective, the charm must be the left hind foot of a graveyard rabbit shot by a cross-eyed African American.

Racism and Conjure. Many consider the survival of CONJURE a response to racism. For example, some medical researchers argue that African Americans' continued belief in herbal and magical remedies for sickness can be credited to racist attitudes that limited blacks' access to higher education and that helped create the poverty that limited their ability to pay doctors' bills. At the same time, racial concepts led to attempts to suppress HOODOO during the late nineteenth and twentieth centuries. For example, laws against the sale of charms and practicing medicine without a license have resulted in the prosecution of many African American practitioners of conjure. Significantly, southern state legislatures passed most such laws only after African Americans had gained their freedom from slavery. Thus although these laws often make no reference to race, one may safely conclude that their designers intended them to control the actions of their former human property. *see* MEDICAL EFFECTS OF CONJURE *and* PSYCHOLOGICAL EFFECTS OF CONJURE.

Railroad Bill. a black Alabama outlaw, known for his penchant of riding on freight trains. He had a reputation for magical powers, most notably the ability to take on the forms of animals.

Rattlesnake. In Missouri HOODOO, Grandfather Rattlesnake is a powerful and threatening conjurer. Although he is not one of the VOODOO GODS, his exalted position probably reflects the importance of Blanc Dani to VOODOO in Louisiana. As with other SNAKES, rattlesnakes or portions of rattlesnakes can also be used in hoodoo charms and spells.

Reader. a type of African American conjurer who practices DIVINATION and diagnoses magical ailments but does not typically make charms, cast spells, or otherwise produce magical products.

Red Flannel. a material featured prominently in African American CONJURE. It is one of the most common materials used for the outer casing of HANDS. The color is most often used for charms designed to bring power to their possessors.

Reed, Ishmael. influential African American poet who uses the CONJURE man as a symbol of black subversion of white society and culture. For examples of his work in this vein, see *Conjure: Selected Poems, 1963–1970* (1972) and *Mumbo Jumbo* (1972). *see* MORRISON, TONI *and* WALKER, ALICE.

Religious Societies. a common feature of African and African-derived religions, including VODU, VODOU, SANTERÍA, and NAÑIGO. Typically, these societies are religiously based and divide along gender lines. Religious societies, often called "secret societies" because their rituals are not open to the outside world, are particularly common in the BIGHT OF BENIN and GOLD COAST regions of Africa. Membership is achieved through INITIATION, and members can advance to higher ranks by taking part in further CEREMONIES. Similar societies survived the Atlantic crossing and exist in virtually every area settled by significant numbers of Africans. In the United States, the word *Nañigo* refers to an African American religion confined to Florida, but in Cuban *Santería*, the term refers to a society. Based on the linguistic evidence and the accounts of witnesses, believers in the Floridian faith saw themselves as members of a religious society. Many accounts of New Orleans VOODOO also describe initiations into a similar group. Unfortunately, most of the evidence for Voodoo societies comes from comparatively unreliable sources, usually composed by unsympathetic whites.

Robinson, Stephaney. *see* DOCTOR BUZZARD.

Rootwork. a synonym for *CONJURE* and *HOODOO* common in the Sea Islands and coastal areas of South Carolina and Georgia. Practitioners from the area are commonly known as rootworkers. The term refers to the prominence of roots in African American magic.

Russell, Chloe. first known African American author of a HOODOO DREAMBOOK. She lived in the Boston area during antebellum times.

Sacrifice. common in VODU, VODOU, and VOODOO. Goats, chickens, and other domestic animals are the usual victims. Their deaths are usually required by lesser GODS, SPIRITS, or ancestors who desire sacrifices as a form of worship or in exchange for their supernatural services. Sometimes the sacrifices serve more pragmatic purposes, as in the ritual to obtain a BLACK CAT BONE. Cases of animals being killed so that their spirits will guard hidden treasure have also been reported. Although most sacrifices are domestic animals, SNAKES and other wild animals sometimes take their place. In parts of Africa, humans have done the same, although rarely for community rituals. Instead, most humans fall victim to sorcerers, understood as being antithetical to good society by most Africans. Rumors of human sacrifice are common in the folklore surrounding Haitian Vodou and U.S. Voodoo. Actual cases have been rare but are not unknown.

Saint John's Eve. the most important VOODOO ceremony in Louisiana. St. John's Eve encompasses the night of June 23 and 24. By the antebellum era, African Americans had begun to celebrate the holiday near where St. John's Bayou joins Lake Pontchartrain. Descriptions of the ceremonies vary greatly. White observers almost invariably portrayed them as debauched orgies. At least one African American described them as simply a time to honor St. John. The most reliable accounts mention rituals that involved bathing in the lake and feasting. VOODOO QUEENS, the most famous of which was MARIE LAVEAU, presided over the rituals. In fact, it may be that Voodoo queens' primary role was to preside over these ceremonies, which is a practice in keeping with African-derived traditions throughout the New World. The ceremonies once attracted large crowds of both participants and spectators, but they gradually died out during the late nineteenth century.

Saints. figure prominently in VODOU and VOODOO. Many honor saints in their own right, but they are also linked to specific African-derived GODS. Believers often consider the saints to be the same beings as the deities. For instance, the nineteenth-century Voodoo faithful believed Saint Michael and BLANC DANI to be the same being. Others, however, think of saints as merely corresponding to or communicating with the gods. The saint-deity link likely developed from the contact between Catholicism and AFRICAN TRADITIONAL RELIGIONS in the New World, although some scholars have recently suggested that it may have an earlier origin in WEST CENTRAL AFRICA, where many people were already nominal Christians. Saints may be called on for a variety of pursuits, including love, protection, and money drawing.

Santería. an Afro-Cuban folk religion. The most evident influences on the faith are YORUBA traditional religion and Roman Catholicism. Some modern authors prefer the term *Lukumí*, although most believers and observers prefer *Santería,* a term referring to the importance of Catholic SAINTS/African GODS to the faith. Since the Cuban

Revolution, the influence of this faith on HOODOO has become increasingly evident. *see* CANDLES.

Senegambia. the westernmost region of Africa, usually described as the area centered on the Senegal and Gambia Rivers, although recent scholars have used the term *Greater Senegambia* to describe a considerably broader region. Many New World slaves arrived from there, having a particularly strong impact on the Mississippi Valley, where they introduced the term *GRIS-GRIS,* among other things.

Seven Sisters. a set of legendary New Orleans CONJURE women who flourished in the early twentieth century. Some claim that there was only one person who pretended to be seven people by using disguises. The name was also adopted by Ida Carter of Lower Alabama during the late nineteenth or early twentieth century.

Sierra Leone. a region of Africa stretching from Guinea-Bissau to the Ivory Coast. Africans from this region were a small but ever-present part of slave population throughout the South. The peoples of this region may have introduced the concept of secret SOCIETIES to the American South.

Silver Dimes. a popular protective item when worn on a string around an ankle. According to some, the dime will turn black whenever someone becomes the victim of evil HOODOO.

Similarity. the magical belief that "like produces like." For example, HOODOO practitioners use LODESTONES in money-DRAWING spells because of their natural magnetic properties. Along with belief in SPIRITS and the principle of CONTAGION, sympathy is a defining feature of magic in general. In herbalism, the principle of sympathy is often called the doctrine of signatures, reflecting the belief that plants' physical appearance indicates the body part or illness they will treat.

Slavery and Conjure. slavery helped stamp out the religions from which CONJURE emerged but also helped preserve many spells designed for individual protection. Many masters actively suppressed the practice of AFRICAN TRADITIONAL RELIGIONS, rightly viewing them as a rallying point for slave resistance. At the same time, slaves carried magical roots to protect themselves from beatings by harsh masters. The famous escaped slave and abolitionist, Frederick Douglass, did so on at least one occasion. Likewise, magical POWDERS applied to the feet supposedly gave runaways the ability to elude slave-tracking dogs. In this respect, conjure was one among many tactics used to resist white dominance. At least one conjurer, GULLAH JACK, used his reputation to build support for a slave revolt. Based on archaeological evidence, the practice of conjure was widespread within black society. Some authors argue that virtually every large plantation had at least one practitioner.

Smith, Theophus. author of *Conjuring Culture: Biblical Formations of Black America* (1994). Smith argues that modern African American theology is based on the concept of conjuring God to work for the good of believers.

Snakes. figure prominently in VODU, VODOU, VOODOO, and CONJURE. In parts of Africa, snakes were the symbols or even embodiments of GODS. This was especially true among peoples of the BIGHT OF BENIN region of Africa, which contributed significantly to both Haitian Vodou and U.S. Voodoo. According to most accounts of New Orleans SAINT JOHN'S EVE CEREMONIES, MARIE LAVEAU used a snake as a means of communicating with a deity variously called Voodoo Magnian, GRAND ZOMBI, or BLANC DANI. Snakes also have an important part in African American magic. For instance, snake infestation is one of the most prominent versions of LIVE THINGS IN YOU.

"Sold as a Curio Only." *see* DISCLAIMERS.

Souls. during the nineteenth century and before, some conjurers claimed to have gained their powers because they possessed two souls. The belief in multiple souls is common in many regions of Africa including those areas where Europeans purchased most of their slaves.

Spirits. many practitioners of CONJURE and VOODOO believe in a wide range of spirits. These range from the Christian God to the lesser GODS of African VODU to the ghosts of ancestors. Spirits are frequently useful in the performance of magic, most notably through their presence in GOOPHER DUST and because of their central role in Voodoo ceremonies.

Spiritual Churches. nominally Christian churches that are widespread across the country, although they are especially associated with New Orleans. These loosely linked churches appear to have emerged from mainstream SPIRITUALISM during the early twentieth century. Spiritual churches tend to be small and are often dominated by women. Although most congregations deny links to VOODOO, HOODOO is clearly an integral part of the denomination, as evidenced by the magic rituals associated with their services, the incorporation of numerous non-Christian SPIRITS in their belief, and the fact that many of their ministers also operate SPIRITUAL SUPPLY SHOPS. In addition to the influences of Spiritualism and hoodoo, Pentecostalism helped shape the churches, to the extent that some researchers consider Spiritual churches a subset of this family of denominations. In the New Orleans area, Roman Catholic influence is also evidenced by the prominence of SAINTS, elaborate ALTARS, holy water, and other Catholic paraphernalia. *see* BLACK HAWK, UNCLE/UNKUS, *and* ANDERSON, LEAFY.

Spiritual Supplies. the name for modern HOODOO items. These are usually sold in shops called spiritual supply shops, religious supply stores, or CANDLE SHOPS. These stores carry traditional items like JOHN THE CONQUEROR roots and DEVIL'S SHOE STRING alongside items of more recent adoption, such as OILS, INCENSE, and even magical aerosol sprays. Many of the modern items have brand names that refer to traditional items. For example, one can buy JOHN THE CONQUEROR aerosol spray, which promises the same results as the root.

Spiritualism. a religion founded on a belief in communication with the dead. In 1848, Kate and Margaret Fox of Hydesville, New York, supposedly began communicating with the ghost of a murdered peddler. The Fox sisters and their followers developed the séance to facilitate communication with the SPIRITS of the deceased. During séances, females usually act as mediums for spirit communication, allowing the dead to use them to communicate with the living. By the time of the Civil War, the new faith had gained an extensive following, with numbers probably reaching into the hundreds of thousands or perhaps even millions. Most researchers point to Spiritualism as the parent faith of the modern SPIRITUAL CHURCHES. The latter have diverged widely from their origins, however, and the original links are recognizable only because of their shared belief in spirits. After the Civil War, Spiritualism declined in the United States.

String. used in many CONJURE practices, particularly healing spells. Louisianan TRAITEURS tie strings around portions of the body afflicted with injury or disease. After the strings fall off, the ailment is supposed to accompany them.

Syncretism. the process of blending elements from diverse cultures, which is evident in all New World CREOLE belief systems.

Tallant, Robert. author of the folkloric *Voodoo in New Orleans* (1946) and *The Voodoo Queen* (1956), a fictionalized biography of MARIE LAVEAU. Tallant was an author of the mid-twentieth century who showed an immense interest in HOODOO and VOODOO. Scholars have relied heavily on his books for decades, but he has recently fallen under harsh and somewhat deserved criticism for sensationalizing Voodoo and embellishing or fabricating his sources. Despite recent attacks, Tallant was sympathetic, if disapproving, in his treatment of African American supernaturalism and was certainly more reliable than his contemporary, ZORA NEALE HURSTON.

Titles. adopted by many conjurers to enhance their prestige. Typical titles used by practitioners include *doctor, madame,* and *reverend.* In some areas, most notably coastal South Carolina, practitioners have also adopted a totemic animal name as well. DOCTOR BUZZARD was by far the best example of this practice.

Tituba. a slave who figured prominently in the Salem Witch Crisis of 1692. A group of girls who claimed to be suffering the effects of diabolic witchcraft made their first accusations against Tituba, who reportedly had some knowledge of magic and divination. Oddly enough, Tituba had herself tried to free the girls from witchcraft by making a "witch cake," with the active ingredient being the girls' urine. She then fed the cake to a dog, with no perceptible benefits for the afflicted children. Tituba escaped death by confession but unfortunately went on to point out other supposed witches. Researchers have traditionally portrayed Tituba as African American, but recent research indicates that she was more likely of Native American descent. A mixed Native American and African heritage is quite possible.

Toby. a good-luck charm. The term probably derives from the KONGO term *tobe,* which also refers to a charm.

Traiteur/Traiteuse. male and female synonyms, respectively, for *rootworker* in the lower Mississippi Valley. The words translate as "treater," emphasizing the predominantly folk medical focus of these practitioners.

Treater. *see* TRAITEUR/TRAITEUSE.

Tricking. a synonym for *CONJURE,* most popular in the Upper South, particularly Virginia. Conjurers in the area have in the past been known as *trick doctors* and their spells called *tricks.* Few use the term today.

Tro. a synonym for VODU when used to refer to a specific god.

Tull, "Aunt Zippy." a well-known conjurer of the late nineteenth century. She lived near the Maryland-Virginia border on the Delmarva Peninsula.

Turning Back. after DIAGNOSIS and CURES, the final phase in removing evil CONJURE. Turning back a spell causes the one who initially cast it to suffer its effects. According to some early sources, turning back is required to bring about cures. By the twentieth century, however, turning back had become optional according to many believers and served simply as an easy way to avenge one's wrongs.

Two Head. *see* DOUBLE HEAD.

Tying. tying knots figures prominently in CONJURE, especially in the making of MOJOS. Knots are a means of empowering magical objects, probably by symbolically tying a spirit or magical force to it. Tying has long been a common feature of charm making in both WEST CENTRAL AFRICA and the BIGHT OF BENIN region.

Ubia. a term, sometimes given as *ubi, obi, obia,* or *ober,* occasionally used as a synonym for *CONJURE* in the South during the nineteenth century and before or as a name for an African-derived deity. Both Ubia and the better-known Caribbean equivalent Obeah appear to derive from one or more of the following: the Ashanti word *obaye,* the Efik *ubio,* or the Igbo *abia.* Each term refers to elements of supernaturalism. If Ashanti in origin, ubia may have been a rare Gold Coast contribution to conjure. Unfortunately, the prevalence of the word among African Americans is unknown, as the few sources that mention it were all written by whites.

Uncle/Unkus. the name for an important spirit in New Orleans's SPIRITUAL CHURCHES. Some churches honor what they call the "Kind Uncle" by placing a bucket of sand holding three American flags near the rear of the church building. The origins of the Uncle are obscure. Some claim he represents the principle of affectionate uncles in the BIBLE. Others argue that he was a Confederate soldier or is identical to St. George. One early Spiritual leader, Mother Price, simply stated that he was one of her own uncles who died in battle, a possibility supported by the use of American flags in making an Uncle Bucket. Some, most notably Eoghan Ballard, suggest that the term derives from the KONGO *nkisi,* the singular form of *MINKISI.* That a few believers refer to the spirit as Unkus makes this interpretation possible.

Van Van Oil. the most famous of HOODOO OILS. Strongly linked to New Orleans, Van Van Oil has been used for a wide variety of positive pursuits since at least the early twentieth century.

Vèvè. sacred images drawn on the earth as part of Haitian VODOU ceremonies. These appear to be of KONGO origin.

Vodou. the folk religion of Haiti, which incorporates elements of Catholicism blended with underlying African beliefs. Most scholars have stressed the religion's strong West African roots, although recent researchers have begun to argue that WEST CENTRAL African influences, most notably from the KONGO, were also profoundly important in shaping the religion. The flight of Haitian refugees to New Orleans during the late eighteenth and early nineteenth centuries influenced American VOODOO, although the degree of their impact remains debatable.

Vodu/Vodun. the name scholars assign the West African Traditional Religion of the FON and EWE peoples. Vodu has a complex spiritual hierarchy involving a supreme deity, lesser GODS (sometimes called *orishas*), ancestral SPIRITS, and a wide variety of animistic spirits that inhabit the natural world. RELIGIOUS SOCIETIES, DIVINATION, and magic are integral parts of the religion. Vodu derives from *vodu,* a term for a spirit used by some cultures of the BIGHT OF BENIN area. Vodu was extremely influential in the development of Haitian VODOU and U.S. VOODOO and HOODOO. Historically, however, CONJURE has been far less influenced by the religion.

Voodoo. an African American folk religion—often erroneously equated with Haitian Vodou—which flourished in the Mississippi River Valley from colonial times to the last decades of the nineteenth century and perhaps beyond. It included an African-derived pantheon of GODS and complex CEREMONIES. The most important influences on the faith appear to have been West African traditional religions, followed by Roman Catholicism. *see* VOODOO QUEEN.

Voodoo Queen. a title often applied to prominent VOODOO priestesses in New Orleans and during the eighteenth century to VODOU manbos in Haiti. Such TITLES are common throughout the AFRICAN DIASPORA and are typically conferred on ceremonial leaders. In the United States, MARIE LAVEAU of New Orleans became by far the best known Voodoo Queen. *see* LATOUR, MALVINA *and* DÉDÉ, SANITÉ.

Walker, Alice. a popular African American writer. A CONJURE woman features prominently her *Third Life of Grange Copeland* (1970), where she is a symbol of strong black womanhood. *see* MORRISON, TONI *and* REED, ISHMAEL.

Wanga. a term for an evil charm found in the lower Mississippi Valley. Most maintain that the word originated in WEST CENTRAL AFRICA.

Wangateur/Wangateuse. masculine and feminine terms for HOODOO and VOODOO practitioners in the lower Mississippi Valley. The words derive from their use of WANGA charms in their practice.

Ward, Martha. author of *Voodoo Queen: The Spirited Lives of Marie Laveau* (2004). Ward's work was designed to appeal to both scholarly and popular readers. *Voodoo Queen* was the first reasonably reliable biography of Laveau to appear, making it a groundbreaking work. In keeping with trends in African American literature, Ward uses Laveau's reputed powers to make her a representative of black feminine power. *see* FANDRICH, INA; LONG, CAROLYN MORROW; MORRISON, TONI; *and* WALKER, ALICE.

West Central Africa. the region of western Africa south of the BIGHT OF BIAFRA. The largest number of slaves to reach North America and much of the rest of the New World appear to have come from this area. The most prominent places of origin for slaves were the Kingdom of the KONGO and Angola.

Witchcraft. a term often used as a synonym for *CONJURE* or *HOODOO*. Many African Americans, however, believed witches to be supernatural beings rather than simply humans who had learned magic.

Woodpecker. a powerful conjurer in the folklore of Missouri blacks, as recorded by MARY ALICIA OWEN.

Yoruba. a major people group of the BIGHT OF BENIN region of West Africa. Wars between the Yoruba and FON Kingdom of Dahomey contributed many captives to the slave trade. Yoruba slaves influenced both VODOU and VOODOO, although their contributions to the faiths were less prominent than those of the EWE, FON, and KONGO. Yoruba Traditional Religion had an even smaller impact on CONJURE. In contrast, Yoruba elements have been central to Cuban SANTERÍA and Floridian NAÑIGO.

Zinzin. a term for a magical amulet in Louisiana HOODOO and VOODOO. The term arrived in the New World during the colonial era along with slaves from SENEGAMBIA. In the Bamana (also known as Bambara) language, *zinzin* has an identical meaning to the American version of the word.

Zombie. in VODOU belief, the body of a dead person, reanimated by a sorcerer or secret society for use as forced labor or to punish a transgression, or a captured disembodied soul set various tasks by its master.

Bibliography

GENERAL WORKS ON CONJURE AND HOODOO

Anderson, Jeffrey E. *Conjure in African American Society.* Baton Rouge: Louisiana State University Press, 2005.

Bacon, A. M. "Conjuring and Conjure-Doctors." *Southern Workman* 24 (1895): 193–194, 209–211.

Bass, Ruth. "The Little Man." *Scribner's Magazine* 97 (1935): 120–123.

———. "Mojo: The Strange Magic That Works in the South Today." *Scribner's Magazine* 87 (1930): 83–90.

"Believed in North Carolina Also." *The Daily Equator-Democrat,* July 10, 1889.

Bell, Michael E. "Pattern, Structure, and Logic in Afro-American Hoodoo Performance." Ph.D. diss., Indiana University, 1980.

Bendenbaugh, J. W. "Folk-Lore and Ethnology: A Contribution from South Carolina." *Southern Workman* 23 (1894): 46–47.

Bims, Hamilton. "Would You *Believe* It . . . Superstition Lives!" *Ebony,* July 1976, 118–122.

Boyle, Virginia Frazier. *Devil Tales.* With illustrations by A. B. Frost. 1900; reprint, Freeport: Books for Libraries Press, 1972.

Brown, David H. "Conjure/Doctors: An Exploration of a Black Discourse in America, Antebellum to 1940." *Folklore Forum* 23 (1990): 3–45.

Chicago Defender, The. July 5, 1924, 2:7.

Chicago Defender, The. July 2, 1927, 1:11.

Chireau, Yvonne. *Black Magic: Religion and the African American Conjuring Tradition.* Berkeley: University of California Press, 2003.

———. "Conjure and Christianity in the Nineteenth Century: Religious Elements in African American Magic." *Religion and American Culture: A Journal of Interpretation* 7 (1997): 225–246.

Clayton, Edward T. "The Truth about Voodoo." *Ebony,* April 1951, 54–61.

Dana, Marvin. "Voodoo: Its Effect on the Negro Race." *The Metropolitan Magazine* 28 (1908): 529–538.

Davis, Daniel Webster. "Conjuration." *Southern Workman* 27 (1898): 251–252.

Davis, Rod. *American Voudou: Journey into a Hidden World.* Denton: University of North Texas Press, 1999.

Elam, William Cecil. "A Case of Hoodoo." *Lippincott's Monthly Magazine* 54 (1894): 138–141.

Granberry, Edwin. "Black Jupiter: A Voodoo King in Florida's Jungle—Black Magic in the Turpentine Forests." With illustrations by Douglas Cleary. *Travel* 58 (1932): 32–35, 54.

Handy, M. P. "Witchcraft Among the Negroes." *Appleton's Journal: A Magazine of General Literature* 8 (1872): 666–667.

Haskell, Joseph A. "Sacrificial Offerings among North Carolina Negroes." *Journal of American Folk-Lore* 4 (1891): 267–269.

Haskins, James. *Voodoo and Hoodoo: The Craft as Revealed by Traditional Practitioners.* New ed. Lanham, New York, and London: Scarborough House, 1990.

Herron, Leonora. "Conjuring and Conjure Doctors." *Southern Workman* 24 (1891): 117–118.

Hurston, Zora Neale. *Folklore, Memoirs, and other Writings,* selected and annotated Cheryl A. Wall. The Library of America. New York: Literary Classics of the United States, Inc., 1995.

———. "Hoodoo in America." *Journal of American Folklore* 44 (1931): 317–417.

Hyatt, Harry Middleton. *Hoodoo-Conjuration-Witchcraft-Rootwork.* 5 vols. Memoirs of the Alma Egan Hyatt Foundation. Hannibal: Western, 1970–1978.

Kulii, Elon Ali. "A Look at Hoodoo in Three Urban Areas of Indiana: Folklore and Change." Ph.D. diss., Indiana University, 1982.

———. "Root Doctors and Psychics in the Region." In *Indiana Folklore: A Reader,* ed. Linda Degh, 120–129. Bloomington: Indiana University Press, 1980.

Lea, M. S. "Two-head Doctors." *The American Mercury* 12 (1927): 236–240.

Long, Carolyn Morrow. "John the Conqueror: From Root-Charm to Commercial Product." *Pharmacy in History* 39 (1997): 47–53.

———. *Spiritual Merchants: Religion, Magic, and Commerce.* Knoxville: University of Tennessee Press, 2001.

McMillan, Timothy J. "Black Magic: Witchcraft, Race, and Resistance in Colonial New England." *Journal of Black Studies* 25 (1994): 99–117.

Owen, Mary Alicia. "Among the Voodoos." In *The International Folk-lore Congress 1891: Papers and Transactions,* 230–248. London: David Nutt, 1892.

———. *Old Rabbit, the Voodoo and Other Sorcerers.* With an Introduction by Charles Godfrey Leland. With Illustrations by Juliette A. Owen and Louis Wain. London: T. Fisher Unwin, 1893; reprint, Whitefish, MT: Kessinger Publishing, 2003.

Park, S. M. "Voodooism in Tennessee." *The Atlantic Monthly* 64 (1889): 376–380.

Pendleton, Louis. "Notes on Negro Folk-Lore and Witchcraft in the South." *Journal of American Folk-Lore* 3 (1890): 201–207.

Pinckney, Roger. *Blue Roots: African-American Folk Magic of the Gullah People.* St. Paul: Llewellyn, 2000.

Puckett, Newbell Niles. *Folk Beliefs of the Southern Negro*. Patterson Smith Reprint Series in Criminology, Law Enforcement, and Social Problems, no. 22. Chapel Hill: University of North Carolina Press, 1926; reprint, Montclair: Patterson Smith, 1968.

R., L., G., and A. "Conjure Doctors in the South." *The Southern Workman* 7 (1878): 30–31.

S. In "Letters from Hampton Graduates." *Southern Workman* 7 (1878): 28.

Skeleton Key, The. Produced by Clayton Townsend. Directed by Iain Softley. 104 min. Brick Dust Productions LLC. DVD.

Snow, Loudell F. "Mail Order Magic: The Commercial Exploitation of Folk Belief." *Journal of the American Folklore Institute* 16 (1979): 44–73.

"Some Conjure Doctors We Have Heard Of." *Southern Workman* 26 (1897): 37–38.

Steiner, Roland. "Braziel Robinson Possessed of Two Spirits." *Journal of American Folk-Lore* 14 (1901): 226–228.

———. "Observations on the Practice of Conjuring in Georgia." *Journal of American Folk-Lore* 14 (1901): 173–180.

Tyler, Varro E. "The Elusive History of High John the Conqueror Root." *Pharmacy in History* 33 (1991): 164–166.

W. and C. "About the Conjuring Doctors." *The Southern Workman* 7 (1878): 38–39.

Whitten, Norman E. "Contemporary Patterns of Malign Occultism among Negroes in North Carolina." *Journal of American Folklore* 75 (1962): 310–325.

Wicker, Christine. *Not in Kansas Anymore: A Curious Tale of How Magic is Transforming America.* New York: HarperCollins, 2005.

GENERAL WORKS ON VOODOO AND NAÑIGO

Anderson, Jeffrey. "Voodoo." In *Encyclopedia of African American Religious Culture*. Santa Barbara, CA: ABC–CLIO, 2009.

———. "Voodoo in Black and White." In a collection of essays. Gainesville: University Press of Florida, forthcoming 2008.

Antippas, A. P. *A Brief History of Voodoo: Slavery & the Survival of the African Gods.* New Orleans: Marie Laveau's House of Voodoo, 1988.

Bodin, Ron. *Voodoo: Past and Present.* Lafayette: University of Southwestern Louisiana, 1990.

"Husbands and Lovers Are Voodoo Sage's Specialty." *New Orleans Times-Democrat,* October 29, 1902, 10.

Kennedy, Stetson. "Ñañigo in Florida." *Southern Folklore Quarterly* 4 (1940): 153–156.

Mulira, Jessie Gaston. "The Case of Voodoo in New Orleans." In *Africanisms in American Culture,* ed. Joseph E. Holloway, 34–68. Blacks in the Diaspora Series, ed. Darlene Clark Hine, John McCluskey, Jr., and David Barry Gaspar. Bloomington and Indianapolis: Indiana University Press, 1990.

Saxon, Lyle. "Voodoo." *The New Republic,* March 23, 1927, 135–139.

Tallant, Robert. *Voodoo in New Orleans.* New York: Macmillan, 1946; reprint, Gretna: Pelican, 1998.

Touchstone, Blake. "Voodoo in New Orleans." *Louisiana History* 13 (1972): 371–386.

"The Voudou-'Fetish'." *Daily Picayune,* June 25, 1873.

Williams, Marie B. "A Night with the Voudous." *Appleton's Journal: A Magazine of General Literature* 13 (1875): 404–405.

GENERAL WORKS ON VODOU, SANTERÍA, AND OTHER AFRO-LATIN FAITHS

Ackermann, Hans-W. and Jeanine Gauthier. "The Ways and Nature of the Zombi." *Journal of American Folklore* 104 (1991): 466–494.

Bellegarde-Smith, Patrick, ed. *Fragments of Bone: Neo-African Religions in a New World.* Urbana: University of Illinois Press, 2005.

Brandon, George. *Santeria from Africa to the New World: The Dead Sell Memories.* Bloomington and Indianapolis: Indiana University Press, 1993.

Cosentino, Donald L., ed. *Sacred Arts of Haitian Vodou.* Los Angeles: University of California Fowler Museum of Cultural History, 1995.

Daniel, Yvonne. *Dancing Wisdom: Embodied Knowledge in Haitian Vodou, Cuban Yoruba, and Bahian Candomblé.* Urbana: University of Illinois Press, 2005.

Davis, Wade. *Passages of Darkness: The Ethnobiology of the Haitian Zombie.* Chapel Hill: University of North Carolina Press, 1988.

———. *The Serpent and the Rainbow: A Harvard Scientist's Astonishing Journey into the Secret Societies of Haitian Voodoo, Zombis, and Magic.* New York: Simon and Schuster, 1986.

Deren, Maya. *Divine Horsemen: The Living Gods of Haiti.* London and New York: Thames and Hudson, 1953.

Desmangles, Leslie G. *Faces of the Gods: Vodou and Roman Catholicism in Haiti.* Chapel Hill: University of North Carolina Press, 1992.

Geggus, David. "Haitian Voodoo in the Eighteenth Century: Language, Culture, Resistance." *Jahrbuch für Geschichte von Staat, Wirtschaft und Gesellschaft Lateinamerikas* 28 (1991): 21–51.

Gorov, Lynda. "The War on Voodoo." *Mother Jones,* June 1990, 12.

Grimm, Fred. "Ritual Sacrifices Turn Miami River Red." *The Miami Herald,* May 30, 1981, 1B-2B.

Herskovits, Melville J. *Life in a Haitian Valley.* New York: Alfred A. Knopf, 1937.

———. "African Gods and Catholic Saints in New World Negro Belief." *American Anthropologist* 39 (1937):635–643.

Heusch, Luc de. "Kongo in Haiti." *Man,* New Series, 24 (1989): 290–303.

Humes, Edward. *Buried Secrets: A True Story of Murder, Black Magic, and Drug-Running on the U.S Border.* New York: Penguin, 1991.

Hurston, Zora Neale. *Tell My Horse: Voodoo and Life in Haiti and Jamaica.* With a Foreword by Ishmael Reed and Afterword by Henry Louis Gates, Jr. New York: Harper and Row, 1990.

Loederer, Richard A. *Voodoo Fire in Haiti.* Translated by New York: Doubleday, 1936.

Métraux, Alfred. *Voodoo in Haiti.* Translated by Hugo Charteris and with an Introduction by Sidney W. Mintz. New York: Schocken, 1972.

Moreau de Saint-Méry, Médéric Louis Élie. *Description topographique, physique, civile, politique et historique de la partie française de l'île de Saint-Domingue.* 2 vols. Philadelphia, 1797.

Murphy, Joseph M. *Santería: African Spirits in America.* With new Preface. Boston: Beacon Press, 1993.

———. *Working the Spirit: Ceremonies of the African Diaspora.* Boston: Beacon Press, 1994.

Newell, William W. "Myths of Voodoo Worship and Child Sacrifice in Hayti." *The Journal of American Folk-Lore* 1 (1888): 16–30.

———. "Reports of Voodoo Worship in Hayti and Louisiana." *Journal of American Folk-Lore* 2 (1889): 41–47.

Olmos, Margarite Fernández and Lizbeth Paravisini-Gebert. *Creole Religions of the Caribbean: An Introduction from Vodou and Santería to Obeah and Espiritismo.* New York University Press, 2003.

———, eds. *Sacred Possessions: Vodou, Santería, Obeah, and the Caribbean.* Piscataway, NJ: Rutgers University Press, 1997.

Pluchon, Pierre. *Vaudou, Sorciers, Empoissoneurs: De Saint-Domingue à Haïti.* Paris: Karthala, 1987.

Renda, Mary A. *Taking Haiti: Military Occupation and the Culture of U.S. Imperialism, 1915–1940.* Chapel Hill: University of North Carolina Press, 2001.

Rigaud, Milo. *Secrets of Voodoo.* Translated by Robert B. Cross. New York: Arco, 1969; reprint, San Francisco: City Lights, 1985.

Saint-Louis. *Le Vodou Haïtien: Reflet d'une Société Bloquée.* Paris: L'Harmattan, 2000.

Seabrook, William B. *The Magic Island.* New York: Harcourt, Brace, 1929.

Simpson, George Easton. *Black Religions in the New World.* New York: Columbia University Press, 1978.

St. John, Spencer. *Hayti or the Black Republic.* London: Smith, Elder, and Company, 1884.

Tivnan, E. "The Voodoo That New Yorkers Do." *New York Times Magazine* 182 (December 2, 1979): 182–192.

Turlington, Shannon R. *The Complete Idiot's Guide to Voodoo.* Indianapolis: Alpha, 2002.

Wetli, Charles V. and Rafael Martinez. "Brujeria: Manifestations of Palo Mayombe in South Florida." *Journal of the Florida Medical Association* 70 (1983): 629–634.

BIOGRAPHICAL WORKS FOCUSED ON INDIVIDUALS INVOLVED IN CONJURE, HOODOO, AND VOODOO

Bibbs, Susheel. *Heritage of Power: Marie Laveau—Mary Ellen Pleasant.* Revised edition. San Francisco, CA: MEP, 1998.

Brown, Karen McCarthy. *Mama Lola: A Vodou Priestess in Brooklyn.* Updated and expanded. Berkeley: University of California Press, 2001.

Burns, Khephra. "The Queen of Voodoo." *Essence* 23 (May 1992): 80.

Colby, Vineta. "Robert Tallant." *Wilson Library Bulletin* 27 (April 1953): 594.

"Death of Marie Laveau." *The Daily Picayune.* May 17, 1881, 8.

Fandrich, Ina Johanna. *The Mysterious Voodoo Queen, Marie Laveaux: A Study of Powerful Female Leadership in Nineteenth-Century New Orleans.* Studies in African American History and Culture. New York: Routledge, 2005.

Gandolfo, Charles M. *Marie Laveau of New Orleans, the Great Voodoo Queen.* New Orleans: New Orleans Historical Voodoo Museum, 1992.

Hearn, Lafcadio. "The Last of the Voudoos." *Harper's Weekly Magazine* 29 (1885): 726–727.

Hurston, Zora Neale. "Uncle Monday." In *Folklore, Memoirs, and other Writings,* selected and annotated Cheryl A. Wall. The Library of America. New York: Literary Classics of the United States, Inc., 1995.

Johnson, F. Roy. *The Fabled Doctor Jim Jordan: A Story of Conjure.* Murfreesboro: Johnson, 1963.

Long, Carolyn Morrow. *A New Orleans Voudou Priestess: The Legend and Reality of Marie Laveau.* Gainesville: University Press of Florida, 2006.

McTeer, James Edwin. *High Sheriff of the Low Country.* With an Introduction by William L. Rhodes, Jr. Columbia: JEM Company, 1970.

———. *Fifty Years as a Low Country Witch Doctor.* Beaufort: Beaufort Book Company, 1976.

Peterson, Tracey. "The Witch of Franklin." *Southern Folklore Quarterly* 33 (1969): 297–312.

Rhodes, Jewell Parker. "Marie Laveau, Voodoo Queen." *Ms.* 28 (1983): 28–31.

Ward, Martha. *Voodoo Queen: The Spirited Lives of Marie Laveau.* Jackson: University Press of Mississippi, 2004.

Winslow, David J. "Bishop E. E. Everett and Some Aspects of Occultism and Folk Religion in Negro Philadelphia." *Keystone Folklore Quarterly* 14 (1969): 59–80.

Wolf, John Quincy. "Aunt Caroline Dye: The Gypsy in the 'Saint Louis Blues'." *Southern Folklore Quarterly* 33 (1969): 339–346.

ARCHAEOLOGICAL WORKS ADDRESSING CONJURE AND HOODOO

Brown, Kenneth L. and Doreen C. Cooper. "Structural Continuity in an African-American Slave and Tenant Community." *Historical Archaeology* 24 (1990): 7–19.

Fennell, Christopher C. "Conjuring Boundaries: Inferring Past Identities from Religious Artifacts." *International Journal of Historical Archaeology* 4 (2000): 281–313.

Ferguson, Leland G. "'The Cross is a Magic Sign': Marks on Eighteenth-Century Bowls from South Carolina." In *"I, Too, Am America": Archaeological Studies of African-American Life,* ed. Theresa A Singleton, 116–131. Charlottesville and London: University Press of Virginia, 1999.

———. "Looking for the 'Afro' in Colono-Indian Pottery." In *Archaeological Perspectives on Ethnicity in America,* ed. R. L. Schulyer, 14–28. Amityville: Baywood, 1980.

Galke, Laura J. "Did the Gods of Africa Die? A Re-examination of a Carroll House Crystal Assemblage." *North American Archaeologist* 21 (2000): 19–33.

Klingelhofer, Eric. "Aspects of Early Afro-American Material Culture: Artifacts from the Slave Quarters at Garrison Plantation, Maryland." *Historical Archaeology* 21 (1987): 112–119.

Leone, Mark P. and Gladys-Marie Fry. "Conjuring in the Big House Kitchen: An Interpretation of African American Belief Systems Based on the Uses of Archaeology and Folklore Sources." *Journal of American Folklore* 112 (1999): 372–403.

Orser, Charles E., Jr. "The Archaeology of African-American Slave Religion in the Antebellum South." *Cambridge Archeological Review Journal* 4 (1994): 33–45.

Patten, M. Drake. "Mankala and Minkisi: Possible Evidence of African-American Folk Beliefs and Practices." *African-American Archaeology* 6 (1992): 5–7.

Stine, Linda France, Melanie A. Cabak, and Mark D. Groover. "Blue Beads As African-American Cultural Symbols." *Historical Archaeology* 30 (1996): 49–75.

Wilkie, Laurie A. "Magic and Empowerment on the Plantation: An Archaeological Consideration of African-American World View." *Southeastern Archaeology* 14 (1995): 136–148.

MEDICAL AND PSYCHOLOGICAL WORKS RELEVANT TO CONJURE, HOODOO, AND VOODOO

Baer, Hans. "Toward a Systematic Typology of Black Folk Healers." *Phylon* 43 (1982): 327–343.

Brown, Jeremy. "Vital Signs: A Deadly Specter." *Discover Magazine,* September 1995, 48–51.

Cannon, Walter B. "Voodoo Death." *American Anthropologist* 44 (1942); reprinted in *Psychosomatic Medicine* 19 (1957): 182–190.

Colligan, Douglas. "Extreme Psychic Trauma is the Power Behind Voodoo Death." *Science Digest,* August 1976, 44–48.

Conklin, Edmund S. "Superstitious Belief and Practice among College Students." *The American Journal of Psychology* 30 (1919): 83–102.

Crellin, John K. and Jane Philpott. *A Reference Guide to Medicinal Plants: Herbal Medicine Past and Present.* Durham and London: Duke University Press, 1990.

Eastwell, Harry D. "Voodoo Death and the Mechanism for Dispatch of the Dying in East Arnhem, Australia." *American Anthropologist* 84 (1982): 5–18.

Fett, Sharla. *Working Cures: Healing, Health, and Power on Southern Slave Plantations.* Chapel Hill: University of North Carolina Press, 2002.

Flannery, Michael A. "Good for Man or Beast: American Patent Medicines from 1865 to 1938." *Alabama Heritage,* Winter 2001, 8–17.

Fontenot, Wonda L. *Secret Doctors: Ethnomedicine of African Americans.* Westport and London: Bergin & Garvey, 1994.

Foster, Steven and James A. Duke. *A Field Guide to Medicinal Plants and Herbs of Eastern and Central North America.* 2nd ed. Boston: Houghton Mifflin, 2000.

Grieve, M. *A Modern Herbal: The Medical, Culinary, Cosmetic and Economic Properties, Cultivation, and Folk-Lore of Herbs, Grasses, Fungi, Shrubs & Trees with All Their Modern Scientific Uses.* With an Introduction by C. F. Leyel and an Index of Scientific Names by Manya Marshall. New York: Dover, 1971.

Hall, Arthur L. and Bourne, Peter G. "Indigenous Therapists in a Southern Black Urban Community." *Archives of General Psychiatry* 28 (1973): 137–142.

Hamel, Paul B. and Mary U. Chiltoskey. *Cherokee Plants and Their Uses—A 400 Year History.* Sylva: Herald, 1975.

Hand, Wayland. "Plugging, Nailing, Wedging, and Kindred Folk Medical Practices." In *Folklore & Society: Essays in Honor of Benjamin A. Botkin,* ed. Bruce Jackson, 63–75. Hatboro: Folklore Associates, 1966.

Harris, Marvin. "Death by Voodoo." *Psychology Today,* August 1984, 16–17.

Howard, James H. in collaboration with Willie Lena. *Oklahoma Seminoles: Medicines, Magic, and Religion.* Civilization of the American Indian Series, vol. 5. Norman: University of Oklahoma Press, 1984.

Hutchens, Alma R. *Indian Herbalogy of North America.* Boston: Shambhala, 1991.

Jordan, Wilbert C. "Voodoo Medicine." In *Textbook of Black-Related Diseases,* ed. Richard Allen Williams. New York: McGraw-Hill Book Company, 1975.

Kimball, Chase Patterson. "A Case of Pseudocyesis Caused by 'Roots'." *American Journal of Obstetric Gynecology* 107 (1979): 801–803.

Maduro, Renaldo J. "Hoodoo Possession in San Francisco: Notes on Therapeutic Aspects of Regression." *Ethos* 3 (1975): 425–447.

Michaelson, Mike. "Can a 'Root Doctor' Actually Put a Hex On?" *Today's Health* March 1972: 38–41, 58, 60.

Millspaugh, Charles F. *American Medicinal Plants: An Illustrated and Descriptive Guide to Plants Indigenous to and Naturalized in the United States Which Are Used in Medicine.* Philadelphia: John C. Yorston and Company, 1892; republication, New York: Dover, 1974.

Mitchell, Faith. *Hoodoo Medicine: Gullah Herbal Remedies.* Columbia: Summerhouse Press, 1999.

Moerman, Daniel E. "Anthropology of Symbolic Healing." *Current Anthropology* 20 (1979): 59–80.

Mooney, James. "Cherokee Theory and Practice of Medicine." *Journal of American Folk-Lore* 3 (1890): 44–50.

———. *Myths of the Cherokee and Sacred Formulas of the Cherokees.* Nashville: Charles and Randy Elder, 1982.

Moss, Kay K. *Southern Folk Medicine, 1750–1820.* Columbia: University of South Carolina Press, 1999.

Neal, James C. "Legalized Crime in Florida." In *Proceedings of the Florida Medical Association: Session of 1891,* 42–50. Jacksonville: Times-Union, 1891.

"The Negro Cesar's Cure for Poison." *The Massachusetts Magazine* 4 (1792): 103–104.

Nickell, J. M. *J. M. Nickell's Botanical Ready Reference.* With new material. Beaumont, CA: Trinity Center Press, 1976.

Saphir, J. Robin, Arnold Gold, James Giambrone, and James F. Holland. "Voodoo Poisoning in Buffalo, NY." *The Journal of the American Medical Association* 202 (1967): 437–438.

Savitt, Todd L. *Medicine and Slavery: The Diseases and Health Care of Blacks in Antebellum Virginia.* Blacks in the New World Series, ed. August Meier. Urbana, Chicago, and London: University of Illinois Press, 1978.

Smith, Peter. *The Indian Doctor's Dispensatory.* Cincinnati: Browne and Looker, 1813.

Snow, Loudell F. "Sorcerers, Saints, and Charlatans: Black Folk Healers in Urban America." *Culture, Medicine and Psychiatry* 2 (1978): 69–106.

Straight, William M. "Throw Downs, Fixin, Rooting and Hexing." *The Journal of the Florida Medical Association, Inc.* 70 (1983): 635–641.

Tinling, David C. "Voodoo, Root Work, and Medicine." *Psychosomatic Medicine* 5 (1967): 483–490.

Vogel, Virgil J. *American Indian Medicine.* Civilization of the American Indian Series, vol. 95. Norman: University of Oklahoma Press, 1970.

"Voodoo Kills by Despair." *Science News Letter* 67 (1955): 294.

Watson, Wilburn H., ed. *Black Folk Medicine: The Therapeutic Significance of Faith and Trust.* New Brunswick and London: Transaction, 1984.

Webb, Julie Yvonne. "Superstitious Influence—Voodoo in Particular—Affecting Health Practices in a Selected Population in Southern Louisiana." New Orleans, Louisiana: By the author, 1971.

Wintrob, Ronald M. "The Influence of Others: Witchcraft and Rootwork As Explanations of Behavior Disturbances." *Journal of Nervous and Mental Disease* 156 (1973): 318–326.

Young, James Harvey. *American Self-Dosage Medicines: An Historical Perspective.* Lawrence: Coronado Press, 1974.

———. *The Toadstool Millionaires: A Social History of Patent Medicines in America before Federal Regulation.* Princeton: Princeton University Press, 1961.

AFRICAN AMERICAN MAGIC AND CRIME/CHARLATANRY

Berendt, John. *Midnight in the Garden of Good and Evil: A Savannah Story.* New York: Random House, 1994.

Catterall, Helen Tunnicliff, ed. *Judicial Cases Concerning American Slavery and the Negro.* 5 vols. New York: Negro Universities Press, 1926; reprint, 1968.

"Magazine: Jackson Resorts to Voodoo." *MSNBC* Website. 2003. http://www.msnbc.com/news/880422.asp (March 11, 2003).

McCall, George J. "Symbiosis: The Case of Hoodoo and the Numbers Racket." *Social Problems* 10 (1963): 361–371.

"Md. Woman Facing Murder Charges Again." *The Washington Post,* January 5, 2002, B1.

Porteous, Laura L. "The Gri-gri Case." *Louisiana Historical Quarterly* 17 (1934): 48–63.

"'Root Doctor' Held in Murder of His Former Wife." *Jet,* June 1, 1987, 29.

"Special Judge Hears Case: Two Blacks Face Murder Charges in Voodoo Scheme." *Jet,* July 17, 1989, 52–53.

White, Jaclyn Weldon. *Whisper to the Black Candle: Voodoo, Murder, and the Case of Anjette Lyles.* Macon, GA: Mercer University Press, 1999.

LITERARY, ARTISTIC, AND MUSICAL WORKS WITH STRONG ELEMENTS OF CONJURE AND HOODOO

Baker, Houston A., Jr. *Workings of the Spirit: The Poetics of Afro-American Women's Writing.* Chicago and London: University of Chicago Press, 1991.

Blair, Jayson. "X-ray Vision Is Needed to Find Black Superheroes." *The New York Times,* May 5, 2002, 4.16.

Cable, George Washington. "Creole Slave Songs." With illustrations by E. W. Kemble. *The Century Magazine* 31 (1886): 807–828.

———. "The Dance in Place Congo." With illustrations by E. W. Kemble. *The Century Magazine* 31 (1886): 517–532.

———. *The Grandissimes: A Story of Creole Life.* New York: Charles Scribner's Sons, 1891.

Chesnutt, Charles W. *The Conjure Woman.* With an Introduction by Robert M. Farnsworth. Ann Arbor: University of Michigan Press, 1969.

Clar, Mimi. "Folk Belief and Custom in the Blues." *Western Folklore* 19 (1960): 173–189.

Hurston, Zora Neale. *Moses, Man of the Mountain.* Philadelphia: J. B. Lippincott, 1939.

Jaskoski, Helen. "Power Unequal to Man: The Significance of Conjure in Works by Five Afro-American Authors." *Southern Folklore Quarterly* 38 (1974): 91–108.

Lindroth, James. "Images of Subversion: Ishmael Reed and the Hoodoo Trickster." *African American Review* 30 (1996): 185–196.

Morrison, Toni. *Sula.* New York: Knopf, 1974.

Naylor, Gloria. *Mama Day.* New York: Ticknor and Fields, 1988.

Page, Thomas Nelson. *Red Rock: A Chronicle of Reconstruction.* Charles Scribner's Sons, 1898.

Peterkin, Julia. *Scarlet Sister Mary: A Novel.* With a Foreword by A. J. Verdelle. Athens: University of Georgia Press, 1998.

Pitkin, Helen. *An Angel by Brevet: A Story of Modern New Orleans.* Philadelphia and London: J. B. Lippincott Company, 1904.

Pryse, Marjorie and Hortense J. Spillers, ed. *Conjuring: Black Women, Fiction, and Literary Tradition.* Bloomington: Indiana University Press, 1985.

Reed, Ishmael. *Conjure: Selected Poems, 1963–1970.* Amherst: University of Massachusetts Press, 1972.

———. *Mumbo Jumbo.* Garden City: Doubleday, 1972.

Rhodes, Jewell Parker. *Voodoo Dreams: A Novel of Marie Laveau.* New York: Picador USA, 1993.

———. *Voodoo Season: A Marie Laveau Mystery.* New York: Atria, 2005.

Sandburg, Carl. *The American Songbag.* New York: Harcourt, Brace, and Company, 1927.

Schroeder, Patricia R. "Rootwork: Arthur Flowers, Zora Neale Hurston, and the 'Literary Hoodoo' Tradition." *African American Review* 36 (2002): 263–272.

Tallant, Robert. *The Voodoo Queen.* New York: Putnam, 1956; reprint, Gretna: Pelican, 2000.

Tsuzuki, Kyoichi. *Sam Doyle.* Books Nippan, 1990.

Tucker, Lindsey. "Recovering the Conjure Woman: Texts and Contexts in Gloria Naylor's *Mama Day.*" *African American Review* 28 (1994): 173–188

Walker, Alice. *The Third Life of Grange Copeland.* New York: Harcourt, Brace, Jovanovich, 1970.

Wilson, Judith. "Down to the Crossroads: The Art of Alison Saar." *Callaloo* 14 (1991): 107–123.

Yates, Irene. "Conjures and Cures in the Novels of Julia Peterkin." *Southern Folklore Quarterly* 10 (1946): 137–149.

Zamir, Shamoon. "An Interview with Ishmael Reed." *Callaloo* 17 (1994): 1131–1157.

WORKS PRIMARILY ADDRESSING OTHER TOPICS BUT WITH SIGNIFICANT MATERIAL ON CONJURE, HOODOO, AND VOODOO

Asbury, Herbert. *The French Quarter: An Informal History of the New Orleans Underworld.* New York: Alfred A. Knopf, Inc., 1936.

Bailey, Cornelia Walker, with Christena Bledsoe. *God, Dr. Buzzard, and the Bolito Man: A Saltwater Geechee Talks about Life on Sapelo Island, Georgia.* New York: Random House, 2001.

Bennett, John. *The Doctor to the Dead: Grotesque Legends and Folk Tales of Old Charleston.* With an Introduction by Thomas Johnson. Columbia: University of South Carolina Press, 1995.

Buel, James William. *Sunlight and Shadow of America's Great Cities.* Philadelphia: West Philadelphia, 1889.

Cappick, Marie. *The Key West Story, 1818–1950.* Serialized in *The Coral Tribune,* May 2, 9, 16, 23; June 6, 1958.

Carmer, Carl. *Stars Fell on Alabama.* With an Introduction by J. Wayne Flynt. Tuscaloosa, AL and London: University of Alabama, 1985.

Castellanos, Henry C. *New Orleans As It Was: Episodes of Louisiana Life.* New Orleans: L. Graham & Son, Ltd., 1895.

Coleman, William H., ed. *Historical Sketch Book and Guide to New Orleans and Environs.* New York: Will H. Coleman, 1885.

Combs, Josiah Henry. "Sympathetic Magic in the Kentucky Mountains: Some Curious Folk-survivals." *Journal of American Folk-Lore* 27 (1914): 328–330.

Cross, Tom Peete. "Witchcraft in North Carolina." *Studies in Philology* 16 (1919): 217–287.

Domenech, Emmanuel Henri Dieudonné. *Missionary Adventures in Texas and Mexico: A Personal Narrative of Six Years' Sojourn in Those Regions.* London: Longman, Brown, Green, Longmans, and Roberts, 1858.

Dorson, Richard M., ed. *American Negro Folklore.* Greenwich: Fawcett, 1967.

———. *Negro Folktales in Michigan.* Cambridge: Harvard University Press, 1956.

Du Pratz, Le Page. *The History of Louisiana or of the Western Parts of Virginia and Carolina.* Two vols. Translation. London: Becket and De Hondt, 1763.

Fields, Mamie Garvin with Karen Fields. *Lemon Swamp and Other Places: A Carolina Memoir.* New York: The Free Press, 1983.

Fry, Gladys-Marie. *Night Riders in Black Folk History.* Knoxville: University of Tennessee Press, 1975.

Genovese, Eugene. *Roll, Jordan, Roll: The World the Slaves Made.* New York: Random House, 1972.

Georgia Writers' Project, Savannah Unit. *Drums and Shadows: Survival Studies among the Coastal Negroes.* With an Introduction by Charles Joyner and photographs by Muriel and Malcolm Bell, Jr. Athens and London: University of Georgia Press, 1986.

Handy, Sara M. "Negro Superstitions." *Lippincott's Monthly Magazine* 48 (1891): 735–739.

Harris, Joel Chandler. *Uncle Remus: His Songs and His Sayings.* New and revised ed. With illustrations by Arthur Burdette Frost. New York: Grosset and Dunlap, 1921.

———. *The Complete Tales of Uncle Remus.* Compiled by Richard Chase. With illustrations by Arthur Burdette Frost, Frederick Stuart Church, J. M. Condé, Edward Windsor Kemble, and William Holbrook Beard. Boston: Houghton Mifflin, 1955.

Hearn, Lafcadio. "New Orleans Superstitions." *Harper's Weekly Magazine* 30 (1885): 843.

Izard, George. "Diary of a Journey by George Izard, 1815–1816." *The South Carolina Historical Magazine* 53 (1952): 67–76, 155–160, 223–229.

Johnson, F. Roy. *Witches and Demons in History and Folklore.* Murfreesboro: Johnson, 1969.

Jones, Charles Colcock Jr. *Gullah Folktales from the Georgia Coast.* With a Foreword by Susan Miller Williams. Athens and London: University of Georgia Press, 2000.

Kennedy, Stetson. *Palmetto Country.* 1942; Tallahassee: Florida A & M University Press, 1989.

Livermore, Mary A. *The Story of My Life, or the Sunshine and Shadow of Seventy Years.* Hartford: A. D. Worthington and Company, 1897.

McGown, Pierre. *The Gullah Mailman.* Illustrated by Nancy Ricker Rhett. Raleigh: Pentland Press, Inc., 2000.

Miller, Elaine Hobson. *Myths, Mysteries, and Legends of Alabama.* Birmingham: Seacoast, 1995.

Noll, Joyce Elaine. *Company of Prophets: African American Psychics, Healers, and Visionaries.* St. Paul, MN: Llewellyn, 1991.

Norris, Thaddeus. "Negro Superstitions." *Lippincott's Monthly Magazine* 6 (1870): 90–95.

Percy, William Alexander. *Lanterns on the Levee: Recollections of a Planter's Son.* With an Introduction by Walker Percy. Baton Rouge: Louisiana State University Press, 1941.

Perry, Richard S. *Vas You Ever in Zinzinnati?: A Personal Portrait of Cincinnati.* Garden City: Doubleday, 1966.

Randolph, Beverly Paschal. *Seership! The Magnetic Mirror.* Toledo, OH: K. C. Randolph, 1896.

Saxon, Lyle. *Fabulous New Orleans.* New York and London: Century Company, 1928.

Saxon, Lyle, Robert Tallant, and Edward Dreyer. *Gumbo Ya-Ya: A Collection of Louisiana Folk Tales.* New York: Bonanza, 1945.

Shepard, Eli. "Superstitions of the Negro." *Cosmopolitan Magazine* 5 (1888): 47–50.

Smiley, Portia. "Folk-lore from Virginia, South Carolina, Georgia, Alabama, and Florida." *Journal of American Folk-Lore* 32 (1919): 357–383.

Steiner, Roland. "Superstitions and Beliefs from Central Georgia." *Journal of American Folk-Lore* 12 (1899): 261–271.

Warner, Charles Dudley. *Studies in the South and West, with Comments on Canada.* New York: Harper & Brothers, 1889.

RELEVANT WORKS ON AFRICAN AMERICAN HISTORY

Andrews, William L. and Henry Louis Gates, Jr., eds. *Slave Narratives.* Library of America Series, no.114. New York: Literary Classics of the United States, Inc., 2000.

Baker, T. Lindsay and Julie P. Baker, eds. *The WPA Oklahoma Slave Narratives.* Norman and London: University of Oklahoma Press, 1996.

Bibb, Henry. *Narrative of the Life and Adventures of Henry Bibb, an American Slave.* 3rd ed. With an Introduction by Lucius C. Matlack. New York: Privately printed, 1850.

Blassingame, John. *The Slave Community: Plantation Life in the Antebellum South.* 2nd ed. New York and Oxford: Oxford University Press, 1979.

Botkin, B. A., ed. *Lay My Burden Down: A Folk History of Slavery.* Athens and London: University of Georgia Press, 1945.

Branch, Taylor. *Parting the Waters: America in the King Years, 1954–1963.* New York: Simon and Schuster, 1988.

Brown, William Wells. *My Southern Home: Or, the South and Its People.* A. G. Brown and Company, 1880; reprint, Upper Saddle River, New Jersey: The Gregg Press, 1968.

———. *Narrative of the Life of William Wells Brown, an American Slave.* London: Charles Gilpin, 1850.

Bruce, Philip A. *The Plantation Negro as a Freedman: Observations on His Character, Condition, and Prospects in Virginia.* New York and London: G. P. Putnam's Sons, 1889.

Carmichael, Stokely and Charles V. Hamilton. *Black Power: The Politics of Liberation America.* New York: Random House, 1967.

Chafe, William Henry. *Civilities and Civil Rights: Greensboro, North Carolina and the Black Struggle for Freedom.* New York: Oxford University Press, 1980.

Chambers, Douglas B. *Murder at Montpelier: Igbo Africans in Virginia.* Jackson: University Press of Mississippi, 2005.

Chappell, David L. *Inside Agitators: White Southerners in the Civil Rights Movement.* Baltimore: Johns Hopkins University Press, 1994.

Cronon, E. David. *Black Moses: The Story of Marcus Garvey and the Negro Improvement Association.* With a Foreword by John Hope Franklin. Madison: The University of Wisconsin Press, 1955.

Dalfiume, Richard. *Desegregation of the U.S. Armed Forces.* Columbia: University of Missouri Press, 1969.

Dessens, Nathalie. *From Saint-Domingue to New Orleans: Migration and Influences.* Gainesville: University Press of Florida, 2007.

Douglass, Frederick. *Narrative of the Life of Frederick Douglass.* With an Introduction by William Lloyd Garrison, a letter from Wendell Phillips, and a new introductory note. New York: Dover, 1995.

Dunning, William Archibald. *Reconstruction, Political and Economic, 1865–1877.* New York and London: Harper and Brothers, 1907.

Frazier, Edward Franklin. *Black Bourgeoisie.* Glencoe: Free Press, 1957.

Gomez, Michael A. *Exchanging Our Country Marks: The Transformation of African Identities in the Colonial and Antebellum South.* Chapel Hill and London: University of North Carolina Press, 1998.

Grossman, James R. *Land of Hope: Chicago, Black Southerners, and the Great Migration.* Chicago: University of Chicago Press, 1989.

Hall, Gwendolyn Midlo. *Africans in Colonial Louisiana: The Development of Afro-Creole Culture in the Eighteenth Century.* Baton Rouge: Louisiana State University Press, 1992.

———. *Slavery and African Ethnicities in the Americas: Restoring the Links.* Chapel Hill: University of North Carolina Press, 2005.

Herskovits, Melville J. *The Myth of the Negro Past.* With a new Introduction by Sidney W. Mintz. Boston: Beacon Press, 1990.

Heywood, Linda M., ed. *Central Africans and Cultural Transformations in the American Diaspora.* Cambridge and New York: Cambridge University Press, 2002.

Huggins, Nathan Irvin. *Harlem Renaissance.* London, Oxford, and New York: Oxford University Press, 1971.

Hughes, Louis. *Thirty Years a Slave: From Bondage to Freedom.* Milwaukee: South Side Printing Company, 1897.

Hutchinson, George. *The Harlem Renaissance in Black and White.* Cambridge: Harvard University Press, 1995.

Jones, Jacqueline. *Labor of Love, Labor of Sorrow: Black Women, Work, and the Family from Slavery to the Present.* New York: Vintage, 1995.

Joyner, Charles. *Down by the Riverside: A South Carolina Slave Community.* Urbana and Chicago: University of Chicago Press, 1984.

Kelley, Robin D. G. "'We Are Not What We Seem': Rethinking Black Working-Class Opposition in the Jim Crow South." *The Journal of American History* 80 (1993): 75–111.

Korstad, Robert and Nelson Lichtenstein. "Opportunities Found and Lost: Labor, Radicals, and the Early Civil Rights Movement." *Journal of American History* 75 (1988): 786–811.

Kramer, Victor A. and Robert A. Russ, eds. *Harlem Renaissance Re-examined: A Revised and Expanded Edition.* Troy: Whitston, 1997.

Landers, Jane. *Black Society in Spanish Florida.* With a Foreword by Peter H. Wood. Urbana: University of Illinois Press, 1999.

Lawson, Steven F. *Black Ballots: Voting Rights in the South, 1945–1969.* New York: Columbia University Press, 1976.

———. *In Pursuit of Power: Southern Blacks and Electoral Politics, 1965–1982.* New York: Columbia University Press, 1985.

Levine, Lawrence W. *Black Culture and Black Consciousness: Afro-American Thought from Slavery to Freedom.* New York: Oxford University Press, 1977.

Major, Clarence. *Dictionary of Afro-American Slang.* New York: International, 1970.

———. *Juba to Jive: A Dictionary of African-American Slang.* New York: Penguin, 1994.

Mishkin, Tracy. *The Harlem and Irish Renaissances: Language, Identity, and Representation.* With a Foreword by George Bornstein. Gainesville and Tallahassee: University of Florida Press, 1998.

Morgan, Philip D. *Slave Counterpoint: Black Culture in the Eighteenth-Century Chesapeake and Low Country.* Chapel Hill: University of North Carolina Press, 1998.

Mullins, Paul R. *Race and Affluence: An Archaeology of African American and Consumer Culture*. New York: Kluwer Academic/Plenum, 1999.

Naison, Mark. *Communists in Harlem During the Depression*. Urbana: University of Illinois Press, 1983.

Nelson, Bruce. *Workers on the Waterfront*. Urbana: University of Illinois Press, 1988.

Norrell, Robert J. *Reaping the Whirlwind: The Civil Rights Movement in Tuskegee*. New York: Knopf, 1985.

Owen, Nicholas. *Journal of a Slave Dealer: A View of Some Remarkable Axcedents in the Life of Nics. Owen on the Coast of Africa and America from the Year 1746 to the Year 1757*. Edited and with and Introduction by Eveline Martin. London: George Routledge and Sons, Ltd., 1930.

Perdue, Charles, Thomas Barden, and Robert Phillips. *Weevils in the Wheat: Interviews with Virginia Ex-slaves*. Charlottesville: University Press of Virginia, 1976.

Pollitzer. William S. *The Gullah People and Their African Heritage*. With a Foreword by David Moltke-Hansen. Athens: University of Georgia Press, 1999.

Rawick, George P., ed. *The American Slave: A Composite Autobiography*. Westport: Greenwood, 1972–78.

Smalley, Eugene V. "Sugar-Making in Louisiana." *The Century* 35 (1887): 100–120.

Stoyer, Jacob. *My Life in the South*. 4th ed. Salem: Newcomb and Gauss, 1898.

Suttles, William C., Jr. "African Religious Survivals as Factors in American Slave Revolts." *Journal of Negro History* 56 (1971): 97–104.

Wilson, Joan Hoff, ed. *The Twenties: The Critical Issues*. Boston: Little, Brown and Company, 1972.

Woodward, C. Vann. *The Strange Career of Jim Crow*. New York: Oxford University Press, 1957.

X, Malcolm with the assistance of Alex Haley. *The Autobiography of Malcolm X*. With an Introduction by M. S. Handler and an Epilogue by Alex Haley. New York: Grove Press, 1965.

AFRICAN HISTORY, TRADITIONAL RELIGION, AND FOLKLORE

Blier, Suzanne Preston. *African Vodun: Art, Psychology, and Power*. Chicago and London: University of Chicago Press, 1995.

Bowen, T. J. *Adventures and Missionary Labors in Several Countries in the Interior of Africa, from 1849 to 1856*. Charleston: Southern Baptist Publication Society, 1857.

Brown, Charles S. and Yvonne R. Chappelle. "African Religions and the Quest for Afro-American Heritage." In *African Religions: A Symposium,* ed. Newell S. Booth, Jr., 241–254. New York, London, and Lagos: NOK, 1977.

Courlander, Harold. *A Treasury of African Folklore: The Oral Literature, Traditions, Myths, Legends, Epics, Tales, Recollections, Wisdom, Sayings, and Humor of Africa*. New York: Crown, 1975.

Ellis, A. B. *The Ewe-Speaking Peoples of the Slave Coast of West Africa: Their Religion, Manners, Customs, Laws, Languages, &c*. London: Chapman and Hall, 1890.

———. "On Vŏdu Worship." *The Popular Science Monthly* 38 (1891): 651–663.

———. *The Tshi-Speaking Peoples of the Gold Coast of West Africa: Their Religion, Manners, Customs, Laws, Language, Etc.* London: Chapman and Hall, 1887.

———. *The Yoruba-Speaking Peoples of the Slave Coast of West Africa: Their Religion, Manners, Customs, Laws, Language, Etc.* Chicago: Benin P, Ltd., 1964.

Farrow, Stephen S. *Faith, Fancies and Fetich, Or Yoruba Paganism: Being an Account of the Religious Beliefs of the West African Blacks, Particularly of the Yoruba Tribes of Southern Nigeria.* Society for Promoting Christian Knowledge, 1926; reprint Athelia Henrietta Press, 1996.

Folk-Lore and Ethnology. *Southern Workman* 22 (1893): 180–181.

Harris, Joseph E. *Africans and Their History.* Revised ed. New York: Penguin Group, 1987.

Haskins, James and Joann Biondi. *From Afar to Zulu: A Dictionary of African Cultures.* New York: Walker and Company, 1995.

Kingsley, Mary. *Travels in West Africa: Congo Français, Corisco and Cameroons.* 5th ed. With an Introduction by Elizabeth Claridge. London: Virago Press, 1982.

MacGaffey, Wyatt. *Religion and Society in Central Africa: The BaKongo of Central Zaire.* Chicago and London: The University of Chicago Press, 1986.

Oliver, Roland and J. D. Fage. *A Short History of Africa.* 6th ed. London: Penguin Group, 1988.

Olupona, Jacob K., ed. *African Spirituality: Forms, Meanings and Expressions.* With a Foreword by Charles Long. New York: Crossroad, 2000.

Opoku, Kofi Asare. *West African Traditional Religion.* Accra, London, *et al:* FEP International Private Limited, 1978.

Parrinder, Geoffrey. *West African Religion: A Study of the Beliefs and Practices of Akan, Ewe, Yoruba, Ibo, and Kindred Peoples.* 2nd ed. With a Foreword by Edwin Smith. London: Epworth Press, 1961.

Rosenthal, Judy. *Possession, Ecstasy, and Law in Ewe Voodoo.* Charlottesville and London: University Press of Virginia, 1998.

Thompson, Robert Farris. *Face of the Gods: Art and Altars of Africa and the African Americas.* New York: The Museum of African Art, 1993.

———. *Flash of the Spirit: African and Afro-American Art and Philosophy.* New York: Random House, 1983.

Umeh, John Anenechukwu. *After God is Dibia: Igbo Cosmology, Divination and Sacred Science in Nigeria.* 2 vols. London: Karnak House, 1997, 1999.

RELEVANT EUROPEAN AND EURO-AMERICAN HISTORY, RELIGION, AND FOLKLORE

Boggs, Ralph Steele. "Spanish Folklore from Tampa Florida." *Southern Folklore Quarterly* 1 (1937): 1–12.

Dues, Greg. *Catholic Customs and Traditions: A Popular Guide.* Revised ed. Mystic: Twenty-third, 1992.

Farmer, David Hugh. *The Oxford Dictionary of Saints*. 3rd ed. Oxford and New York: Oxford University Press, 1992.

Fischer, David Hackett. *Albion's Seed: Four British Folkways in America*. New York and Oxford: Oxford University Press, 1989.

Grimm, Jacob and Wilhelm Grimm. *The Complete Fairy Tales of the Brothers Grimm*. Translated and with an Introduction by Jack Zipes. With illustrations by John B. Gruelle. New York: Bantam, 1992.

Hauptmann, O. H. "Spanish Folklore from Tampa Florida: (No. VII) Witchcraft." *Southern Folklore Quarterly* 3 (1939): 197–200.

Hughes, Pennethorne. *Witchcraft*. Longmans, Green, 1952; Hammondsworth and Baltimore: Penguin, 1973.

Institoris, Henricus. *Malleus Maleficarum*. Translated and with an Introduction, bibliography, and notes by Montague Summers. New York: Benjamin Blom, Inc., 1928.

Levack, Brian P. *The Witch-hunt in Early Modern Europe*. London and New York: Longman, 1987.

Russell, Jeffrey Burton. *Witchcraft in the Middle Ages*. Ithaca and London: Cornell University Press, 1972.

Scot, Reginald. *The Discoverie of Witchcraft*. With an Introduction by Hugh Ross Williamson. Carbondale: Southern Illinois University Press, 1964.

Thomas, Keith. *Religion and the Decline of Magic*. New York: Charles Scribner's Sons, 1971.

Waite, Arthur Edward. *The Book of Ceremonial Magic: The Secret in Goëtia*. With a Foreword by John C. Wilson. New York: Citadel Press, 1994.

Wedeck, Harry E. *A Treasury of Witchcraft*. New York: Philosophical Library, 1961.

Weyer, Johann. *Witches, Devils, and Doctors in the Renaissance*. Translated by John Shea, Introduction and notes by George Mora, and with a Foreword by John Weber. Binghampton: Medieval & Renaissance Texts and Studies, 1991.

NATIVE AMERICAN HISTORY, RELIGION, AND FOLKLORE

Benson, Henry Clark. *Life among the Choctaw Indians and Sketches of the South-west*. With an Introduction by T. A. Morris. Cincinnati: L. Swormstedt & A. Poe, 1860; reprint, Johnson Reprint Corporation, 1970.

Carmody, Denise Lardner and John Tully Carmody. *Native American Religions: An Introduction*. New York and Mahwah: Paulist Press, 1993.

Hamel, Paul B. and Mary U. Chiltoskey. *Cherokee Plants and Their Uses—A 400 Year History*. Sylva: Herald, 1975.

Hudson, Charles. *The Southeastern Indians*. Knoxville: University of Tennessee Press, 1976.

Hultkrantz, Åke. *Belief and Worship in Native North America*. Ed. and with an Introduction by Christopher Vecsey. Syracuse: Syracuse University Press, 1981.

———. *The Religions of the American Indians*. Translated by Monica Setterwall. Berkeley, Los Angeles, and London: University of California Press, 1979.

Lankford, George E., ed. *Native American Legends: Southeastern Legends: Tales from the Natchez, Caddo, Biloxi, Chickasaw, and Other Nations.* American Folklore Series, ed. W. K. McNeil. Little Rock: August House, 1987.

McReynolds, Edwin C. *The Seminoles.* Norman: University of Oklahoma Press, 1957.

SPIRITUALISM, SPIRITUAL CHURCHES, AND OTHER AFRICAN-INFLUENCED AMERICAN RELIGIONS

Baer, Hans A. *The Black Spiritual Movement: A Religious Response to Racism.* 2nd ed. Knoxville: University of Tennessee Press, 2001.

Bell, Caryn Cossé. *Revolution, Romanticism, and the Afro-Creole Protest Tradition in Louisiana, 1718–1868.* Baton Rouge: Louisiana State University Press, 1997.

Berry, Jason. *The Spirit of Black Hawk: A Mystery of Africans and Indians.* Jackson: University Press of Mississippi, 1995.

Cox, Robert S. *Body and Soul: A Sympathetic History of American Spiritualism.* Charlottesville: University of Virginia Press, 2003.

Du Bois, William Edward Burghardt. "The Religion of the American Negro." *New World* 9 (1900): 614–625.

Frey, Sylvia R. and Betty Wood. *Come Shouting to Zion: African-American Protestantism in the American South and British Caribbean to 1830.* Chapel Hill and London: University of North Carolina Press, 1998.

Jacobs, Claude F. and Andrew J. Kaslow. *The Spiritual Churches of New Orleans: Origins, Beliefs, and Rituals of an African-American Religion.* Knoxville: University of Tennessee Press, 1991.

MacRobert, Iain. "The Black Roots of Pentecostalism." In *African-American Religion: Interpretive Essays in History and Culture,* ed. Timothy E. Fulop and Albert J. Raboteau, 295–309. New York and London: Routledge, 1997.

Raboteau, Albert J. *Slave Religion: The "Invisible Institution" in the Antebellum South.* Oxford and New York: Oxford University Press, 1978.

"The Religious Life of the Negro Slave." *Harper's New Monthly Magazine* 27 (1863): 479–485, 676–682, 816–825.

Smith, Theophus H. *Conjuring Culture: Biblical Formations of Black America.* New York and Oxford: Oxford University Press, 1994.

Synan, Vinson. *The Holiness-Pentecostal Tradition: Charismatic Movements in the Twentieth Century.* 2nd ed. Grand Rapids and Cambridge: William B. Eerdmans, 1997.

Wacker, Grant. *Heaven Below: Early Pentecostals and American Culture.* Cambridge and London: Harvard University Press, 2001.

Wehmeyer, Stephen C. "Indian Altars of the Spiritual Church: Kongo Echoes in New Orleans." *African Arts* 33 (2000): 62–69, 95–96.

Weisberg, Barbara. *Talking to the Dead: Kate and Maggie Fox and the Rise of Spiritualism.* New York: HarperCollins, 2004.

Wicker, Christine. *Lily Dale: The True Story of the Town that Talks to the Dead.* HarperCollins, 2004.

THE NEW AGE MOVEMENT, PARAPSYCHOLOGY, AND RELATED TOPICS

Auerbach, Loyd. *ESP, Hauntings and Poltergeists: A Parapsychologist's Handbook.* New York: Warner, 1986.

Baker, Melody. *A New Consciousness: The True Spirit of the New Age.* Duluth: New Thought, 1991.

Basil, Robert. *Not Necessarily the New Age: Critical Essays.* Buffalo: Prometheus, 1988.

Erickson, Millard J. *Postmodernizing the Faith: Evangelical Responses to the Challenge of Postmodernism.* Grand Rapids, MI: Baker, 1998.

Faber, Mel D. *New Age Thinking: A Psychoanalytic Critique.* Religion and Beliefs Series, no. 5. University of Ottawa Press, 1996.

Harvey, David. *The Condition of Postmodernity: An Enquiry into the Origins of Cultural Change.* Cambridge and Oxford: Blackwell, 1990.

Heelas, Paul. *The New Age Movement: The Celebration of the Self and the Sacralization of Modernity.* Oxford and Cambridge: Blackwell, 1996.

Kyle, Richard. *The New Age Movement in American Culture.* Lanham, New York, and London: University Press of America, Inc., 1995.

Lewis, James R. and J. Gordon Melton, eds. *Perspectives on the New Age.* Albany: State University of New York Press, 1992.

Mead, Margaret. *Coming of Age in Samoa: A Psychological Study of Primitive Youth for Western Civilization.* With a Foreword by Franz Boas. New York: Blue Ribbon, 1932.

Melton, J. Gordon, Jerome Clark, Aidan A. Kelly, Dell deChant, Johnny Flynn, James R. Lewis, Suzanne Riordan, and Steve Shafarman. *New Age Encyclopedia: A Guide to the Beliefs, Concepts, Terms, People, and Organizations That Make up the New Global Movement Toward Spiritual Development, Health and Healing, Higher Consciousness, and Related Subjects.* Detroit and London: Gale Research, Inc., 1990.

Wolman, Benjamin B., ed. *Handbook of Parapsychology.* New York: Van Nostrand Reinhold Company, 1977.

SOME PROMINENT HOW-TO CONJURE WORKS AND BOOKS USED BY CONJURERS

Aunt Sally's Policy Players' Dream Book. New York: H. J. Wehman, 1889; reprint, Los Angeles: Indio Products, Inc.

Best, Michael R. and Frank H. Brightman. *The Book of Secrets of Albertus Magnus of the Virtues of Herbs, Stones and Certain Beasts—Also a Book of the Marvels of the World.* Studies in Tudor and Stuart Literature series, ed. F. H. Mares and A. T. Brissenden, vol. 2. Oxford and New York: Oxford University Press.

Black, S. Jason and Christopher S. Hyatt. *Urban Voodoo: A Beginner's Guide to Afro-Caribbean Magic.* Tempe: New Falcon, 1995.

Canizares, Raul. *The Life and Works of Marie Laveau: Gris-gris, Cleansings, Charms, Hexes.* Plainview: Original, 2001.

Claremont, Lewis de. *Legends of Incense, Herb & Oil Magic.* Revised ed. Arlington: Dorene, 1966.

The Complete Book of Fortune: How to Reveal the Secrets of the Past, the Present and the Future. Associated Newspapers, Ltd., 1936; republication, New York: Crescent, 1990.

DeLaurence, Lauren William. *The Great Book of Magical Art, Hindu Magic, and East Indian Occultism.* 1902.

Gamache, Henri. *The Magic of Herbs Throughout the Ages.* Plainview: Original, 1985.

———. *The Master Book of Candle Burning.* Revised ed. Plainview: Original, 1998.

Gandolfo, Charles M. *Voodoo Vé-Vé's & Talismans and How to Use Them.* New Orleans: New Orleans Historical Voodoo Museum, [unknown publication date].

Hohman, John George. *Pow-Wows, or Long Lost Friend: A Collection of Mysterious and Invaluable Arts and Remedies for Man As Well As Animals—With Many Proofs.* 1855; reprint Brooklyn: Fulton Religious Supply.

Jim, Papa and James e Sickafus. *Papa Jim Magical Herb Book.* 2nd ed. San Antonio: Papa Jim II, Inc., 1985.

The Key of Solomon the King (Clavicula Salomonis). Translated and ed. by S. Liddell MacGregor Mathers. With a Foreword by Richard Cavendish. York Beach: Samuel Weiser, Inc., 1972.

Lampe, H. U. *Famous Voodoo Rituals & Spells: A Voodoo Handbook.* New ed. Minneapolis: Marlar, 1982.

Laveau, Marie [pseudonym]. *Original Black and White Magic.* Los Angeles: International Imports, 1991.

Malbrough, Ray T. *Charms, Spells, and Formulas: For the Making and Use of Gris-Gris, Herb Candles, Doll Magick, Incenses, Oils and Powders . . . To Gain Love, Protection, Prosperity, Luck, and Prophetic Dreams.* Llewellyn's Practical Magick Series. St. Paul: Llewellyn, 1986.

Rucker, Herman. *Black Herman's Secrets of Magic, Mystery, and Legerdemain.* New York: Dorene, 1938.

Selig, Godfrey A. *The Secrets of the Psalms.* New ed. Arlington: Dorene, 1982.

The 6th and 7th Books of Moses, or Moses' Magical Spirit Art. New ed. Arlington: Dorene.

Snake, Doktor. *Doktor Snake's Voodoo Spellbook: Spells, Curses and Folk Magic for All Your Needs.* New York: St. Martin's Press, 2000.

Sonny Boy Blue Book Guide to Success Power. 6th ed. Birmingham, Alabama: By the author, 1715 3rd Avenue N, 2000.

Yronwode, Catherine. *Hoodoo Herb and Root Magic: A Materia Magica of African-American Conjure and Traditional Formulary Giving the Spiritual Uses of Natural Herbs, Roots, Minerals, and Zoological Curios.* Forestville: Lucky Mojo Curio Company, 2002.

———. *Hoodoo Rootwork Correspondence Course.* Forestville, CA: Lucky Mojo Curio Company, 2006.

IMPORTANT ACCESSIBLE MANUSCRIPTS

Breaux, Hazel and Robert McKinney, Federal Writers Project. "Hoodoo Price List." In Robert Tallant Papers, 320–321. City Archives, New Orleans Public Library, New Orleans.

Cannella, Felix with F. Hilton Crowe. "Nañigo," May 26, 1936. In "American Guide: Ybor City." Tampa: Federal Writers Project, [1939]. P. K. Yonge Library of Florida

History, Department of Special and Area Studies Collection, George A. Smathers Libraries, University of Florida, Gainesville.

Dillon, Catherine. "Voodoo, 1937–1941." Louisiana Writers' Project, folders 118, 317, and 319. Federal Writers' Project. Cammie G. Henry Research Center, Watson Memorial Library, Northwestern State University, Natchitoches, LA.

Hurston, Zora Neale, Federal Writers Project in Florida. "The Negro in Florida, 1528–1940." Zora Neale Hurston Collection, Department of Special and Area Studies Collection, George A. Smathers Libraries, University of Florida, Gainesville.

Lopez, A. L. "Nanigo Dance: Superstitions and Customs of Cuban Negroes in Tampa." In "Tampa." Tampa: Federal Writers Project, [1938]. P. K. Yonge Library of Florida History, Department of Special and Area Studies Collection, George A. Smathers Libraries, University of Florida, Gainesville.

McKinney, Robert, Federal Writers Project. "Popular Gris-gris among Present Day Hoodoo Queens." In Robert Tallant Papers, 302–317. City Archives, New Orleans Public Library, New Orleans.

Richardson, Martin. "Bolita," August 17, 1937. In "Negro Folk Lore and Custom," ed. John A. Simms. In "Florida Folklore & Customs." (Federal Writers Project, [193-]). P. K. Yonge Library of Florida History, Department of Special and Area Studies Collection, George A. Smathers Libraries, University of Florida, Gainesville.

Tallant, Robert. "Chronology of Voodoo." In Robert Tallant Papers, 245–247. Photocopy. City Archives, New Orleans Public Library, New Orleans.

Taylor, Samuel C. "A Hodoo Doctor, 30 April 1890." Photocopy. James S. Schoff Collection, William L. Clements Library, University of Michigan, Ann Arbor.

SUPPORTING HISTORY AND ANTHROPOLOGY

Boas, Franz. *Anthropology and Modern Life.* New and revised ed. New York: W. W. Norton and Company, 1932.

Breslaw, Elaine G. "Tituba's Confession: The Multicultural Dimensions of the 1692 Salem Witch-Hunt." *Ethnohistory* 44 (1997): 535–556.

Conzen, Kathleen Neils, David A. Gerber, Ewa Morawska, George E. Pozzetta, Rudolph J. Vecoli. "The Invention of Ethnicity: A Perspective from the U.S. A." *Journal of American Ethnic History* 12 (1992): 3–41.

Epstein, Cynthia Fuchs. *Woman's Place: Options and Limits in Professional Careers.* Berkeley, Los Angeles, and London: University of California Press, 1970.

Evans, Sara M. *Born for Liberty: A History of Women in America.* New York and London: The Free Press, 1989.

Hobsbawm, Eric and Terence Ranger, eds. *The Invention of Tradition.* Cambridge and New York: Cambridge University Press, 1983.

McCracken, Grant. *Culture and Consumption: New Approaches to the Symbolic Character of Consumer Goods and Activities.* Bloomington and Indianapolis: Indiana University Press, 1988.

Nash, Gary B. *Red, White and Black: The Peoples of Early North America.* 4th ed. Upper Saddle River, NJ: Prentice Hall, 2000.

Penkower, Monty Noam. *The Federal Writers Project: A Study in Government Patronage of the Arts.* Urbana, Chicago, and London: University of Illinois Press, 1977.

Ritzer, George. *The McDonaldization of Society.* New Century ed. Thousand Oaks: Pine Forge Press, 2000.

Roller, David C. and Robert W. Twyman, eds. *The Encyclopedia of Southern History.* Baton Rouge and London: Louisiana State University Press, 1979.

Said, Edward W. *Orientalism.* New York: Vintage, 1979.

Schlesinger, Arthur M., Jr. *The Disuniting of America.* New York and London: W. W. Norton and Company, 1992.

Scott, Anne Firor. *The Southern Lady: From Pedestal to Politics, 1830–1930.* Chicago and London: University of Chicago Press, 1970.

Warner, Coleman. "N.O. Headcount Gains Steam." *Times-Picayune.* August 9, 2007. http://www.nola.com/news/t-p/frontpage/index.ssf?/base/news-8/1186642536113410.xml&coll=1 and http://www.nola.com/news/t-p/frontpage/index.ssf?/base/news-/1186642536113410.xml&coll=1&thispage=2 (November 6, 2007).

Weinstein, James. "Radicalism in the Midst of Normalcy." *Journal of American History* 52 (1966): 773–790.

Winkelman, Michael. "Magic: A Theoretical Reassessment." *Current Anthropology* 23 (1982): 37–66.

Wyatt-Brown, Bertram. *Southern Honor: Ethics and Behavior in the Old South.* New York and Oxford: Oxford University Press, 1982.

SUPPORTING FOLKLORE AND RELIGION

Bergen, Fanny D., ed. *Animal and Plant Lore: Collected from the Oral Tradition of English Speaking Folk.* With an Introduction by Joseph Y. Bergen. Vol. 7, *Memoirs of the American Folk-Lore Society.* Boston and New York: Houghton, Mifflin and Company, 1899.

———. "Some Bits of Plant-Lore." *Journal of American Folklore* 5 (1892): 19–22.

Bronner, Simon. *American Folklore Studies: An Intellectual History.* Lawrence: University Press of Kansas, 1986.

Bronner, Simon, ed. *Folklife Studies in the Guilded Age: Object Rite, and Custom in Victorian America.* Ann Arbor and London: University Microfilms, 1987.

Cocchiara, Giuseppe. *The History of Folklore in Europe.* Translated by John N. McDaniel. Translations in Folklore Studies, Dan Ben-Amos, ed. Philadelphia: Institute for the Study of Human Issues, 1981.

Conway, David. *The Magic of Herbs.* New York: E. P. Dutton and Company, Inc., 1973.

Frazer, James G. *The Golden Bough: A Study in Magic and Religion.* 1922; reprint, New York: Macmillan, 1951.

"Folk-Lore and Ethnology: Hags and Their Ways." *Southern Workman* 23 (1892): 26–27.

Gainer, Patrick W. *Witches, Ghosts, and Signs: Folklore of the Southern Appalachians.* Morgantown: Seneca, 1975.

Hand, Wayland, ed. *Popular Beliefs and Superstitions from North Carolina.* Vol. 7, *The Frank C. Brown Collection of North Carolina Folklore,* ed. Newman Ivey White. Durham: University of North Carolina Press, 1952–1964.

Hughes, Langston and Arna Bontemps, eds. *The Book of Negro Folklore.* New York: Dodd, Mead, and Company, 1959.

Hyatt, Harry Middleton. *Folk-Lore from Adams County Illinois.* New York: Memoirs of the Alma Egan Hyatt Foundation, 1935.

Jackson, Bruce, ed. *The Negro and his Folklore in Nineteenth-Century Periodicals.* American Folklore Society, Biographical and Special Series, ed. Kenneth S. Goldstein, vol. 18. Austin and London: University of Texas Press, 1967.

McNeil, W. K., ed. *Ghost Stories from the American South.* Little Rock: August House, 1985.

Opie, Iona and Moira Tatem, eds. *A Dictionary of Superstitions.* Oxford and New York: Oxford University Press, 1989.

Prahlad, Anand. *The Greenwood Encyclopedia of African American Folklore.* 3 vols. Westport, CT: Greenwood Press, 2006.

Propp, Vladimir I. *Morphology of the Folktale. International Journal of American Linguistics,* vol. 24, no. 3, part 3. Bloomington: 1958.

Waring, Philippa. *The Dictionary of Omens & Superstitions.* 1986 ed. Secaucus: Chartwell, Inc., 1986.

Whitney, Annie Weston and Caroline Canfield Bullock. *Folk-Lore from Maryland.* New York: American Folk-Lore Society, 1925.

Web Resources

INTRODUCTION

As with almost any topic, there is substantial online material that addresses conjure, hoodoo, and Voodoo. Unlike other subjects of historical and folkloric interest, however, their study had been limited until the last few decades. Because of the underdeveloped nature of this field of study, much of the information available online is suspect. As with any Internet site, readers should carefully weigh the data they find before judging it to be factually accurate. The following is a helpful, although far from exhaustive, list of sites valuable for their research potential and/or reliability. In this section, Web site names will appear in bold type to distinguish them from book titles.

SEARCH ENGINES

To save time by avoiding outdated Web addresses and to get a quick idea of the materials available for research, search engines are indispensable. On most of them words entered into the search field are treated as individual units unless placed within quotation marks. Thus a search for the words *hoodoo* and *Voodoo* will locate any Web sites containing both words. Entering "*hoodoo and Voodoo*" will locate sites containing the phrase *hoodoo and Voodoo,* however. Using multiple search engines can lead to better results. Try starting with the following:

- **Alta Vista** (http://www.altavista.com).
- **Ask** (http://www.ask.com/).
- **DMOZ** (http://www.dmoz.org).
- **Google** (http://www.google.com).
- **Excite** (http://www.excite.com).

- **Lycos** (http://www.lycos.com).
- **Webcrawler** (http://www.webcrawler.com).
- **Yahoo!** (http://www.yahoo.com).

REFERENCE WORKS

There are several reference works available online as well. These serve the dual purpose of providing surveys of topics, as well as pointing to sources with greater depth. Those with links to additional Web sites are particularly useful. Some of the better ones are as follow:

- **Highbeam Encyclopedia** (http://www.encyclopedia.com).
- **Infoplease** (http://www.infoplease.com).
- **Wikipedia.** Although much maligned, it is reasonably accurate, and its links to additional sources can be extremely valuable (http://www.wikipedia.org).

ONLINE DOCUMENT REPOSITORIES

These resources include wide arrays of primary sources, with significant material about African American magic and religion or about their African ancestors. Many of these sites are searchable, rendering the location of specific information easy to find. The following are some of the best for the study of African American supernaturalism.

- **Bartleby.com.** A useful collection of online texts, including reference books (http://www.bartleby.com).
- **Born in Slavery: Slave Narratives from the Federal Writers' Project, 1936–1938, from the Library of Congress, American Memory Project.** An exceptionally valuable collection of ex-slave oral histories (http://memory.loc.gov/ammem/snhtml/snhome.html).
- **Chicken Bones.** Although addressing primarily literary and artistic themes, this Web site has significant material on hoodoo (http://www.nathanielturner.com/index.html).
- **Documenting the American South.** A large collection of books and pamphlets on many aspects of southern life, including some materials on African American folk beliefs (http://docsouth.unc.edu).
- **Internet Sacred Texts Archive.** A collection of sacred texts from a vast array of world religions, including studies of both African and African American belief systems (http://www.sacred-texts.com).
- **Making of America.** An extensive collection of nineteenth-century periodicals and books assembled by the University of Michigan and Cornell University. Many references to Voodoo, hoodoo, and conjure can be found here (http://quod.lib.umich.edu/m/moa) and (http://moa.cit.cornell.edu/moa).

- **Project Gutenberg.** A massive collection of online books (http://www.gutenberg.org).
- **Sacred Magick Esoteric Library.** A commercial site with fees for use. Although it is potentially handy, many of its materials can be found elsewhere for free (http://www.sacred-magick.com).
- **Southern Spirits: Ghostly Voices from Dixie Land.** The Internet's best collection of conjure- and hoodoo-specific primary documents. Each text is accompanied by commentary written by Catherine Yronwode, a hoodoo practitioner and proprietor of the Lucky Mojo Curio Company (http://www.southern-spirits.com).

In addition to these sites, some university libraries have their own online document collections. Almost all have catalogs that are searchable online. Although acquiring a source might require a visit to campus, knowing ahead of time whether the item in question is available can save time.

ONLINE PERIODICALS

Many periodicals now have online editions, which can be purchased directly by individuals. Moreover, several compendiums of multiple journals are now available, most readily through a college campus. Two of the most useful of these are the following:

- **J STOR.** A collection of online scholarly journals available on most university campuses (http://www.jstor.org).
- **Project Muse.** An online collection of scholarly humanities and social science journals (http://muse.jhu.edu).

College and university Web sites frequently have links to additional online periodicals. These can usually be accessed on campus, although using them from home typically requires enrollment in the school or at least a password.

PRACTITIONERS AND ONLINE SHOPS SELLING CONJURE, HOODOO, AND/OR VOODOO PARAPHERNALIA

One of the best resources for information on hoodoo, conjure, and Voodoo as practiced today are the Web sites of practitioners. The following are a few that promise interesting factual data. Also available from these sites are magical and religious goods and in some cases professional hoodoo consultations.

- **Angel Spiritual Consultant.** The Web site of Savannah, Georgia-based Angel Hakim (www.angelmindbodyspirit.com).
- **Botanica de Los Orishas.** A botanica with substantial information on the religion of Santería. Available in both Spanish and English (http://www.botanica-de-los-orishas.com).

- **Botanica Elegua.** A Houston, Texas, botanica with an emphasis on Afro-Latin religion (www.botelegua.com).
- **Dr. Kioni.com.** The Web site of Dr. Kioni, a well-known hoodoo practitioner. This site also links to his online radio show (http://drkioni.com/70801.html).
- **Erzulie's Authentic Voudou.** A New Orleans Voodoo shop (http://www.erzulies.com/).
- **Indio Products.** Currently the world's largest hoodoo manufacturer (www.indio-products.com).
- **Island of Salvation.** The botanica of Sallie Ann Glassman, a white Vodou priestess who lives in New Orleans (www.mindspring.com/~cfeldman/bot2).
- **Lucky Mojo Curio Company.** An exceptionally impressive site with extensive informational pages, a wide array of hoodoo goods, books, and even a correspondence course (http://www.luckymojo.com).
- **Maria Burton Voodoo Talk Radio Show.** A Voodoo call-in show (http://www.spellslove.com/home).
- **Miller's Rexall Drugs.** A well-known pharmacy and spiritual supply store in Atlanta, Georgia (http://www.millersrexall.com).
- **Papa Jim's Botanica.** A spiritual supply shop based in San Antonio, Texas (http://www.papajimsbotanica.com).
- **Planet Voodoo.** An online Voodoo shop specializing in Voodoo dolls, with significant information on their history and their similarity to magical items of non-African origin (http://www.planetvoodoo.com).
- **Temple of Yehwe.** A Haitian Vodou congregation (http://www.vodou.org).
- **VodouSpirit.** A Vodou congregation from Snellville, Georgia (http://www.vodouspirit.com).
- **Voodoo and Yoruba Priestess Ava Kay Jones.** An African American convert to Haitian and West African religion (http://yorubapriestess.tripod.com).
- **Voodoo Authentica.** A New Orleans Voodoo shop specializing in Haitian Vodou (http://www.voodooshop.com).
- **Voodoo Spiritual Temple.** A New Orleans Spiritual Congregation incorporating concepts from Haitian Vodou (http://www.voodoospiritualtemple.org/).

INFORMATIONAL WEB SITES

There are many useful informational sites addressing Haitian Vodou and other African and Afro-Latin faiths. The following are but a tiny fraction of the total number. Web sites on African American practices are comparatively uncommon. Many practitioners' Web sites, however, are packed with valuable data. Most useful of such dual-purpose sites is Catherine Yronwode's Lucky Mojo Curio Company, referenced previously.

While researching, one should remain aware that many of the following are designed to promote particular belief systems. In consequence, they come with all the drawbacks of partiality, as well as its benefits.

- **About.com: Alternative Religions.** Contains a link to information on Vodou, Santería, and other African derived religions (http://altreligion.about.com/?once=true).
- **African-Based Religions.** Web site with informational on a wide variety of African Diasporic faiths and numerous links to similar sites (http://sparta.rice.edu/~maryc/AfroCuban.html).
- **African Traditional Religions.** A Web site made up of numerous topical essays on various aspects of faiths from across sub-Saharan Africa (http://afrikaworld.net/afrel).
- **Everything Haitian.com.** As the name implies, a catch-all site for information on Haiti, including a Kreyol (Creole) dictionary (http://www.everythinghaitian.com/index.asp).
- **Haiti: Voodoo.** A highly informative sight addressing Haitian Vodou (www.webster.edu/~corbetre/haiti/voodoo/voodoo.htm).
- **Haitian Creole.** Provides information on the language of the average Haitian (http://j_zyric.tripod.com/book.htm).
- **Kreyol/Haitian Creole.** A dictionary of Haitian Kreyol (http://www.kreyol.com/dictionary.html).
- **Internet African History Sourcebook.** A collection of sources addressing topics in African history from the ancient world to the present (http://www.fordham.edu/halsall/africa/africasbook.html).
- **Mami Wata West African and Diasporic Vodoun.** As the name indicates, the Web site focuses on West African religion and its influence in the New World (http://www.mamiwata.com).
- **Official Oyotunji Village Web Site.** Created by the inhabitants of Oyotunji Village, an ongoing attempt to build a Yoruba-based religion and culture. Located in South Carolina, it is a self-proclaimed independent country that promotes African American cultural nationalism, including a return to traditional African religion (http://www.oyotunjiafricanvillage.org).
- **OrishaNet.** Web site devoted to the religions that incorporate the orishas (http://www.orishanet.org).
- **Roots Without End Society.** A society for adherents of Haitian Vodou, with significant informational resources (http://www.rootswithoutend.org/index.php).
- **Sacred Arts of Haitian Vodou.** A Web site sponsored by the American Museum of Natural History (www.amnh.org/exhibitions/vodou/index.html).
- **This Far by Faith.** Part of the Public Broadcasting System's Web site, it is a brief introduction to African and African American faiths (http://www.pbs.org/thisfarbyfaith).
- **Vodou.** An informational website prepared by a Vodou manbo (http://members.aol.com/racine125/index1.html).
- **Vodoun Culture.** Available in French and English, this Web site gives insight into Haitian Vodou and calls on believers to preserve their culture (http://www.geocities.com/Athens/Delphi/5319/).

- **World History Archives: The Culture History of the Republic of Haiti.** Includes numerous links on many aspects of Haitian life, including Vodou (http://www.hartford-hwp.com/archives/43a/index-f.html).

USEFUL WEB SITES FOR TOURISTS

Some aspects of Voodoo and hoodoo require visits to specific locations, most often cities along the Mississippi River or the South Carolina and Georgia Lowcountry. Thorough study of Haitian Vodou or African Traditional Religions requires considerably more extensive travel. The following Web sites offer some useful information for those who would visit places outside of cyberspace. Of course, these represent only some of the locations prominently associated with African diasporic religions.

Some of these destinations can be unsafe for researchers and/or tourists. Please consider carefully the political, economic, and social situation at the location under consideration before making any travel plans.

- **Beale Street.** A guide to Memphis, Tennessee's Beale Street, a hotbed for music and hoodoo (http://www.bealestreet.com).
- **Gullah Tours.** Locations associated with Dr. Buzzard are part of this Charleston, South Carolina, tour company's repertoire (http://www.gullahtours.com).
- **New Orleans Cemetery and Voodoo Pages.** Web site addressing Voodoo and other aspects of the supernatural in the Crescent City (www.geocities.com/BourbonStreet/6157).
- **New Orleans Convention and Visitors' Bureau.** Includes a wide range of information on the city, including contact information for Voodoo establishments and companies that conduct Voodoo-related tours (http://www.neworleanscvb.com).
- **New Orleans Historic Voodoo Museum.** A small museum dedicated to New Orleans Voodoo and Haitian Vodou (http://www.voodoomuseum.com).
- **New Orleans Online.** Another valuable Web site for those interested in visiting New Orleans (http://www.neworleansonline.com).
- **New Orleans Pharmacy Museum.** Contains collections from some of New Orleans old-fashioned hoodoo drugstores (http://www.pharmacymuseum.org).
- **Republic of Haiti Tourism Site.** Site designed to promote tourism in Haiti. Contains links to valuable tour books, including travel warnings (http://www.haititourisme.com).
- **Virtual Tourist: Haiti Travel Guide.** Provides information on popular destinations, hotel rates, and other additional travel information (http://www.virtualtourist.com/travel/Caribbean_and_Central_America/Haiti/TravelGuide-Haiti.html).

DISCUSSION GROUPS

One of the best ways to learn about hoodoo and Voodoo is talking with believers and practitioners. The following are some online ways to do so through discussion boards. Although these and similar groups generally require membership, they allow for interaction among a wide range of interested individuals. Please note that the following represent only a small fraction of the available discussion groups.

- **Hoodoo-in-Texas: The Study and Practice of Hoodoo.** A discussion group on hoodoo and similar magical practices (http://groups.yahoo.com/group/Hoodoo-In-Texas).
- **hrc: Hoodoo Rootwork Course.** The discussion group linked to Catherine Yronwode's Hoodoo Rootwork Correspondence Course. Taking the course is required for membership (http://groups.yahoo.com/group/hrcourse/).
- **HyattSpells.** Discusses the spells found in interviews conducted by Harry Middleton Hyatt during the 1930s and 1940s (http://groups.yahoo.com/group/HyattSpells/).
- **Mambo Racine's Vodou Forum.** A Vodou discussion group that also covers related African Creole Religions and magic (http://groups.yahoo.com/group/Mambo_Racines_Vodou_Forum).
- **Santeria.** Dedicated to the discussion of Santería and open to both initiates and non-initiates (http://groups.yahoo.com/group/santeria).
- **Santeria Cubana.** Predominantly Spanish-language site covering Santería and related practices (http://espanol.groups.yahoo.com/group/SanteriaCubana).
- **Voodoo-L.** A discussion group focused on U.S. hoodoo and Voodoo (http://groups.yahoo.com/group/voodoo-l).

Index

About the Author

JEFFREY E. ANDERSON currently resides in Monroe, Louisiana, where he has been an assistant professor of history at the University of Louisiana-Monroe since fall 2007. His writings include several articles of varying types and the book *Conjure in African American Society*. As part of his research, Anderson has interviewed practicing conjurers and Voodoo priestesses in Florida, Georgia, South Carolina, Alabama, Tennessee, California, Pennsylvania, and Louisiana.